FOCUS 5

SECOND EDITION

B2+/C1
WORKBOOK

Pearson Education Limited
KAO Two
KAO Park
Hockham Way,
Harlow, Essex,
CM17 9SR England
and Associated Companies throughout the world.

www.english.com/focus

© Pearson Education Limited 2020

Focus 5 Second Edition Workbook

The right of Daniel Brayshaw, Tomasz Siuta, Beata Trapnell, Dean Russell and Gregory Manin to be identified as authors of this Work has been asserted by them in accordance with the Copyright, Designs and Patents Act 1988.

First published 2020
Tenth impression 2024

ISBN: 978-12-9228-840-6

Set in Avenir LT Pro
Printed in Slovakia by Neografia

Acknowledgements
The publishers and authors would like to thank the following people for their feedback and comments during the development of the material:
Kinga Auguścińska, Katarzyna Babiarz, Anna Brewińska, Joanna Buczkowska, Kamila Chojnacka-Kwatek, Maciej Doksa, Jolanta Dziewulska, Dorota Gajda, Agnieszka Gajewska, Kamila Gałek, Ewa Goldnik-Ciok, Dominika Gostyńska, Renata Gramowska, Anna Maria Grochowska, Maria Górna, Katarzyna Guess, Barbara Henke, Dariusz Jankowski, Krystyna Jasińska, Monika Jaworska, Agnieszka Karolak, Urszula Kębrowska, Aleksandra Kolasińska-Bin, Małgorzata Kowal, Anna Kraśko, Sylwia Kurdek, Magdalena Loska, Katarzyna Maciejewska, Monika Mierczyńska, Joanna Mirońska, Justyna Mirowska, Anna Mirowska-Przybył, Marcin Morawski, Katarzyna Mrozowska-Linda, Marzena Nalewajek, Andrzej Nejman, Romana Otto-Kubot, Mariola Palcewicz, Anna Pawelczyk, Marta Piróg-Riley, Roksana Rajkowska, Anita Rogozińska-Parmee, Beata Roth, Joanna Różańska, Maria Ruczyńska, Anna Rux-Szewczuk, Alicja Sadowska, Ewa Schubert, Tomasz Siuta, Anna Sochacka, Patrycja Studzińska-Korpowska, Agnieszka Szlachciak, Beata Szot, Renata Tomaka-Pasternak, Beata Trapnell, Magdalena Wachowska, Anna Waluch, Grażyna Wilczyńska, Dorota Wojsznarowicz, Magdalena Wróblewska, Ewa Wrzesińska.

Text

Extracts on page 18 adapted from "Bird Brains", *The Telegraph*, 13/05/2012, and "Crows may be smarter than apes" by Roger Highfield, *The Telegraph*, 17/09/2008, copyright © Telegraph Media Group Limited 2008, 2012; Extract on page 18 adapted from "Bird Brains" by Gareth Huw Davies, http://www.pbs.org/lifeofbirds/brain/. Reproduced by permission of Gareth Huw Davies; Extract on page 21 from "Schools that ban mobile phones see better academic results" by Jamie Doward, *The Guardian*, 16/05/2015, copyright © Guardian News & Media Ltd 2016; Extract on page 30 adapted from "The bitter truth about sugar" by William Leith, *The Telegraph*, 27/03/2012; Extract on page 42 "Print out digital photos or risk losing them, Google boss warns" by Sarah Knapton, *The Telegraph*, 13/02/2015, copyright © Telegraph Media Group Limited 2012, 2015; Extract on page 42 adapted from "The eternity drive: Why DNA could be the future of data storage" by Peter Shadbolt, Updated February 25, 2015, http://edition.cnn.com/ Reproduced courtesy of CNN; Extracts on page 78 adapted from "Lorde interview: the Royals singer on her sudden fame and being boring" by Craig McLean, *The Telegraph*, 07/12/2014, and "Lorde interview: Dream Teen" by Bernadette McNulty, *The Telegraph*, 26/01/2014, copyright © Telegraph Media Group Limited 2014; Extract on page 100 from "I went vegan for 60 days - and it changed my life" by Craig McLean, *The Telegraph*, 01/08/2015, copyright © Telegraph Media Group Limited 2015; Extract on page 102 from www.trashisfortossers.com, reproduced with kind permission of Lauren Singer. Extract on page 113 adapted from "Eating breakfast helps teens lose weight, says US study" by Jerome Taylor, *The Independent*, 05/03/2008, copyright © The Independent, 2008, www.independent.co.uk; Extract on page 114 adapted from "Space 'smells like fried steak'", *The Telegraph*, 16/10/2008, copyright © Telegraph Media Group Limited 2008; Extract on page 114 adapted from "Behind The Scenes - Before the curtain goes up", http://www.rsc.org.uk. Reproduced by permission of RSC; Extract on page 114 adapted from "On the expedition", http://www.earthwatch.org/europe/exped/burns_teen.html. Reproduced with permission from Earthwatch Institute, www.earthwatch.org/europe; Extract on page 115 adapted from "Why isn't slow food taking off faster?" by Stuart Gillies, *The Guardian*, 24/10/2008, copyright © Guardian News & Media Ltd 2016; Extract on page 115 adapted from "Beware of salesmen who offer you a warm drink" by Steve Connor, *The Independent*, 24/10/2008 copyright © The Independent, 2008, www.independent.co.uk; Extract on page 115 adapted from "At last, light is shed on secrets of dark matter" by Steve Connor, *The Independent*, 07/11/2008, copyright © The Independent, 2008, www.independent.co.uk; Extract on page 116 adapted from "500 places to see before they die" by Amelia Hill, *The Observer*, 26/10/2008, copyright © Guardian News & Media Ltd 2016; Extract on page 116 adapted from "A brief history of film music", http://www.mfiles.co.uk/film-history.htm. Reproduced with permission of Music Files Ltd.

Images

123RF.com: Eleonora Konnova 33, Graham Oliver 108, Ian Allenden 83, maridav 91, ostill 89, rawpixel 64, 90, Stefan Ember 66; **Alamy Stock Photo:** National Geographic Creative 64, Onoky - Photononstop 71, Rgb Reporter 35, Roger Bamber 54, Westend61 GmbH 71; **Fotolia:** Adwo 64, Alex 95, Anna Kucherova 28, Artem Shadrin 30, Bestphotostudio 28, Davis 55, Deagreez 95, Denisgo 107, Destina 42, Dionisvera 28, Dpeteshin 43, Drubig-Photo 96, Elena Belyaeva 102, Feng Yu 47, Frenk58 64, Gpointstudio 6, Highwaystarz 55, Iulianvalentin 59, James Thew 72, Jdwfoto 102, Jiri Hera 29, Jörn Buchheim 55, Josfor 64, Jpldesigns 102, Kzenon 97, Leungchopan 46, LoloStock 102, Lucky Images 88, Margo555 28, Mates 28, Michael Jung 64, Miguel Garcia Saaved 28, Mila Supynska 29, Monkey Business 6, 7, 71, Monticellllo 28, Onepony 28, Otsphoto 64, Patpitchaya 109, Photographee.eu 59, Pure-Life-Pictures 64, Rawpixel.com 60, Robert Kneschke 55, Sergey Kamshylin 48, Syda Productions 12, Thodonal 103, Toa555 36, Valerii Zan 28, Zenstock 64; **Getty Images:** Alberto E. Rodriguez 30, Franziska Krug 76; **Lauren Singer:** 102; **Shutterstock.com:** 11, 13, 100, 3000ad 107, arek_malang 40, GaudiLab 11, M Morton / 20th Century Fox / Kobal 84, Masatoshi Okauchi 77, Motortion Films 5, Phuong D. Nguyen 71, Richard Isaac 78

Illustrations

Illustrated by Ewa Olejnik pp. 25, 52, 57, 58, 81, 100, 105, 106.

All other images © Pearson Education Limited.

CONTENTS

Unit 1   The ties that bind

1.1   Vocabulary 4
1.2   Reading 6
1.3   Grammar 8
1.4   Use of English 9
1.5   Listening Language Practice 10
1.6   Speaking 11
1.7   Writing 12
1.8   Self-check 14

Unit 2   Learning for life

2.1   Vocabulary 16
2.2   Reading 18
2.3   Grammar 20
2.4   Use of English 21
2.5   Listening Language Practice 22
2.6   Speaking 23
2.7   Writing 24
2.8   Self-check 26

Unit 3   Let's eat

3.1   Vocabulary 28
3.2   Reading 30
3.3   Grammar 32
3.4   Use of English 33
3.5   Listening Language Practice 34
3.6   Speaking 35
3.7   Writing 36
3.8   Self-check 38

Unit 4   The new thing

4.1   Vocabulary 40
4.2   Reading 42
4.3   Grammar 44
4.4   Use of English 45
4.5   Listening Language Practice 46
4.6   Speaking 47
4.7   Writing 48
4.8   Self-check 50

Unit 5   All in a day's work

5.1   Vocabulary 52
5.2   Reading 54
5.3   Grammar 56
5.4   Use of English 57
5.5   Listening Language Practice 58
5.6   Speaking 59
5.7   Writing 60
5.8   Self-check 62

Unit 6   Journeys

6.1   Vocabulary 64
6.2   Reading 66
6.3   Grammar 68
6.4   Use of English 69
6.5   Listening Language Practice 70
6.6   Speaking 71
6.7   Writing 72
6.8   Self-check 74

Unit 7   Express yourself

7.1   Vocabulary 76
7.2   Reading 78
7.3   Grammar 80
7.4   Use of English 81
7.5   Listening Language Practice 82
7.6   Speaking 83
7.7   Writing 84
7.8   Self-check 86

Unit 8   Text me!

8.1   Vocabulary 88
8.2   Reading 90
8.3   Grammar 92
8.4   Use of English 93
8.5   Listening Language Practice 94
8.6   Speaking 95
8.7   Writing 96
8.8   Self-check 98

Unit 9   Future generations

9.1   Vocabulary 100
9.2   Reading 102
9.3   Grammar 104
9.4   Use of English 105
9.5   Listening Language Practice 106
9.6   Speaking 107
9.7   Writing 108
9.8   Self-check 110

Use of English 112

Writing Bank 121

Speaking Bank 126

Self-check Answer Key 128

1 The ties that bind

VOCABULARY
1.1
Personality and relationships
• adjectives • collocations • phrases

SHOW WHAT YOU KNOW

1 Complete the letter with the words from the box. There are three extra words.

> depend   fall   feel   get   grow
> live   look (x2)   put   take

HOW MOVING ABROAD TRANSFORMED MY FAMILY

Two years ago, my parents announced that we were moving to North Africa, where they had both accepted research jobs. Of course my sister and I were worried. We would be leaving friends, school and everything familiar behind. But because we *looked* up to and admired our parents, we tried to be enthusiastic.
I know now that this move was the best thing that ever happened to our family. In the UK, my sister and I were pretty distant, but after moving we began to ¹_____ on each other more. We also learned to ²_____ on together much better instead of arguing, and we began to ³_____ after each other in stressful situations. This has helped both of us to ⁴_____ up and act less like dependent children.
Another change is that our parents became more relaxed about our social lives and academic achievements. In the UK, they did not want us to ⁵_____ up with classmates who were not serious about school, and it was hard to ⁶_____ up to their high expectations. Now they are happy to see us making all kinds of new friends, and this has brought us much closer together as a family.

2 Complete the sentences with the correct prepositions.

> Thrust into power by the untimely death of his father, the young Emperor was required to grow *up* overnight.

1 Of course, the monarchy has to put ____ with intrusions into its private affairs; that's the price of privilege.
2 Although my cousin and her fiancé split ____ last month, they made it up and we're going to their wedding this summer.
3 It took my grandmother ages to agree to go ____ with my grandfather.
4 Our teacher has fallen ____ with Mrs Bayram over her son's behaviour.
5 In his generosity, Mr Perez takes ____ his much-admired grandfather.

WORD STORE 1A | Personality adjectives

3 Complete Lena's message with the correct forms of the words in brackets.

> Maggie,
>
> Although I'm reluctant to admit it, I think our friendship is over. Ever since you started hanging out with 'you-know-who', you've gone from *down-to-earth* (earth) and ¹_____ (consider) to selfish and ²_____ (obstinacy). Probably because of her and the other 'populars' you now spend all your time with, you've become two-faced and no longer ³_____ (faith) to your former friends. I used to regard you as one of the ⁴_____ (sharp) girls in our year and to admire your ⁵_____ (prejudice) attitude towards others, but these days you seem to have lost that accepting side and become completely ⁶_____ (reverence) towards anyone who doesn't look, speak and dress the same as you and your new 'best friends'. You've changed, and I miss my old friend. Have a nice life.
>
> Lena

WORD STORE 1B | Collocations

4 Complete the sentences. The first letters are given.

> Peter wanted to take a break, but his **i**ron **w**ill prevented him from joining the others outside.

1 Despite its **d**_____ **s**_____ , the pygmy marmoset, the world's smallest monkey at just eleven to fifteen centimetres long, can leap up to five metres between branches.
2 Soldiers of the time **s**_____ many **h**_____ including intense hunger and long periods without sleep.
3 Don't be fooled by the elephant's **u**_____ **m**_____ . It will attack if it feels threatened.
4 Julia's floral perfume **c**_____ up **m**_____ of his mother, which made him think of home.
5 The Queen **n**_____ in **a**_____ at the consul's suggestion.
6 My favourite part of the festival is the never-ending supply of **h**_____-**b**_____ treats.
7 Only six more months of mopping floors and you could be promoted to the **d**_____ **h**_____ of hygiene supervisor.

WORD STORE 1C | EXTRA Collocations

5 Choose the correct words to complete the sentences.

1 Meditation often helps troubled patients to *put / blot / nod* out dark memories.

2 Mike took his brother to dinner as a birthday *party / invitation / treat*, but forgot his wallet.

3 Clifford is huge, but his *imposing / irreverent / unassuming* stature hides a chronic shyness.

4 A controversial new study has suggested that *free / thoughtful / flexible* will is actually an illusion.

5 Animals living at such altitudes *do / face / meet* great hardships during the winter months.

6 After reaching the *eager / lofty / respectful* heights of amateur league four, the team fell apart when five of the players went off to university.

7 Membership applications require *approval / approving / accept* from the site moderator.

8 The president's forthright *habit / manner / memory* can make diplomacy difficult.

WORD STORE 1D | Common phrases

6 Complete each pair of sentences with the same word.

a If the mangoes are green and hard, you can be sure that they are not *ripe* yet.

b At the *ripe* old age of eighty-six, Bert is the oldest in the race.

1 a Everyone makes mistakes but by lying about it, you've let yourself _____ and upset your parents.

b No more excuses. I'm putting my foot _____ . Hand in your essay tomorrow or fail the class.

2 a Welcome to Wimbledon. Today, Williams and Wang _____ each other in the women's semi-finals.

b Cindy was terrified of thunder but she put on a brave _____ in front of her little brother.

3 a His mother only sees the _____ in him. She doesn't realise how difficult he can be.

b I think it would be for the _____ if you had an early night. The exam starts at 8 a.m.

4 a Whether we get there depends _____ the traffic.

b Stop complaining and get _____ with cutting the lawn.

5 a With the accident and then the robbery, Scott has had more than his _____ share of bad luck recently.

b _____-skinned visitors in particular should use cream as the walking route offers little shade.

6 a Despite the cost of the graduation dinner, Oliver's proud parents didn't bat an _____ when the bill arrived.

b It was Fiona's first attempt at doing her make up and most of the mascara ended up on her upper _____ rather than on her eyelashes.

SHOW WHAT YOU'VE LEARNT

7 Complete the dialogue with the words from the box. There are two extra words.

> best brave ~~earth~~ fair nodding
> respectful share sharp

M: Adele, we met your brother's girlfriend last night. They work together, you know? They came over for dinner.

A: Finally! And?

M: Very nice. For someone so successful, she was very down-to-*earth*. Your father liked her.

A: Did he?

M: Instantly. She listened to more than her fair ¹_____ of train spotting stories and managed to appear genuinely eager to hear about the 1987 cup final.

A: Ha! I'm sure she was just putting on a ²_____ face, but it sounds like she scored some points at least.

M: Oh, absolutely. By the time we got to dessert, your father was ³_____ in approval at all she said.

A: Clever girl. Very ⁴_____ . Get in with the father and everything will be OK.

M: Oh really? And, what about the mother?

A: Oh, Mum. You never have a bad word to say about anyone anyway. She could be a complete dropout and you'd still see the ⁵_____ in her.

8 Correct the mistakes.

The minister's comments were ~~unrespectful~~ to the people of the North. *disrespectful*

1 Revisiting the village after so long conjured so many childhood memories. _____

2 After six months of backbreaking work, Henry reached the lofting heights of assistant box carrier. _____

3 At the ripe old year of ninety-four, Edna is the oldest skydiver we've ever met. _____

4 Those who are faithless to the King will be suitably rewarded. _____

5 Those students wishing to go on the school trip require the written approvement of their parents. _____

| /10 |

WISE WORDS

A Every nation has its own proverbs which are repeated across the generations in order to pass on advice about the basic truths of life. In Germany, it is said that 'a country can be judged by the quality of its proverbs', while an Arabic saying suggests that 'a proverb is to speech what salt is to food'. In my view, a well-chosen proverb used at the right time can flavour a person's communication with wit and wisdom, but, to continue the Arabs' dinner-table analogy, it is important not to 'over-season' the meal. Speech or writing peppered with proverbs soon begins to sound patronising and contrived. Proverbs are a truly global phenomenon and, while their exact origins may not always be easy to **pinpoint**, by their very nature they **transcend** geographical, religious and cultural differences by focusing on broad topics such as family matters, friendship and affairs of the heart. Thus a proverb which has its roots in Asian culture may still convey a relevant wisdom for someone from a completely different corner of the world.

B Regardless of our nationality, most of us are similar in appearance or behaviour to one or both of our parents. Despite our protestations, my father and I are consistently told by those who know the family that the older I get, the more like him I become. 'What a load of rubbish!' say Dad and I in unison, with perfectly matched dismissive gestures and identical looks of scorn*. As appears to be the case for me, the combined influences of our genes and our upbringing mean that often 'the apple doesn't fall far from the tree'. Here, the tree **symbolises** the parents and the fruit their offspring. Probably of Turkish origins, this saying has its Western equivalents in 'like father, like son' or 'like mother, like daughter'. Similarly, a child who **resembles** one or the other of his or her parents, or indeed **exhibits** similarities of character is often described as being 'a chip off the old block'. Though bitter personal experience may lead significant numbers of us to doubt the assertion, it is nevertheless widely believed that no bond is stronger than the one that exists between family members. In Africa, people say that 'a family tie* is like a tree: it can bend but it cannot break'. Similarly, the proverb 'blood is thicker than water', which is thought to have **originated** in Germany, places family above all others, including close friends.

C 'To be without a friend is to be poor indeed' according to a Tanzanian proverb. Of course, nothing comes for free in this world, and that includes friendship. German wisdom advises us that 'friendship is a plant we must often water' or, in other words, effort is required to maintain relationships and avoid finding ourselves friendless. A popular way to achieve this is through the sharing of food: 'warm food, warm friendships' suggest the Czechs. In the same way, an Arabian proverb assures us that 'so long as the pot is boiling, friendship will stay warm'. Conveniently then, whereas some might say I was simply too lazy to hit the gym three times a week as promised every New Year's Day for the last five years, I blame my ever-expanding waistline on my friends and the 'sacrifices' required to keep our relationships suitably warm. **Maintaining** friendships over the long term seems particularly important in Russia, where 'an old friend is much better than two new ones'. Perhaps this is because those who we have known for many years can usually be relied on to tell us the truth about ourselves, or as the Irish say, 'a friend's eye is a good mirror'. Should you need any further persuasion as to the importance of your mates, pals or buddies, then remember the Egyptian advice that 'friendship doubles joy and halves grief'.

D 'Love is blind', they say, which is of great comfort when you look like I do. The idea that love can 'blind' us to the negative in each other is recognised globally. In Germany, 'love sees roses without thorns*' and for the Chinese 'even water is sweet'. Love-related proverbs also exist to remind us that we must accept our partners for what they are and try to love every aspect of them. In Africa, 'he who loves the vase loves also what is inside'. Often stereotyped as romantics, the French say that 'real love is when you don't have to tell each other' and to this, the famously gastronomic nation adds that 'the torch of love is lit in the kitchen'. Wise words indeed, though based on personal experience, I can't be sure whether they are talking about love between two people or the love of one man for the contents of his fridge. When it comes to neighbourly love, the Chinese remind us that there are limits: 'love your neighbour, but don't pull down the fence'. Finally, returning to the natural world, the people of Burundi warn those who feel loved by their canine* companions that 'dogs don't love people, they love the place where they are fed'.

Although the human experience varies greatly according to our geographical and cultural origins, it seems proverbial wisdoms almost always ring true no matter where they originate.

GLOSSARY

scorn (n) – the feeling that someone or something is stupid and does not deserve respect

tie (n) – a strong connection or relationship between people, groups or nations

thorn (n) – a sharp point that grows on the stem of a plant

canine (adj) – relating to dogs

1 Read the article quickly and match a title to each section.

1 Family Features ◯
2 Best Mates ◯
3 True Love ◯
4 Worldly Wisdom ◯

2 Read the article again. For questions 1–10, choose from sections A–D. The sections may be chosen more than once.

In which section of the article does the writer

1 refer to certain proverbs as a justification for not achieving a personal goal? ◯
2 illustrate the truth of a proverb by citing a personal relationship? ◯
3 offer a scientific and a social explanation for a particular proverb? ◯
4 suggest a desirable quality in a platonic relationship? ◯
5 offer an explanation for pets' apparent devotion to their owners? ◯
6 explain the universal relevance of proverbs? ◯
7 suggest that food plays an important part in romantic attachment? ◯
8 comment on the importance of using proverbs in moderation? ◯
9 imply that he does not consider himself physically attractive? ◯
10 question the underlying assumption behind certain proverbs? ◯

3 Match the verbs in bold in the text to the definitions. Write the infinitive form without *to*.

a formal verb meaning to show a particular quality, emotion or ability *exhibit*

1 to locate or identify exactly _____
2 to come from a certain place or begin in a particular situation _____
3 to go beyond the usual limits of something _____
4 to make something continue in the same way as previously _____
5 to represent a quality, belief, feeling, etc. _____
6 to look similar to something else _____

4 Complete the sentences with the verbs from Exercise 3. Change the form if necessary.

The book, translated into over thirty languages, *transcends* cultural barriers to delight all kinds of readers.

1 This GPS system is particularly accurate and can _____ the user's location to within a few metres.
2 Victims of the illness usually _____ symptoms such as headaches, fever and insomnia.
3 Inexperienced runners often find it difficult to _____ their initial pace for the whole race.
4 The flower of this orchid closely _____ the insect that pollinates it.
5 The soaring eagle on the country's new flag _____ the newfound freedom of its people.
6 Svetlana's family _____ from Novosibirsk in Siberia, but she has never actually been there.

WORD STORE 1E | Word pairs

5 Complete the sentences with the correct forms of the words in brackets followed by a noun. The first letters are given.

Advertising should not *condone* (condone) the i*dea* that people are in some way inferior because they don't own the latest version of an expensive gadget.

1 Unfortunately, according to those who knew Jobs, Fassbender gives a largely _____ (accuracy) p_____ of the Apple founder in this biopic.
2 With its _____ (compel) n_____ and break-neck pace, it is impossible to put Jameson's new novel down.
3 As a proud father, Kenneth _____ (song) his daughter's p_____ to anyone who will listen.
4 Unlike the PM, we don't all come from a _____ (privilege) b_____ where wealth is taken for granted.
5 _____ (spoil) a_____ ! If you haven't watched the season finale yet, don't read this.
6 The documentary _____ (offering) an i_____ into the realities of family life in Spain.
7 This book offers the reader neither a _____ (captivate) s_____ , nor engaging characters.
8 This comic novel imagines a _____ (poor)-s_____ royal family living in a caravan behind a supermarket.

6 Look at the vocabulary in lesson 1.2 in the Student's Book. Choose the correct prepositions to complete the sentences.

1 Judges must examine every facet *in / with / of* the case before giving their verdict.
2 In our case, the supposed strong bond *over / between / through* siblings simply wasn't there.
3 Youngsters associated *with / on / in* gangs often drop out of school.
4 Faced *to / with / by* the prospect of his parents separating, Scott decided to keep calm.
5 Ross was envious *of / to / about* his parents' relationship with his sister. In their eyes, she could do no wrong.
6 As your best friend I promise to stand *by / to / for* you through thick and thin.

SHOW WHAT YOU KNOW

1 Complete the questions with the correct forms of the verbs from the box. The number of words you need to use in each question is given in brackets.

domesticate   make   ~~own~~   replace   wake

Have you ever *owned* a pet? (1)

1 Jill, if someone asked you what animal _____ a good pet, what would you say? (1)

2 My cat _____ forever _____ me up in the middle of the night for food. (2)

3 Did you know that as early as 3500 B.C. Egyptians _____ wild cats from Africa on a regular basis? (2)

4 _____ robot pets ever _____ real pets as man's best friends? (2)

2 ★ Choose the most suitable option to complete the sentences.

1 This summer the shelter on the outskirts of our town *will have taken care / will have been taking care* of injured animals for twenty-five years.

2 Since the release of the film *101 Dalmatians*, the number of people buying this breed of dog on impulse *has risen / has been rising* by almost 10 percent, according to the Animal Society's recent estimates.

3 Before retiring last month, Bertha revealed that she *had worked / had been working* with animals continuously for over fifty years and was now looking forward to spending more time with her own cat.

4 In June my little nephew, Freddie, *will have had / will have been having* his little green turtle for five years.

5 By 2015 the fad for exotic pets *had led / had been leading* to some tragic consequences.

3 ★★ Complete the dialogue with the correct forms of the verbs in brackets. Use no more than four words in each gap.

A: Ben, *have you read* (you/read) the story about those two missing dogs?

B: Not yet.

A: Well, they ¹_____ (be) missing for a week before a walker ²_____ (find) them in the woods.

B: What ³_____ (they/do) there?

A: Apparently, at some point one of them ⁴_____ (get) trapped in a hole and the other one ⁵_____ (stand) by its side since the unfortunate incident to keep it company and only ⁶_____ (leave) it for a few minutes each day to go for help. In the meantime the owners ⁷_____ (post) messages on Facebook like crazy. Finally, someone ⁸_____ (spot) that dog and it ⁹_____ (lead) them to its trapped friend.

B: Wow, what a story! Listen, Andy, ¹⁰_____ (you/read) this magazine much longer?

A: I think I ¹¹_____ (finish) by lunchtime. Why? ¹²_____ (you/think) of reading the story yourself?

4 ★★★ Complete the text with the correct forms of the verbs from the box.

accept   cause   ~~compete~~   get back
live   make   not change   pick   reveal

MY WORST FRIEND

For the past six months two hundred pets *have been competing* for the crown in the Naughtiest Pet Competition organised by Train Your Pet, a London-based company offering training courses for dogs.

The winner's owner, Sarah Cook, aged thirty, who is a sales assistant from Edinburgh, ¹_____ at the prize-giving ceremony that up till that moment her beloved pet ²_____ hundreds of pounds worth of damage to her garden. 'When I ³_____ from work one day and first saw the mess Buddy ⁴_____ , I was in shock! I actually thought he had dug up all the plants in my herb garden, but it turned out it was only the rosemary and lavender. The remains were scattered everywhere and I ⁵_____ them up for two hours that afternoon.' Mrs Cook claims that the incident ⁶_____ her affection for her German Shepherd.

While she ⁷_____ the prize, a dog training voucher worth £800, Miss Cook said: 'Next month Buddy ⁸_____ with me for eight years and although he has cost me much more than expected, he is my closest friend and I couldn't imagine living without him.'

SHOW WHAT YOU'VE LEARNT

5 Complete the second sentence so that it means the same as the first. Do not change the words in capitals. Use between four and six words in each gap.

How long ago did they buy her the guinea pig? **BOUGHT**
How long *is it since they bought* her the guinea pig?

1 Harry and Will's great friendship ended after twenty-five years with a quarrel over copyright ownership. **HAD**
Harry and Will _____ twenty-five years before they had a quarrel over copyright ownership.

2 My dog went missing in the middle of our daily walk in the forest. **WHILE**
My dog went missing _____ our daily walk in the forest.

3 Megan's best friend got his pet snake in May. **SINCE**
Megan's best friend _____ May.

4 Over the next month the charity near Londonderry will house about a hundred stray animals. **HOUSED**
By the end of next month the _____ about a hundred stray animals.

5 The guide dog began helping Tim four years ago. **FOR**
Next year the guide dog _____ five years.

6 After working with her for ten years, I was proud to be able to call Beth a loyal friend. **BEEN**
We _____ ten years and I was proud to be able to call Beth a loyal friend.

/6

1 Choose the correct answer A–C.

1 My brother said he __ to the party with his friends, but he came alone.
   A was going to come   B will be coming
   C was about to come
2 Jeff promised he __ us a postcard from Tenerife.
   A was sending   B is going to send
   C would send
3 Nina __ the wheel herself when she saw another car.
   A would change   B was going to change
   C was due to change

2 Complete the sentences with the words from the box. There are two extra words.

> about   due   intended   going
> planning   ~~point~~   supposed   verge

Jason was on the _point_ of giving up when he found a solution to his problems.

1 We've just found out by chance you're changing schools. When were you _____ on telling us this?
2 What was I _____ to do? Everything was happening so quickly – I couldn't just stand there doing nothing so I called the police.
3 At 9:45 the students were already standing in front of the school because the trip was _____ to start fifteen minutes later. And it did, at 10 sharp.
4 The band's gig was on the _____ of being cancelled but, luckily, a big group of people showed up to watch.
5 We got the text message about our flight just as we were sitting in the taxi and _____ to leave for the airport.

REMEMBER THIS

- We use **was/were to + infinitive** or **was/were due to + infinitive** to talk about things destined to happen, e.g. *The new teacher was (due) to start work in May.*
- We use these structures with **perfect infinitive** to show that a planned event didn't happen, e.g. *The committee was (due) to have announced the results at 9 p.m. but the conference was delayed.*

3 Correct the mistakes.

Philip was planning ~~on do~~ his homework before watching a film on DVD. _to_

1 We were getting anxious because it was time to leave and Tom hadn't arrived yet, but just as we were due to text him, we saw him crossing the street. _____
2 One of the actors taking part in the performance had emailed them the day before to let them know that they were to have met him right after the show. _____
3 Martha couldn't go to her friend's birthday party as she would go on holiday with her parents that day. _____
4 Sunday was the ultimate deadline, so the principal knew that by the end of that week the registration process for the new courses would be finishing. _____

4 Complete the article with the phrases from the box. There are two extra phrases.

> decided to invite   was calling   was due to happen
> was due to marry   was going to die
> was to have married   was on the verge of having
> ~~was supposed to be~~   were planning on spending
> were to go   would be   wouldn't be taking
> would have stayed   would stay   would take

WHO NEEDS A GROOM?

It _was supposed to be_ the wedding of her dreams, but one week before it [1]_____ , Jessica Hudson, a twenty seven year old banker from Nottingham, found out there [2]_____ no ceremony. 'Last Friday my fiancé announced that he [3]_____ everything off,' Ms Hudson told us. She [4]_____ her college sweetheart in Nottingham cathedral yesterday. Afterwards the newlyweds [5]_____ with their guests to the posh Four Seasons restaurant in the city centre. 'At first I believed I [6]_____ ,' said Ms Hudson. 'My mum thought I [7]_____ a nervous breakdown, but then she had an idea,' Ms Hudson explains. 'Instead of cancelling the restaurant and catering, the Hudson family [8]_____ the city's homeless and those in need to take part in the reception.' The would-be bride's mother Vera Hudson, aged fifty-five, told us: 'When I found out that the wedding [9]_____ place, I said I [10]_____ away something good from the whole experience.' On Monday she put up invitations on lamp-posts around the city centre and anxiously waited until Saturday.
Although her heartbroken daughter decided she [11]_____ at home, Mrs Hudson watched as her new guests arrived.
'I was really touched to see complete strangers: single people, families, the elderly, all coming up to me, thanking me for the invitation,' she said.
The newlyweds [12]_____ their honeymoon in Mexico. The trip is non-refundable so Mrs Hudson and her daughter chose to go on it together.

SHOW WHAT YOU'VE LEARNT

5 Complete the sentences with the words in brackets in the correct forms. Do not change the word order. Use between four and six words in each gap.

I thought you _would be able to come to_ (would/able/come) our performance last Friday.

1 You _____ (suppose/call/I) yesterday. Why didn't you?
2 Last time we met, Kelly _____ (go/take/she) driving test. How did it go?
3 My English teacher told me that I _____ (be/talk) the head of the school immediately about my inappropriate behaviour.
4 The company rep couldn't talk much longer because _____ (he/be/leave) Paris on business in a matter of hours.
5 Ted _____ (just/about/close) the window when he saw a man climbing over his neighbour's balcony.
6 Kim _____ (on/verge/drop) out of school this time last month.

/6

9

1 Complete the extract from the recording with the missing prepositions.

Extract from Student's Book recording 🔊 **1.8**

Jen: Last week, I took part in an interesting experiment and thought that maybe you'd like to hear *about* it. I got involved ¹_____ one of my psychology lecturers. She explained that her team was looking ²_____ the factors involved ³_____ forming first impressions and was looking ⁴_____ volunteers. Well, I was intrigued as that's the topic of my major assignment this semester. And I had some free time as I'd just finished an essay so I signed ⁵_____ . The experiment was simple. Basically we had to sit in front of a computer and watch a slideshow. The slides showed photos of people's faces accompanied ⁶_____ information about the person, for example, that they'd been convicted ⁷_____ a minor crime, or that they frequently did charity work. We had to study the photos for a couple of minutes and then try to recall them. I found this easy, as I'm good ⁸____ remembering faces.
We were then told to come back three days later. I chatted ⁹_____ the experiment ¹⁰_____ a friend and we both wondered what the next step would be.

2 Complete the phrasal verbs with *look* with the missing letters. Use the definitions to help you.

LOOK

f**o**r something – to try to find something

¹ __**nt**__ something – to examine the possibility of doing something

² __**n** something – to watch something as a spectator

³**t**__ somebody – to depend on someone for something

⁴ __**v**__**r** something – to inspect something in order to check its quality

⁵**d**__**wn** __**n** somebody – to consider somebody/something inferior

⁶**b**__**ck** __**n** something – to think about something in one's past

⁷**thr**__ __**gh** somebody – to ignore somebody by pretending not to see them

⁸**r**__ __**nd** something – to visit a place or building as a tourist or guest

⁹ __**p fr**__**m** something – to interrupt what you are doing to focus on something else

¹⁰ __**n** __**n** somebody – to pay a short visit to somebody

3 Choose the correct prepositions to complete the sentences.

1 James was so proud to score the winning goal with his family looking *on / over / round* that he ran round the whole pitch twice waving his arms in celebration.

2 If you need help with your dissertation, I wouldn't look *through / to / down on* Arthur. He's completely unreliable and his knowledge is sketchy at best.

3 I couldn't believe it when my own sister looked *into / through / to* me like I wasn't even there. I do hope she's not embarrassed by me.

4 Jules said he'd have a good look *from / into / over* my assignment before I hand it in.

5 Margaret's uncle Tim has offered to look *round / back on / into* her getting some experience at his accountancy firm next summer.

6 When I told my father I was thinking of leaving Poland to live in Spain for a year, he didn't even do so much as look *up from / down on / into* his newspaper.

7 Bella said they had some people looking *over / round / through* their house last week. She's worried that her parents are really going to sell up and move.

8 You really shouldn't look *back on / down on / on* your last relationship so much. It's self-defeating and it's definitely time you moved on.

9 Why don't we look in *at / on / to* Hannah on the way home? I hear she's not been feeling very well of late.

10 Just because Adam never went to university doesn't mean you should look down *at / by / on* him. He's actually one of the brightest people I know.

WORD STORE 1F | Collocations

4 Complete the sentences with the correct form of the words in the box. There are two extra words.

> break   crime (x2)   charitable   move
> react   splitting   upstand

Did you know that having a *criminal* record can exclude you from getting certain jobs?

1 When I saw Patrick coming, I have to admit my gut _____ was to hide. Call me a coward – I don't care.

2 One minute my sister was standing next to me and a _____ second later she was gone.

3 Marianne said she's seriously thinking of doing some _____ work. Something involving mistreated animals by all accounts.

4 Jono swears he's the perfect _____ citizen. Can you believe he's never paid a single bill late?!

5 Even being convicted of a minor _____ can result in a permanent black mark next to your name.

1 Match phrases 1–7 to descriptions A–G.

free and easy   H

1 aloof and distant
2 fun-loving and content
3 has got all the time in the world
4 introspective and thoughtful
5 pensive and melancholic
6 takes themself too seriously
7 uptight and anxious

A The guy opposite me in the waiting room was biting his nails and tapping his foot and he kept on letting out these massive sighs. Guess he must've been waiting for some test results or something.

B I can safely say I've never seen such a satisfied-looking dog. It adores tearing around the back garden fetching sticks and balls.

C Carly has looked really down lately. Sort of slow and unhappy like she hasn't slept and is preoccupied with some problem or other.

D The new girl doesn't say much, does she? I tried to get her chatting but she didn't seem interested.

E Half an hour late and we're all sat on the coach waiting to leave, and the driver is still standing, drinking coffee and chatting to his mate as if there's no rush.

F Since she did that 'modelling' for the local hairdresser, she thinks she's the next Cara Delevingne. It wasn't exactly the cover of *Vogue*, was it?

G He was sat alone at a corner table. I don't know what he was thinking about but now and again he would raise his eyebrows and smile to himself.

H He looks like he's escaped the corporate grind and left all his responsibilities far behind him.

2 Put the words in order to make phrases.

photo / saw / I / first / when / the <u>When I first saw the photo</u>, I thought she looked rather pensive.

1 about / way / there's / he's / something / the

_____
smiling that makes him look a bit dodgy.

2 may / she / said / having / be / that
_____ the kind of girl who always comes across as a bit melancholic.

3 be / can't / certain / I _____
but I think he's probably had plastic surgery.

4 to / as / looks / it / if / me _____
_____ she hasn't got a care in the world.

5 just / than / more / it's / his _____
hair; his clothing also suggests he's a geeky type.

6 wrong / again / then / could / I / be
She doesn't look my type of person. _____
_____ . We shouldn't judge too much by appearances.

3 Choose the correct words to complete the description.

OK, so my ¹*initial / closer* impression was that this is a man trying to comfort his friend because she's upset about something she's seen on social media, but now it looks to me ²*that / as* if he might be her teacher or tutor and she's having trouble understanding a difficult problem. ³*Mind you / Again*, I could be wrong. It's ⁴*hard / more* to say why the student seems so frustrated, but ⁵*judging / guessing* by her expression she's been trying to solve the problem for some time. ⁶*Feeling / Going* purely on appearance, I'd say she's in her early twenties, so I suppose this has to do with a university class that's challenging for her. By the look of her, I'd say this is more ⁷*than / of* just a trivial issue.

4 Complete the description of the photo below. The first letters are given.

Well, he looks like a ¹**b**_____ of a character, doesn't he? You know, the deep-thinking type who wants to be taken seriously. At first ²**g**_____ , he appears older than he actually is, I think – it probably has something to ³**d**_____ with his beard and glasses. I'm ⁴**a**_____ he's an artist or a musician because of his serious but 'cool' vibe. In fact, on closer ⁵**i**_____ , his unusual hat and large glasses make him seem like someone who likes to be noticed. I could be ⁶**w**_____ about him, of course – it wouldn't be the first time – but my ⁷**g**_____ feeling is that this guy would be interesting to spend time with. I'm only ⁸**g**_____ , but I think you could pick up a lot of new ideas by hanging out with him.

WRITING

1.7

A formal email/letter

1 Complete the advice. The first and last letters are given.

When writing to organisations or people you don't know, it is common to use formal style. To achieve a higher level of formality in your writing, consistently use ¹f_u_ll forms rather than contractions and opt for single verbs rather than ²p_____l verbs. In general, avoid ³c_____l phrases and where possible use formal quantifiers and ⁴q_____s. Do not use ⁵s_____n discourse markers such as *well* or *actually* but do aim to address the reader ⁶i_____y. Finally, always use ⁷c_____e sentences and never use question ⁸t_____s.

2 Match the examples to tips 1–8 in Exercise 1. Then rewrite them to make them more formal. Sometimes more than one answer is possible.

1   We couldn't be more pleased that you've agreed to assist us.   Tip ①
    We could not be more pleased that you have agreed to assist us.

2   Event will start 9 a.m. and finish 4 p.m.   Tip ○
    _____

3   We would be over the moon if you were able to join us for the day.   Tip ○
    _____

4   Well anyway, we hope you will actually consider our request.   Tip ○
    _____

5   We plan to go on holding these charity events as they bring in significant amounts of money.   Tip ○
    _____

6   Would you be available to take part on the date specified?   Tip ○
    _____

7   We understand you have been involved in such schemes in the past, haven't you?   Tip ○
    _____

8   As the waterslide is kind of expensive to hire, we were hoping you could offer us a bit of a discount.   Tip ○
    _____

3 Read the task and underline the information mentioned in points 1–3.

The Minister for Education in your country is planning to visit a school in your region to see a successful European student exchange programme in action and to speak to the students involved. You have been asked to write to the minister and invite him/her to visit your school, where a successful exchange programme has been in operation for a number of years. There are students from several European countries attending English classes and studying other subjects in English at your school. You should explain:

• why the minister should choose to visit your school and its exchange programme in particular.
• how both visiting and local students benefit from the exchange programme at your school.
• what the school and its students would gain from the minister's visit.

1   Who you should write to.
2   The purpose of the letter.
3   Three main points the letter should address.

4 Read the letter on page 13 and underline information relating to the three main points in the task in Exercise 3.

5 Complete the letter with the adjectives from the box.

current   diverse   entire   grateful   ideal
substantial   ~~thrilled~~   unique   willing

REMEMBER THIS

In formal writing, conditional sentences with the inverted pattern **should** (instead of *if*) **+ subject + verb** are common. Include examples in your letters and emails to increase the level of formality.

(**If you should be willing**) → **Should you** be willing to select our school, we would like to …

(**If you should wish**) → **Should you** wish to contribute, please contact us …

---

6 Match the formal words and expressions in bold from the letter to the less formal items below.

	signed up for	*enrolled in*
1	think about	_____
2	choose	_____
3	to give a few examples	_____
4	existed	_____
5	places	_____
6	because of	_____
7	parts	_____
8	for everyone	_____
9	so/therefore	_____
10	plan	_____
11	show that we appreciate you being there	_____

Dear Minister,

My name is Tiago Cruz and I am a student from Portugal currently **enrolled in** the European exchange programme at King Bartholomew's Secondary School, in Newcastle. My classmates and I were _thrilled_ to hear that you **intend** to visit our region and I am writing **on everyone's behalf** to explain why we feel our school would be the ¹_____ choice for your visit.

The exchange programme at King Bartholomew's is ²_____ in the region **due to** the ³_____ range of nationalities involved. Over the ten years it has **been in existence**, students from such ⁴_____ European **locations** as Slovenia, Latvia, Norway and Austria, **to name but a few**, have benefited from the opportunities presented by the programme. These opportunities include linguistic and social immersion, of course, but also regular events where exchange students present **aspects** of the culture of their countries to both local and visiting students. In this way, the ⁵_____ school benefits from the programme.

Should you be ⁶_____ to **select** our school, we would like to **honour your presence** on the day with a series of events including food-tasting, a concert and various sporting and cultural demonstrations organised and presented by our ⁷_____ exchange students. We would also be extremely ⁸_____ if you would **consider** giving us your thoughts on how we might recruit students from beyond Europe and **thus** work towards a truly international exchange in the future.

We look forward to your reply and hopefully to welcoming you at King Bartholomew's in the near future.

Yours faithfully,

Tiago Cruz

7 Read the writing task. Then follow the instructions below.

A former student of your school has just won a gold medal while representing your country in the Olympic Games. Write a letter asking them to visit the school and give a talk to the students to inspire them to lead healthier lifestyles and become more involved in sport. You should:

- congratulate the sportsperson on their achievement and mention how proud the school is.
- explain how the students would benefit from a visit and a talk given by this sportsperson.
- outline how the visit would be organised and what efforts would be made to welcome the sportsperson.

Before you start, follow steps 1–3 below.

1 Identify the key parts of the writing task to focus on what the letter needs to cover.
2 Brainstorm ideas:
   - What are you going to include in the first paragraph?
   - Which ideas might you include in the main body?
   - How are you going to conclude the letter?
3 Remember to use a formal style. Decide which words and phrases from this lesson and the lesson in the Student's Book could be useful for your letter.

SHOW THAT YOU'VE CHECKED

Finished? Always check your writing (especially in the exam!) Can you tick ✓everything on this list?

In my formal letter/email:

• I have used a formal salutation.	☐
• in the first paragraph, I have outlined my reasons for writing.	☐
• in the main body of the letter/email, I have addressed the three main points in the task.	☐
• I have achieved a formal style by:	☐
❯ using full forms rather than contractions.	☐
❯ choosing single verbs rather than phrasal verbs.	☐
❯ avoiding colloquial expressions and incomplete sentences.	☐
❯ avoiding question tags and spoken discourse markers.	☐
❯ addressing the reader indirectly.	☐
❯ using longer, more formal words and phrases.	☐
• I have used a wide range of adjectives to attract and hold the reader's attention.	☐
• I have used a formal sign-off.	☐
• I have checked my spelling.	☐
• I have checked my handwriting is neat enough for someone else to read.	☐

VOCABULARY

1 Complete the text with the correct forms of the words in brackets.

Given that in childhood we spend a high proportion of our free time with our siblings, one would expect that children learn to be <u>considerate</u> (consider) towards each other and that shared memories provide the basis for a good relationship.

However, few people would admit to having always loved and backed their sibling ¹_____ (condition). Children often accuse their parents of not being ²_____ (prejudice) as they are convinced their mother prefers their sister or brother to them. Many also spend their childhood competing for ³_____ (approve) from one or other of their parents.

Nevertheless, no matter how ⁴_____ (respect) you may have been towards one another as children, siblings often get on better as they become older. You could be thankful one day to have someone who is always there during times of ⁵_____ (hard).

/5

2 Complete the sentences with appropriate words. The first and last letters are given.

Lisa is a prolific writer and she always comes up with such **c**aptivatin**g** narratives.

1 Roger's colleagues hate his **f**_____**t** manner! Recently he told somebody how stupid Tina was to have quit working for a big international corporation.

2 Henry VIII's **i**_____**g** stature must have terrified many of his subjects.

3 My younger brother, Alex, was left alone for a **s**_____**t** second but he still managed to break a vase.

4 My dad tends not to rely on his first impressions but his **g**_____**t** reaction to Jen's words was that she was a liar.

5 Mia's classmate is unbelievably **o**_____**e** – he never changes his mind.

/5

3 Match sentence beginnings 1–5 with their endings a–e.

After talking to somebody for only a few minutes, it's rather impossible to give an accurate [f]

1 I was flabbergasted that Betty didn't bat [ ]
2 My grandma keeps singing [ ]
3 Helen has often taken advantage of her privileged [ ]
4 Lots of people have recently fled from the poverty- [ ]
5 This company will never condone [ ]

a her neighbour's praises even though he's been mean to her.
b stricken countryside and settled down in towns.
c using illegal computer programs.
d an eyelid when I told her I was leaving the country.
e background as a manager.
f portrayal of a person's skills and abilities.

/5

GRAMMAR

4 Complete the text with the correct forms of the verbs in brackets.

Living in the middle of nowhere and being an only child meant a fairly lonely life. That was why by the time I turned six, I <u>had invented</u> (invent) an imaginary friend, Gina. As my parents recall it, we ¹_____ (constantly/argue), mainly about toys and games. But both Gina and I hated the mountains and once, on our way there, my parents heard me say to Gina: 'You see, nobody cares what we think, they ²_____ (pack) us in the car again to go hiking, but don't you worry, this time next month we ³_____ (hitchhike) to the seaside.' As I grew older, Gina became a distant memory.

However, my former classmate's own daughter, aged four, has such a friend too. She's not worried because she believes by the time Lizzy goes to school, the girl ⁴_____ (make) enough real friends to replace the imaginary one. She even sees it as a good thing, as now kids ⁵_____ (spend) more and more time staring at screens, and not developing their social skills.

/5

5 Complete the sentences with the words in brackets in the correct forms. Do not change the word order. Use between four and six words in each gap.

Dad, <u>will you be using the car</u> (you/use/car) later today?

1 The students had to wait for the guest speaker for over half an hour because he _____ (not/tell) about the change in the timetable.

2 The roadworks here are usually not too chaotic, but this time _____ (they/cause/lot) traffic problems and people are late for work.

3 Because the kids _____ (rehearse/they/role) before the school play since morning, the room was still darkened when we came in.

4 Next week Tim and his builders _____ (redecorate/we/house) for nearly eight months and it's still far from being ready.

5 I don't believe it! Are you saying that Joshua _____ (manipulate/data) all this time?

/5

6 Complete the text with one word in each gap. The first letters are given.

My older sister Charlotte often repeated that after her university course, she **w**ould work in a large design and building company. We knew she was ¹**g**_____ to do everything she could to make her dream come true.

Soon she found what she believed was her dream job. She was ²**d**_____ to start in two weeks and just could not wait to be part of the team. To her great disappointment, it turned out that she landed herself a job in a rather unfriendly office where her colleagues were ³**s**_____ to be concentrated on their projects only. Charlotte suffered terribly and was really on the ⁴**v**_____ of quitting her career altogether when my dad suggested she should try working in a family-run company. He was right! When she reflects on it now, she often says that she was ⁵**a**_____ to give up doing what she always had dreamt of, but thankfully was pointed in the right direction.

/5

Total /30

7 Choose the correct answer A, B, C or D.

The value of friends

A recent newspaper report claims that something which many successful people have in common is their ability to <u>C</u> people easily.

The explanation given is that if people **1**____ in others, they are more likely to get an **2**____ into human nature, which is an important **3**____ of success in the workplace, whether one is managing staff or working in a team.

4____ these advantages, being popular is not without its dangers, apparently. If this report is to be believed, it is better to have fewer than ten **5**____ friends. More friends than this can drain you of energy if you have to listen to their problems and try to resolve them. Plus one or more of these friends will almost certainly **6**____ at some point and lose your trust.

Some people believe that, as texting and emailing replaces meeting face to face, it is becoming increasingly difficult to form a strong **7**____ with others. In the future it may become more of a rarity to enjoy an **8**____ friendship that would last for a lifetime.

	A associate	B coincide
	Ⓒ befriend	D redress
1	A confide	B reveal
	C confess	D depend
2	A appreciation	B awareness
	C insight	D intuition
3	A side	B angle
	C facet	D point
4	A Instead of	B Apart from
	C On account of	D In spite of
5	A familiar	B close
	C immediate	D accessible
6	A let you down	B put you off
	C take you back	D turn you round
7	A relation	B contact
	C commitment	D bond
8	A upstanding	B undying
	C impetuous	D ambiguous

/8

8 Complete the text with one word in each gap.

An unusual pet

One day, after Jacques Damier had <u>been</u> volunteering in Namibia for around a month, he literally fell over a tiny lion cub on the verge of death. His split second decision to adopt the cub and nurse him back to health was something that **1**_____ change his life dramatically.

Three years on, Jacques still **2**_____ his parental responsibilities very seriously. He has invested a lot of time and energy **3**_____ the upbringing of his cub – regularly accompanying him on walks of nine hours or more through the parks. Sasha, **4**_____ he named the cub, has now grown much bigger and heavier than his 'father,' which means that Jacques must now take care that their play-fighting doesn't get out of hand. **5**_____ this risk, Jacques says that he has never felt scared.

However, Jacques is aware that by this time next year he will **6**_____ left Namibia and returned to his home in France. The task he faces now is to get Sasha used to living independently in the wild.

/6

9 Complete the second sentence so that it means the same as the first. Do not change the words in capitals. Use between three and six words in each gap.

The traffic was so heavy that we missed the beginning of the concert. **BY**
Due to heavy traffic, the concert <u>had already begun/ started by the time</u> we got there.

1 My friend was just about to get on the train when I phoned her with the news. **POINT**
My friend was just _____ on the train when I phoned her with the news.

2 Whenever I look at Tom, I have strong memories of my father. **REMINDS**
Each time I look at Tom, he _____ of my father.

3 My mother was determined not to let me go to the festival. **FOOT**
My mother _____ about my going to the festival.

4 The student only started participating in lessons about three months ago. **PART**
The student _____ in lessons for about three months.

5 I attempted to phone my aunt several times but nobody answered. **TOUCH**
Despite several _____ my aunt, nobody answered the phone.

6 I will be supported by my friend when times get difficult. **STAND**
My friend _____ difficult times.

/6

Total /20

15

2 Learning for life

VOCABULARY

2.1

Studying and exams • synonyms
• phrasal verbs • phrases to
describe being relaxed/stressed

SHOW WHAT YOU KNOW

1 Choose the correct forms to complete the headlines.

Report reveals widespread ¹*plagiarise /
plagiarism* at prestigious university.

Celebrity ²*unrecognisable / recognises*
after plastic surgery nightmare.

Minister for Education claims he has no ³*memorable /
memory* of alleged incident at five-star hotel.

Education supplement: Top tips on
effective ⁴*revision / revise.*

Penguins ⁵*familiarise / familiar* themselves
with new enclosure at city zoo.

**2 Complete the sentences with the correct forms of the
words in brackets.**

To say that all teenagers are awkward and moody is an
unfair *generalisation*. (general)

1 Jenny is so _____ (organise) she is unable to find her
to-do list and can't even find a pen to write a new one.

2 Jeremy found a website where he could order _____
(personal) trainers with his name on.

3 I realise my fear of birds is completely _____
(rational) but I simply can't get over it.

4 Emma, assuming you did your homework, could you
_____ (summary) chapter two for the class, please?

5 The brain's capacity to process _____ (vision)
information is remarkable.

WORD STORE 2A | Synonyms – exaggerated language

**3 Complete the dialogue with the words and phrases
from the box. There is one extra item.**

> all the books under the sun   flit   ~~frazzled~~
> hammer in   looming   manic   minefield
> plastered   regurgitate   swimming in

K: You look tired, Maddie.

M: Well, Kit, you sure know how to make a girl feel good.
But you're right. I'm so *frazzled* I can hardly keep my
eyes open.

K: Well, yeah, you do look pretty awful. How come?

M: Awful? Er, well, life is just ¹_____ at the moment.
I seem to ²_____ between school, hockey team
and babysitting and never actually have a spare moment.

K: You should slow down a bit.

M: Well, I'd love to.

K: Then again, with the exams ³_____ next month
I suppose that's going to be difficult. Soon you'll be
⁴_____ textbooks and your bedroom walls will be
⁵_____ with revision notes. And you're going to
be in the school play, aren't you? That's a ⁶_____ .
All those lines to learn and ⁷_____ on the night –
all that pressure to perform.

M: Well, thanks Kit. If you were trying to ⁸_____ just
how stressful my life is, then you've done a perfect job.

WORD STORE 2B | Phrasal verbs

**4 Complete the sentences with the correct forms of the
words from the box.**

> come   face   kick   lead   notch   set   ~~top~~

Sorry I didn't call you. I forgot to *top* up my phone
credit before I left home.

1 Congratulations to last week's winning contestant who
returns to today's show after _____ up an incredible
score of 131 points.

2 I know it hurts now, but soon the painkillers will
_____ in and you'll feel much better.

3 Experts hope that analysis of the flight recorder will
reveal more about the events _____ up to the crash.

4 When _____ with such a wide choice of handsets, it
can be difficult to choose the best phone for your needs.

5 This is a very rare school textbook from around 1830.
How did you _____ by it?

6 I need four volunteers to help _____ out the desks
in the gym hall for tomorrow's exam.

WORD STORE 2C | EXTRA Phrasal verbs with *up*

5 Complete the television announcements. The first letters are given.

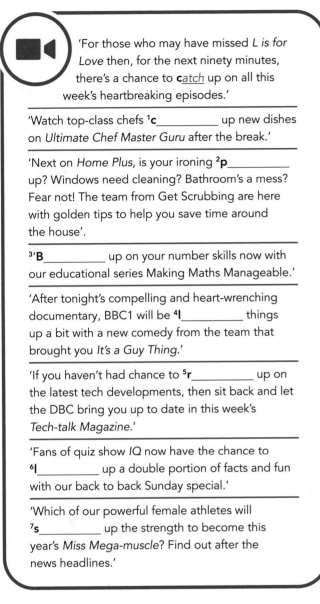

'For those who may have missed *L is for Love* then, for the next ninety minutes, there's a chance to **c**atch up on all this week's heartbreaking episodes.'

'Watch top-class chefs ¹**c**_____ up new dishes on *Ultimate Chef Master Guru* after the break.'

'Next on *Home Plus*, is your ironing ²**p**_____ up? Windows need cleaning? Bathroom's a mess? Fear not! The team from Get Scrubbing are here with golden tips to help you save time around the house'.

³'**B**_____ up on your number skills now with our educational series *Making Maths Manageable*.'

'After tonight's compelling and heart-wrenching documentary, BBC1 will be ⁴**l**_____ things up a bit with a new comedy from the team that brought you *It's a Guy Thing*.'

'If you haven't had chance to ⁵**r**_____ up on the latest tech developments, then sit back and let the DBC bring you up to date in this week's *Tech-talk Magazine*.'

'Fans of quiz show *IQ* now have the chance to ⁶**l**_____ up a double portion of facts and fun with our back to back Sunday special.'

'Which of our powerful female athletes will ⁷**s**_____ up the strength to become this year's *Miss Mega-muscle*? Find out after the news headlines.'

SHOW WHAT YOU'VE LEARNT

7 Choose the correct answer A–D.

1 You can have all the money __ the sun but that doesn't guarantee happiness.
   A through   B under   C of   D by

2 The country is __ in debt and the government can no longer afford to provide free education for all.
   A hammering   B looming   C swimming   D falling

3 Generally speaking, it takes around forty-eight hours for antibiotics to kick __ and for patients to begin feeling better.
   A in   B off   C up   D over

4 Faced __ overwhelming evidence, the defendant finally admitted his guilt.
   A in   B against   C to   D with

5 If you hadn't let your work __ up, you'd be free to enjoy the weekend.
   A read   B notch   C soak   D pile

6 I've read up __ revision methods and I think I know the best way to go about it.
   A on   B with   C in   D to

7 Melanie was a bundle of __ on the day of her driving test.
   A nervous   B nerves   C nervousness   D nervy

8 The first part of the online music production course was so complicated that Simon felt totally out of his __ .
   A depth   B grip   C calm   D mind

9 Selena always gets butterflies in her __ before a visit to the dentist.
   A stride   B stomach   C brain   D legs

10 As her tutor had predicted, Mia sailed __ her piano exam and got a distinction.
   A over   B round   C through   D past

/10

WORD STORE 2D | Relaxed/stressed

6 Complete the diary entries. The number of letters in each missing word is in brackets.

12 June

Exam tomorrow ☹ Can't sleep. I'm a *bundle* (6) of nerves and I've got ¹_____ (11) in my stomach. Trying to remember what I revised but my ²_____ (4) just keeps going blank. Feel completely ³_____ (3) of my depth. Why didn't I study more? I'll never get to sleep. My ⁴_____ (5) is pounding and I'm a ⁵_____ (7) wreck.

13 June

Feel like a ⁶_____ (6) has been lifted. Managed to ⁷_____ (3) a grip last night and finally get some sleep. Breakfast – Dad told me to keep things in ⁸_____ (11) and just do my best. Reminded me that I had sailed ⁹_____ (7) the mock exams. Got there, opened the paper, saw the essay questions and a ¹⁰_____ (4) came over me. Knew what to write – remembered everything. Just as Dad said – took it in my ¹¹_____ (6). Such a relief ☺

—BIRD BRAINS—

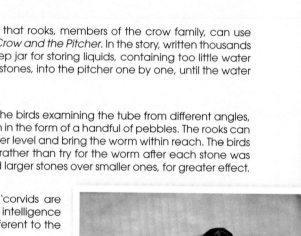

In many cultures, crows have long been thought of in rather negative terms. These large black birds have been regarded as bad omens: dangerous and impure, bringers of bad luck or death. Even in the 21st century, for many the sight of their dark shapes and large, hammering beaks is as unwelcome as their ear-splitting cries, and few of us view them as more than unattractive pests*.

1 ___

One example of such adaptability has been observed among communities of crows living in the urban environment of a Japanese city. There, they have found a way of reaching food that is normally inaccessible. The birds wait patiently at traffic lights for the oncoming traffic to stop at the red light for pedestrians. Next, they hop in front of the waiting cars and place walnuts gathered from nearby trees on the surface of the road. Just before the lights turn green, they fly away and, when the traffic begins to move again, the cars roll over the hard-shelled nuts and crack them open. Finally, once pedestrians regain the right of way, the crows return and collect their delicious snacks.

2 ___

In another revealing demonstration of avian* intelligence, researchers found that rooks, members of the crow family, can use stones to raise the level of water in a container – just like the bird in the tale *The Crow and the Pitcher*. In the story, written thousands of years ago by the Ethiopian slave Aesop, a thirsty crow finds a pitcher, a deep jar for storing liquids, containing too little water for its beak to reach. The bird solves the problem by throwing pebbles, or small stones, into the pitcher one by one, until the water level rises high enough for it to drink.

3 ___

To start with, the tasty treat was out of reach. Videos of the experiments show the birds examining the tube from different angles, appearing to think the problem through. Then the researchers provide a solution in the form of a handful of pebbles. The rooks can be seen picking up the stones and dropping them into the tube to raise the water level and bring the worm within reach. The birds appeared to estimate* how many pebbles were needed from the start and, rather than try for the worm after each stone was dropped, they waited until the water level was high enough. They also selected larger stones over smaller ones, for greater effect.

4 ___

Rooks and crows both belong to the corvid family. According to Mr Bird, 'corvids are exceptionally intelligent, and in many ways rival* the great apes in their physical intelligence and ability to solve problems. This is remarkable considering their brain is so different to the great apes.'

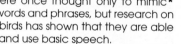

5 ___

'Wild tool use appears to be dependent on motivation,' said Mr Bird. 'Rooks do not use tools in the wild because they do not need to, not because they can't. They have access to other food that can be acquired without using tools.'

Corvids are by no means the only intelligent species of bird. Parrots too demonstrate amazing brain power. Known for their ability to 'talk', parrots were once thought only to mimic* human words and phrases, but research on captive birds has shown that they are able to learn and use basic speech.

6 ___

After tutoring, Alex, as he is known, has learned a vocabulary of over 100 words, which he appears to be able to use meaningfully. Even more impressively, Alex uses phrases such as 'no', 'come here' and 'I want X' in order to engage in what appears to be genuine communication.

The old saying 'bird brain', traditionally used to insult someone who does something stupid, would, it seems, perhaps be better used as a compliment for those who show intelligence.

GLOSSARY

pest (n) – a small animal or insect that destroys crops or food supplies, or annoys other animals or humans in some way

avian (adj) – relating to birds

estimate (v) – to try to judge the value, size, cost, etc. of something without measuring it exactly

rival (v) – to be as good or important as something else

mimic (v) – to copy the behaviour, look or sound of something else

dexterity (n) – skill and speed doing something with a part of your body; in humans, usually the hands

captivity (n) – when an animal is kept in a cage or zoo rather than living in the wild

1 Read the article without looking at the missing paragraphs. What is the main purpose of the text?

1 To highlight the intelligence of a particular species of bird. ⬜

2 To compare avian intelligence to that of other species of animals. ⬜

3 To report a new development in research into avian intelligence. ⬜

2 Read the article again. Complete gaps 1–6 with paragraphs A–G. There is one extra paragraph.

A A similar challenge faced the rooks studied by the appropriately named Cambridge University zoologist, Christopher Bird. In a series of tests, the four rooks named Cook, Fry, Connelly and Monroe were offered a worm floating on the surface of water in a vertical tube.

B Through the work of a professor at the University of Arizona, one such bird is now believed to have the intelligence and emotional make-up of a three- or four-year-old child.

C Crows have been engaged in this remarkable behaviour since the 1990s and have since been observed doing something very similar in California. There, it is thought to be an adaptation of a method used for opening clams. The crows were known to drop the tightly sealed shellfish from a height onto rocks on the seashore in order to crack them and get at the nutritious flesh hidden inside.

D Corvids can tell human beings apart by their voices and recognise people who have fed them. They are also alarmed by the sound of those they have never seen before. Most intriguingly, the scientists speculate that they may be clever enough to cooperate with other bird species.

E Research, however, suggests that the common view of the crow may be wrong. They might not be beautiful, but they are amongst the most intelligent creatures on the planet. For example, they have demonstrated a remarkable ability to change their behaviour according to their surroundings in order to make the most of opportunities presented.

F The only animal believed to have done a similar fluid-mechanics task is the orangutang, said Mr Bird, a PhD student. The orangutangs were reported to have brought a peanut within reach by spitting water into a tube.

G One member of this incredibly bright species, the Caledonian crow, is renowned for its ability to make twig and leaf tools in the wild and adapt them with great dexterity* to extract grubs and caterpillars. However, such behaviour has never been seen in rooks living outside captivity*.

3 Complete the sentences with words from the text. Use the definitions in brackets to help you.

The town of Niagara is _renowned_ **for** (famous for) its huge waterfalls.

1 Giraffes have long necks so they can _____ **at** (gain access to) leaves and fruit in the tallest trees.

2 _____ **the most of** (use something to the best advantage) your visit because you might never have the opportunity to come here again.

3 The book that Kristy needed was **out of** _____ (not near enough to be touched) on the top shelf, so she climbed on Daniel's shoulders.

4 One of the most important road signs to learn before you drive in a foreign country is the one that shows who has **the right of** _____ (the legal right to go before another car or pedestrian, e.g. at a junction).

5 The only way to **tell** the twins _____ (tell the difference between two similar things) is to hear them speak. Lewis has a slightly higher voice than Tyler.

WORD STORE 2E | Collocations

4 Complete the sentences with the correct forms of the words from the box.

> dismiss   meet   ~~monotonous~~
> reserve   stand   think

I need to break the _monotony_ of revision somehow, even if it's just a quick walk with the dog.

1 My parents _____ the idea of a gap year before university saying I should get my qualifications first.

2 I have _____ about doing the science project with Michael because, to be frank, he's lazy.

3 Please give your degree some serious _____ as choosing the wrong subject is the fastest route to failure.

4 I had to stay up all night to do it, but in the end I _____ the deadline for submission of my final assignment.

5 Katarina has always _____ out from the crowd with her unusual height and that frizzy hair.

GRAMMAR

2.3 Speculating

SHOW WHAT YOU KNOW

1 Decide what functions are expressed by the modal verbs in the sentences below.

We could learn together at the weekend. [e]

1 At that time the students of his class could get punished for whatever silly thing they did. ☐

2 Martin and his classmates have been notified that their A-level results may come any time. ☐

3 Sadly, my flatmates and I might not meet again. ☐

4 Back then Rachel could recite very long poems without referring to her poetry book even once. ☐

5 I know I must try harder if I want to get a good job. ☐

6 The lights in Maggie's room are still on. She must be revising for tomorrow's test. ☐

a past possibility
b past ability
c obligation
d speculation
e future possibility

2 ★ Write sentences from the prompts.

probably / difficult / the / will / more / real / be / exam
The real exam will probably be more difficult.

1 scored / harder / work / term / those / next / poorly / definitely / will / much / who

_____

2 slackers / won't / there / the / be / probably

_____

3 well / by / the / might / closed / supermarket / be / now

_____

REMEMBER THIS

We can use **will** to express certainty or confidence about:

• the present: *Don't text her now – she'll be busy revising for tomorrow's test.*

• the past: *Don't text her now – she'll have gone to bed.*

3 ★★ Choose the option that explains each sentence.

1 Most students will have memorised the wordlist by now.
A I'm sure most students have already memorised it.
B It's possible most students have already memorised it.
C Perhaps most students have already memorised it.

2 You could have told me you weren't taking the test.
A Thank you for telling me you weren't taking it.
B Why didn't you tell me you weren't taking it?
C It was possible for you to tell me you weren't taking it.

3 Ben may have annoyed the boss by asking that question.
A Perhaps Ben annoyed the boss by asking it.
B I'm sure Ben annoyed the boss by asking it.
C It's impossible Ben annoyed the boss by asking it.

4 We remember our Maths teacher could be sarcastic.
A We remember he was always sarcastic.
B We remember that he can be sarcastic at times.
C We remember that he was sometimes sarcastic.

4 ★★★ Complete the sentences with the correct form of the verbs in brackets and *may, might, could* or *must*. Sometimes more than one answer is possible.

Ian: Rob, soon we'll have to decide which university we want to apply to. Does MOOCs ring a bell?

Rob: Yeah, I think I *may have come* (come) across an article on them some time ago. You ¹_____ (refer) to Massive Open Online Courses, right?

Ian: Exactly. So what do you think of them?

Rob: Well, the idea of studying for a degree at the most prestigious universities around the world without leaving your home ²_____ (sound) exciting, but I look at university education as a social experience. Besides, there are many concepts which require real-time discussions with fellow students and tutors.

Ian: You ³_____ (be) right, but full-time university fees are really high these days and you ⁴_____ (admit) that the financial benefits of distance learning are quite appealing. Online courses aren't so expensive, many of them are in fact free, plus you ⁵_____ (have) the opportunity to juggle studies with part-time work.

Rob: I can see you ⁶_____ (give) this distance learning idea a lot of thought.

Ian: I'm just beginning, actually. I will definitely do some research before making my final decision.

SHOW WHAT YOU'VE LEARNT

5 Complete the second sentence so that it means the same as the first. Do not change the words in capitals. Use between three and four words in each gap.

It's impossible the cleaner saw Matt yesterday. **CAN'T**
The cleaner *can't have seen* Matt yesterday.

1 It's possible they had been copying answers from each other long before the examiner realised it. **MIGHT**
They _____ answers from each other long before the examiner realised it.

2 I'm convinced that the students themselves removed some of the podcasts from the webpage. **MUST**
Some of the podcasts _____ from the webpage by the students themselves.

3 His English stands no chance of improving because he doesn't do any homework. **DEFINITELY**
His English _____ if he doesn't do any homework.

4 I'm sure you've realised by now that Monica is not very good with modern technology. **WILL**
You _____ by now that Monica is not very good with modern technology.

5 Perhaps you don't know it, but Ned came top of the class in Geography last year. **MIGHT**
You _____ it, but Ned came top of the class in Geography last year.

6 It's possible we're talking to the next Einstein. **COULD**
We _____ to the next Einstein.

/6

1 Complete the pairs of sentences with *a/an* or Ø (no article).

   a If students want to have <u>a</u> good education, they need to be highly motivated.

   b In many countries <u>Ø</u> education is free only until the age of sixteen.

1 a Freedom of speech and ___ belief are fundamental human rights.

   b There is ___ strong belief that every child should have access to education.

2 a Marcia was widely considered as ___ outstanding beauty.

   b Do you know the saying that ___ beauty is in the eye of the beholder?

3 a We all have to suffer___ pain at one time or another.

   b Stop being such ___ pain and start helping us instead!

4 a Last year I did a lot of voluntary work for ___ charity called Sightsavers.

   b Most people think it's a good idea to give money to ___ charity.

REMEMBER THIS

- Some nouns are not preceded by *a/an*, however, putting an adjective in front of them requires using *a/an*:
  have **breakfast** but *have **a big breakfast***
- Putting an adjective in front of a number also requires using *a/an*: **2 percent** but ***a mere 2 percent***
- Most uncountable nouns can never be preceded by *a/an* even if you put an adjective in front of them:
  *All our students have **easy access** to the Internet.*

2 Complete the sentences with *a/an* or Ø.

   My parents are sending me to England because they want me to speak <u>Ø</u> excellent English.

1 In some countries ___ shocking 60 percent of people are illiterate.

2 We're having such ___ beautiful weather right now that it's hard to believe it's autumn.

3 Every student will get ___ packed lunch before the trip.

4 Gina's grandparents enjoy ___ very good health.

5 Most of my classmates do ___ voluntary work.

6 If you sign up for our course now, you'll save ___ amazing 30 percent off the regular price.

3 Find six more mistakes in the text, two in each paragraph, by adding or crossing out *a/an*.

> Most English schools introduced ^a ban on mobile phones during classes a long time ago and now they have conclusive proof that they were right. According to the latest study, not giving students an access to their phones translates into extra week's education in a school year. Researchers also observed that test results in such schools went up by over 6 percent.
>
> The research was conducted at several British schools before and after bans were introduced. 'While it's true that a modern technology used in the classroom engages students and improves a performance, there are also potential obstacles, as it could lead to distractions,' the researchers say.
>
> The findings will definitely provide powerful arguments in the ongoing debate about pupils' access to mobile phones. In the UK, staggering 90 percent of teenagers own smartphone; in the US, almost 75 percent.

4 Read some comments on the article in Exercise 3 and choose the best option.

> Why ban phones? Teachers should teach our children phone etiquette instead. They should be taught from ¹Ø / *a* / *an* early age about responsible use.
>
> My phone means everything to me. It's ²Ø / *a* / *an* tremendous help and I wouldn't want to part with it.
>
> Yeah, it helps you play games or check your Facebook account. Thanks for ³Ø / *a* / *an* great laugh!
>
> What I meant was ⁴Ø / *a* / *an* mobile technology offers useful educational apps that students can use during classes, like graphic display calculators.
>
> Using mobile apps for checking everything is ⁵Ø / *a* / *an* example of overdependence on technology.
>
> Phones are ⁶Ø / *a* / *an* terrible distraction. I wish my school would ban them.

SHOW WHAT YOU'VE LEARNT

5 Complete the gaps with one word wherever necessary.

   None of us seemed to be in a <u>hurry</u> to see the exam results. We were walking there rather hesitatingly.

1 It was _____ great sacrifice for Ruby to give up her place on the football team.

2 They say that money is not the key to _____ happiness.

3 Jon will need to do a lot of preparation before the presentation because he hasn't done anything like it in a _____ .

4 It was _____ real pleasure to train your puppy to fetch a ball, he's really intelligent.

5 Chris was on his way to the airport when all of a _____ he received an urgent call to go back to work.

6 Having ___ good laugh with friends always cheers me up and makes me feel great.

/6

LISTENING LANGUAGE PRACTICE

Verb forms • phrases

1 Complete the conversation between the man and woman and with the correct form of the verbs in brackets.

Extract from Student's Book recording 🔊 **1.20**

W: *Have you ever consulted* (ever/consult) an online video for help with ¹_____ (fix) something? You know, one of these 'how-to' videos? I'm a bit wary of ⑦ them – I'm not sure I trust the advice fully.

M: Yeah, I ²_____ (use) them. When I ³_____ (have) issues with ◯ software, anything like that, I go on these specialist sites or forums. They've got detailed advice and videos there. Like the other day I had a problem ⁴_____ (install) an update for my computer and I went online immediately, and this guy sorted out the whole problem for me in no time ◯!

W: So it's professionals sponsored by tech companies? Otherwise, it seems odd.

M: Not always. It's often ordinary people who ⁵_____ (have) similar problems … or people who are technical geniuses and want to share their expertise. First you type in your problem, and then loads of videos pop up with people who are a lot more technical than you ◯ or me. What they say is really easy ⁶_____ (follow) because they're like tutorials that show you how to fix problems step by step ◯. You ⁷_____ (think) that the videos posted by experts might be too complicated or too difficult for the average person to follow, but they're not.

W: Right. And I guess it doesn't really matter if the videos are a bit amateurish – I mean they're free – and you can always re-watch them if you ⁸_____ (not/get) it the first time ◯. When real experts choose ⁹_____ (share) their knowledge with everyone for free, it's really helpful.

M: Absolutely – it's good ¹⁰_____ (know) help is just a few clicks away ◯.

2 Match definitions 1–6 to the underlined phrases in the text.

1 to do something very quickly
2 to encounter problems with somebody/something
3 to do something methodically by going from one stage to the next
4 to be quickly accessible via a computer program
5 to have greater knowledge regarding technology than somebody else
6 to understand something without needing for it to be repeated
7 to worry about something because it might cause a problem

3 Complete the sentences using the correct form of the underlined phrases from Exercise 1.

James, can you help Dan install this new application? You know that you *are a lot more technical than* he is and his whinging is driving me up the wall.

1 This homework is doing my head in. I've never been good at Maths, but I'm _____ this Algebra problem like you wouldn't believe.
2 Wow! You finished that assignment _____ . Nobody else has even started it yet and you've already handed it in!
3 Don't you just love the Internet? Everything you ever need to know is only _____ . Take Wikipedia®, for example. An absolute fount of knowledge.
4 Tomas admits to not being very good at DIY but when he takes it slowly and does things _____ , he can do a decent enough job.
5 Tamara tends to be _____ doing or saying something wrong when she meets new people. First impressions are really important to her.
6 Alright, alright! You don't have to keep going on about it – I _____ .

WORD STORE 2F | Phrases

4 Complete the sentences with suitable words to make phrases. The first letters are given.

It looks like Marty and Jake will both have to re-sit the test. You could say they're in the same **b**oat now – however unenviable that might be.

1 Ah. There's nothing like a breath of fresh air to help clear your **h**_____ . I reckon I'll be ready to start work again soon.
2 If only you'd told me that you were worried about the school gala. I had no idea that we shared the same **c**_____ and that we could have supported each other.
3 Why doesn't Tom use his **i**_____ for a change and do something without asking first? He might find it very liberating and he'll probably get more recognition for his work.
4 A lot of blogs are all about people wanting to share their **e**_____ in a particular field. There's a great one about 1960's underground rock! It's really informative.
5 Wayne finds it hard to keep his **c**_____ when Barbara talks to him. Everything goes out of his head and he ends up blathering like an idiot. It's quite funny really.
6 You know what? I feel a real **a**_____ with the new History teacher. He seems really cool and it turns out he's a big fan of The Flaming Lips like I am.
7 If you'd only use your **c**_____ sense you'd be able to work it out in no time. It's really not that complicated you know.

1 Put the words in order to make phrases used for giving supporting examples.

my / case / in _In my case_
1 obvious / is / an / example _____
2 is / notable / most / of / the / one / examples _____
_____
3 of / example / a / it's / prime _____
4 a / illustration / is / useful _____
5 mind / the / example / comes / is / graphic / the / that / most / to _____
_____
6 classic / is / a / case _____

2 Complete the sentences with appropriate prepositions or Ø if no preposition is necessary. Sometimes more than one answer is possible.

A case _in_ point is the intriguing story _of_ Laika, one _of_ the first animals ever _to_ orbit _Ø_ the Earth.
1 Consider ____ how many towels are washed unnecessarily each day by the world's hotels and the perceived importance ____ comfort and luxury over environmental responsibility becomes clear.
2 Think ____ last year's Tweed Run cycle event, ____ which around 1,000 people took part, including many cyclists ____ abroad.
3 Take ____ the success of reality shows such ____ _The Great British Bake Off._ It is tempting to conclude that the average TV viewer is not seeking ____ intellectual stimulation ____ part of their primetime entertainment.
4 Look ____ how many people are involved ____ the Park Run movement around the world. Clearly, the popularity of running as a method of keeping fit is ____ the rise.

3 Match arguments 1–5 with supporting examples A–E. Then complete the supporting examples with the words from the box.

case   consider   ~~extreme~~   illustration
instance   look

Parents around the world are trying to ensure their children's future success by signing them up for so many extra activities and classes that they no longer have time to be kids! ⬜ F
1 According to various accounts, the boy became so exhausted mentally and physically that he eventually had to be hospitalised. ⬜
2 In fact, psychologists say that boredom is a key part of growing up. ⬜
3 Children who are kept constantly occupied may never discover their true talents. ⬜
4 Of course it is also true that exposing kids to a variety of activities allows them to discover their real interests. ⬜
5 As with most things in life, finding the right balance is key. ⬜

A For _____ , when children are left with nothing specific to do, they often find or invent an activity to alleviate the boredom, and this helps them to understand their own natural interests.
B _____ at the many cases of childhood over-occupation around you, and then find ways to allow more freedom, and even a bit of boredom, into your own child's life.
C A _____ in point is a friend's child, who was kept constantly busy until the family went on an off-the-grid holiday, when the boy picked up a pencil and paper and revealed an amazing talent for drawing.
D Whether or not this case is factual, it certainly serves as a striking _____ of a real problem, which is that many children are not being allowed to experience the pleasure of inventing their own activities and playing on their own.
E _____ that a child who is never given a music lesson or a dance class may never know they have a real talent, but exposing them to too many activities can lead to confusion and frustration.
F One of the most _extreme_ examples of this is the son of an ambitious family who ended up suffering from severe exhaustion as a result of being occupied fourteen hours per day.

4 Correct the mistakes.

Typical example of such misunderstandings occurred during a teacher-student meeting held last week.
A typical example
1 The most striking example comes to mind is that of Lance Armstrong, who finally admitted using performance enhancing drugs during all seven of his Tour de France victories. _____
2 A useful illustrator is given as part of the discussion on p. 17. _____
3 A case on point is the huge investment that has gone into the city's new concert hall. _____
4 For instant, a UK report from 2012 found that only 27.2 percent of the population aged from sixteen to seventy-four had a degree or equivalent, or higher. _____
5 Consider about how many times people share articles on social media sites without actually having read more than the headline. _____
6 Look to the wonderful work done by specialist animal welfare groups such as the Albino Squirrel Preservation Society. _____

1 **Read the article and choose the most suitable title.**

1 Use it or lose it: how to educate a gifted child. ☐

2 Teaching everyone: how to divide attention in the classroom. ☐

3 Special needs: why gifted pupils need attention too. ☐

Schools and colleges around the world quite rightly devote a great deal of time and effort to helping children and young adults who are deemed to have special educational needs. Nine times out of ten, this effort is focused on those who are struggling to reach a minimum standard and therefore falling behind with their education. However, is it not the case that if you are gifted, you also have distinct educational requirements and just as much right to individual attention in the classroom? Let's consider both sides of the debate.

'The cream always rises to the top', they say, and so it is often assumed that bright children will **excel** at whatever they take on. Don't consistently good grades at school amount to proof of the satisfactory academic progress of those who achieve them? If so, then surely teachers are justified in their decision to concentrate on those who are **lagging** behind. Add to this the claim that labelling certain children as 'gifted' sends an unproductive message to those who don't **measure** up, and there is really nothing left to debate, is there?

Not so fast. Gifted children need attention too! Exceptional pupils should face rigorous challenges at school if they are to remain engaged and realise their full **potential**. Without such challenges to rise to, these pupils soon become bored and then distracted. It is a tall order for them to **thrive** if they are constantly asked to twiddle their thumbs while their peers catch up. According to US researchers, by not stretching the brightest of their students 'teachers could be **squandering** the talent of the most creative minds of a generation'.

Clearly, there is a case for attending more closely to the needs of top pupils, as well as helping those who are struggling to make the **grade**. There will always be competition for teachers' attention and schools' resources and, in my opinion, every child is entitled to their fair share during the time they spend at school or college.

2 **Read the article again and underline examples of the following items:**

- Three direct questions
- A direct address to the reader
- A quotation
- An exclamation

3 **Put the words in order to make phrases for addressing the reader directly in an introduction.**

details / the / at / look

Let's *look at the details*.

1 arguments / examine / the

Let's _____

2 debate / sides / the / both / of / consider

Let's _____

3 the / points / against / clarify / for / and / main

Let's _____

4 the / issue / angles / from / explore / opposing

Let's _____

5 main / view / of / the / elaborate / on / points

Let's _____

4 **Complete the first part of each quotation with the words from the box. Then match the sentence halves.**

according   observed   pointed
quote   ~~said~~   words

It was Benjamin Franklin who *said* 'an investment in knowledge   Ⓕ

1 In the _____ of Oscar Wilde, 'education is an admirable thing, but it is well to remember from time to time   ☐

2 'It is ordinary people who have to be educated'. _____ out Jean-Jacques Rousseau, 'and their education alone can serve   ☐

3 As Arthur Schopenhauer famously _____ 'truth acquired by thinking of our own   ☐

4 To _____ Alexander Pope, 'men must be taught as if you taught them not   ☐

5 _____ to Anatole France, 'the whole art of teaching is   ☐

A only the art of awakening the natural curiosity of young minds'.

B is like a natural limb, it alone really belongs to us'.

C that nothing that is worth knowing can be taught'.

D and things unknown proposed as things forgot'.

E as a pattern for the education of their fellows'.

F always pays the best interest'.

REMEMBER THIS

Avoid overusing exclamations as this can make your writing seem trivial or immature. Also, if you use too many, they will lose their significance. Consider including a maximum of two in your piece of writing.

---

5 Complete the adverts with the words in bold from the article.

> Do you _excel_ at video games?
> Ever thought about becoming a professional gamer?
> Call us to find out more.

> Private science tuition.
> Helping secondary students
> to make the ¹_____
> since 1998.

> Realise your
> full ²_____ with
> our world-renowned
> life-coaching
> programme.

> Are you
> ³_____ behind in English?
> Study privately with a qualified
> native speaker.
> Call 77 804 904.

> **Could you pass your
> child's final exams?**
> Find out how you
> ⁴_____ up against
> the country's brightest
> secondary students.

> **Gifted
> footballer?**
> Avoid ⁵_____ your
> talent. Contact Ellis
> and Marks football
> agents to find out
> how we can help
> you reach your goal.

> Ensure your cacti
> ⁶_____
> with our specially
> formulated food mix.

6 Complete the definitions. Use the article to help you if necessary.

If someone t_widdles_ **their thumbs**, they do nothing while they wait for something to happen.
1 If something happens or is true **nine times out of t_____** , it is almost always the case.
2 If someone is **s_____ to do something**, they are finding it very difficult.
3 If someone **e_____ at something**, they are extremely good at it.
4 **Not so f_____** is an informal way of saying 'wait or think before you do or believe something'.
5 If something is **a t_____ order**, it is an unreasonable or difficult demand.
6 If you **devote supreme e_____ to something**, you try your very hardest at it.

7 Complete the sentences with the correct forms of the phrases in bold from Exercise 6.

Nine times out of ten everything is fine, but just occasionally something unexpected happens.
1 The lifeguards are _____ to reach the stranded couple because the waters are so rough.
2 Collins, last year's world snooker champion, really does _____ at these long corner pocket shots.
3 _____ , buddy! Remember who is in charge here. I'll tell you when we are ready.
4 To win, Simons needs to cover the last ten kilometres in less than thirty minutes. A _____ by anyone's standards.
5 Gordon is late and Sarah has been sitting _____ for nearly an hour.
6 These climbers _____ to their preparations as they know how many lives Everest has claimed in the past.

8 Read the writing task. Then follow the instructions below.

Should physically disabled students be encouraged to study alongside able-bodied students rather than in schools that are specially adapted to their needs?

Write an article for a student website giving arguments for and against and stating your view.
1 Brainstorm arguments for and against.
2 Select the best ideas and make a plan for your article.
3 Add an interesting title.
4 Write your article and remember to use a fairly informal style.

Finished? Always check your writing (especially in the exam!) Can you tick ✓ everything on this list?

In my article:
- I have begun with an eye-catching title. ☐
- I have addressed the reader directly. ☐
- I have asked direct questions. ☐
- I have included at least one quotation. ☐
- I have included an exclamation. ☐
- I have used a fairly informal style. ☐
- I have explored both sides of the issue. ☐
- I have given my own opinion. ☐
- I have checked my spelling. ☐
- I have checked my handwriting is neat enough for someone else to read. ☐

VOCABULARY

1 **Choose the correct words to complete the sentences.**

Having begun university studies at sixteen, Agnes definitely *gets* / *stands* / *walks* out from the crowd.

1 The aftermath of the principal's decision to expel the troublesome students turned out to be quite a/an *minefield* / *composure* / *expertise*.

2 The news about bankruptcy came as a blow so Fiona needed time to clear her *thoughts* / *brain* / *head*.

3 Dan's determination to revise Maths shows he's worried about his *rambling* / *summoning* / *looming* exams.

4 With so few pupils the village school was *venturing* / *teetering* / *mustering* on the edge of closure.

5 Matthew and Libby are going bungee jumping next weekend provided neither gets cold *feet* / *hands* / *legs*.

/5

2 **Match the words from the two boxes to make expressions. Then complete the sentences with the expressions.**

A
> bundle of   common   in the same
> leap into   meet   ~~under~~

B
> boat   nerves   sense   the deadline
> ~~the sun~~   the unknown

Don't you find Zoe tiring? She seems to have an opinion on every subject <u>under the sun</u>.

1 For Harry, going to do voluntary work in Africa was a _____ , as he'd never done it, or even been to Africa.

2 When the parents finally found their daughter, she was a _____ , trembling and crying over her lost dog.

3 Oh, come on. Use some _____ when connecting the printer to the computer. It's not rocket science.

4 There's no point in working until late tonight. You're not going to _____ anyway.

5 Sorry Jen, I can't lend you any money. We're _____ now because I've also lost my job.

/5

3 **Complete the sentences with the appropriate verbs in the correct form. The first letters are given.**

I need to **t**<u>op</u> up my phone before I can call you again.

1 Thanks to Roy's outstanding performance we've **n**_____ up another victory!

2 You'd better **b**_____ up on your Italian before you go to Sicily, as few people speak very fluent English there.

3 It's unbelievably difficult to listen to Luke giving a talk because he just **f**_____ between subjects and rarely sticks to the point.

4 Although the new vinyl shop has an impressive collection of LPs, anything by my favourite composer is hard to **c**_____ by.

5 Can you **s**_____ out the aim of the questionnaire more clearly so that everybody understands why it's necessary to conduct it?

/5

GRAMMAR

4 **Choose the correct options. Sometimes two answers are possible.**

1 You *must* / *will* / *can* be feeling tired after such a long day in the lab. Sit down and I'll make you a cup of tea.

2 Are Tom and Jim sure they've got the right address of the boarding house? They *couldn't* / *mustn't* / *can't* have written it correctly. We're too far from the school.

3 The supervisor definitely *can't* / *may not* / *won't* tolerate any smartphones during the exam.

4 Mr Jenking is often working in the garden now. I guess he *might* / *could* / *can* have lost his job in the bank.

5 A: Why isn't Sue here yet? B: I don't know, but her train *will* / *may* / *must* be running late today.

/5

5 **Complete the sentences with the correct form of the words in brackets. Do not change the word order. Use between three and four words in each gap.**

The owner of the mansion <u>may be staying</u> (may/stay) there now so we can only look around the gardens.

1 Don't worry. I'm sure Sandra _____ (must/borrow) your laptop. She needed one this morning.

2 If you ask me, making Jeff rewrite his assignment definitely _____ (not/help/improve) his handwriting. It's pointless.

3 Since James is so poor at playing the piano, he _____ (can/be/learn) it for very long.

4 Earlier this morning we _____ (might/come) across some snakes in the grass but they were unlikely to be poisonous.

5 It's most probable that class 3B is in the gym. But they _____ (could/prepare) for the final exams in the library right now.

/5

6 **Read the following text and correct five more mistakes with the use of articles. The numbers in brackets indicate the number of mistakes in each paragraph.**

What education is needed nowadays?

It is said that schools should provide students with^{an} excellent education to help them in their career and life choices. But is that really the case?

School leavers emphasise how few subjects offer a practical experience and not just theory. They also feel that their timetables are filled with incredible number of uninspiring subjects rarely allowing them to have good night's sleep. It is obvious that students need a help, but does being given a lot of homework work? (4)

Both educationalists and students claim that there should be less focus on tests and more attention paid to a progress that students make in the course of education. (1)

/5

Total   /30

7 Choose the correct answer A, B, C or D.

Why I prefer teaching myself

Although I'm only sixteen, I'm perfectly capable of *B* my own decisions. I also love doing things on my own and rarely get ¹__ by difficulties I come across. I can be a case in ²__ for all of those who would prefer to go for home schooling rather than formal education.

Everyone has their preferred learning style and I learn more efficiently when I choose what I do rather than when I'm faced ³__ tasks imposed on me. I go at my own speed, taking everything in my ⁴__ . I don't feel isolated, because the goals I set with the help of others are chosen with my ultimate ambitions in mind – like what qualifications I might need for the career I want. Another important point is revision and preparation for exams. I avoid just ⁵__ for exams. The key point is having a good understanding of the subject. If I don't understand something, I look it up – there's no shortage of options around.

I often do more than strictly necessary because I'm self-motivated, and I rarely get frazzled because I can ⁶__ things in perspective. I'm deeply convinced that thinking for myself is worth my ⁷__ because I tend to sail through exams thanks to it and my increased knowledge. Obviously, some might think it's easier to stay in their comfort ⁸__ and be spoon-fed, but the extra effort involved in self-teaching has given me a will to succeed.

	A doing	Ⓑ making
	C getting	D finding
1	A put off	B let down
	C cooked up	D written off
2	A idea	B mind
	C point	D example
3	A to	B with
	C at	D through
4	A stride	B way
	C footstep	D pace
5	A hammering	B regurgitating
	C breezing	D venturing
6	A maintain	B hold
	C carry	D keep
7	A period	B time
	C while	D moment
8	A area	B section
	C place	D zone

/8

---

8 Complete the text with the correct forms of the words in brackets.

Preparing for college

You're all set to make your first *application* (apply) for college - how should you go about it? Unsurprisingly, there are several ¹_____ (administration) hurdles to get over.

Firstly, producing an impressive CV - there should be no irrelevant ²_____ (ramble)! Simply construct a clear summary of your qualifications so far, and remember to ³_____ (rational) your reasons for wanting to do the course. Check if the university website provides any useful ⁴_____ (guide) on how to do this.

Use your ⁵_____ (initiate) - try contacting students already at the college to find out what the course is like. You might get some valuable tips from people who've been through the experience.

Finally, present yourself as a ⁶_____ (depend) and serious person - colleges take students who will maximise their time, and if you're confident, you'll go far.

/6

---

9 Complete the second sentence so that it means the same as the first. Do not change the words in capitals. Use between three and six words in each gap.

It's possible the teacher has already left to prepare the speech. **MAY**
The teacher *may have already left* to prepare the speech.

1 Knowing good Spanish can be useful when travelling around Mexico. **HAVING**
When travelling around Mexico _____ Spanish can be useful.

2 I'm sure he didn't rush doing it and that's why the presentation was so brilliant. **HURRY**
He can't _____ and that's why the presentation was so brilliant.

3 The number of our students rose sharply thanks to some new departments having been opened. **ROOF**
Thanks to some new departments having been opened, the number of our students _____ .

4 Sarah isn't here yet. Maybe the train is running slightly late. **MIGHT**
The train _____ bit late and that's why Sarah isn't here yet.

5 I would have been able to help you there and then if you had asked me to explain the matter. **COULD**
It's a pity you didn't ask me to explain the matter as _____ there and then.

6 I'm sure you have never felt as tired in your life as after such a long and exhausting exam. **FEELING**
You must _____ after such a long and exhausting exam than ever before.

/6

Total /20

27

3 Let's eat

VOCABULARY

3.1

Cooking and eating • food
• kitchen/dining sounds
• collocations

SHOW WHAT YOU KNOW

1 Complete the definitions. The first letters are given.

An oily fish flavoured with smoke. s*moked* m*ackerel*

1 A popular type of shellfish of which there are many varieties. c_____

2 A commonly eaten fish with white flesh (when cooked). c_____

3 A large bird, often white, and capable of swimming, flying and walking on land. g_____

4 The meat of a young cow, in contrast to beef from older cows. v_____

5 The meat of a game animal, usually referring to deer. v_____

6 Originally from Asia, long, thin strips of dough boiled and often eaten with soup. n_____

7 A spice made from dried, powdered chillies. p_____

8 A spice derived from the central part of the crocus flower, known for its expense and its ability to colour food a rich golden yellow. s_____

9 A bright green herb with pointed leaves, common in Europe and often chopped and sprinkled over finished dishes. p_____

10 A green herb with rounded leaves and a perfumed taste, common in Asian cuisine. c_____

11 The organ (a pair) responsible for removing waste products from the body. k_____

12 The organ (single) that regulates the composition of the blood. l_____

13 A collective term for seafood items that have a shell. s_____

WORD STORE 3A | Food

2 Label the pictures. The first letters are given.

b*eetroot*
1 l_____   3 a_____   6 o_____
2 l_____   4 n_____   7 o_____
          5 b_____   8 c_____

---

3 Put the words in the correct groups. Use a dictionary if necessary.

~~acidic~~ bland chewy flaky glutinous honeyed pasty perfumed pungent slimy

Smells/flavours: *acidic* e.g. vinegar, [1]_____ e.g. boiled rice, [2]_____ e.g. baklava, [3]_____ e.g. coriander, [4]_____ e.g. mustard

Textures: [5]_____ e.g. toffee, [6]_____ e.g. fresh croissants, [7]_____ e.g. uncooked dough, [8]_____ e.g. overripe bananas, [9]_____ e.g. oysters

WORD STORE 3B | Kitchen/dining sounds

4 Complete the extract from a memoir with the sound words from the box. There is one extra word.

~~buzzy~~ chink clink crunch hum pop sizzle

Chapter 1 – The Early Years

My love of food and ultimately my career as a restaurateur has its roots in my childhood. My parents ran a small but successful Italian eatery named 'Capaldi's' in the East Village district of Manhattan, New York. We lived in a miniscule apartment perched over the business and our single shared bedroom nestled directly above the bustling dining room. Oddly, it is the myriad sounds rather than the smells which remain with me most vividly some fifty years later. I recall lying alone in bed listening to the *buzzy* conversations of the evening's gathered diners. This comforting constant was punctuated by the rhythmic [1]_____ of cutlery as the customers made their way through the many courses placed before them by Miguel, our long-serving Mexican waiter, and the clear [2]_____ of glass on glass, when the water jugs were being filled, then swiftly distributed, table by table. The sudden [3]_____ of steaks hitting the grill in the kitchen would rouse me when I had almost drifted away and then, during the summer months, the [4]_____ of the ancient air-conditioning system would draw me irresistibly back into the arms of Morpheus. Winters were marked by the [5]_____ of the customers' footsteps on the icy pavement outside as they arrived red-cheeked and empty-bellied, or left rounded and glowing with well-fed satisfaction.

WORD STORE 3C | Collocations

5 Complete the extracts from restaurant reviews. The first letters are given.

'The coffee was served dangerously hot, my **p**_et_ hate. Taste ruined, tongue burnt.'

. . . .

'An overly formal dining room leaves customers sitting stiffly, obliged to talk in **¹h**_____ tones.'

. . . .

'The flexible kitchen staff seem happy to cater for all manner of **²d**_____ requirements.'

. . . .

'Fine **³d**_____ does not get any finer than at this world-class establishment'.

. . . .

'As I enter, a hungry-looking woman seated at a foodless table in the far corner is having a **⁴f**_____ in front of a spotty and sorrowful looking young waiter. Not a good start.'

. . . .

'No **⁵s**_____ tablecloths or silver cutlery here. Instead, a no-nonsense dining room knocking out delicious staples at a reasonable price.'

WORD STORE 3D | **EXTRA** Collocations

6 Complete the recipe with the correct forms of the words from the box.

> clove drop knob lump ~~pinch~~
> sip spoonful sprig stick

```
● ● ●
```

simplestudentrecipes.com

Spicy Veggie Spaghetti (for two)

Add a _pinch_ of salt to boiling water and submerge around 100g of pasta. Chop one or two **¹**_____ of garlic, a large red chilli and a **²**_____ of celery and fry gently for two minutes with a **³**_____ of butter. Chop and add a **⁴**_____ of parsley, a small **⁵**_____ of honey, and a **⁶**_____ of lemon or lime juice and stir continuously over a low heat. Add a can of chopped tomatoes and continue stirring. Remove the pasta from the boiling water after seven minutes and mix with the sauce. Grate a **⁷**_____ of Parmesan (or similar) cheese and sprinkle over the pasta and sauce to serve.

---

7 Complete each pair of sentences with the same answer A–C.

1 a Most of the patients in this particular ward are here because they have __ all their lives.
 b I like fish, but not really strong types such as __ sardines.
 A smoked   B worried   C burned

2 a Our most popular genre of downloads is definitely __ .
 b The balloon went __ and frightened the little dog half to death.
 A bang   B rock   C pop

3 a It is my firm belief that an exotic animal such as a pangolin should never be kept as a __ .
 b One of my __ hates is watching myself in videos.
 A child   B pet   C toy

4 a I'm naturally suspicious of people who'd rather chew on a __ of celery than enjoy an ice cream.
 b The undercover police officer chose simple black clothes in order not to __ out.
 A stand   B bit   C stick

5 a Many students who __ out of university tend to end up in menial jobs.
 b A __ or two of lemon juice will stop the chopped apple from going brown.
 A drop   B squeeze   C lump

8 Choose the correct answer A–C.

1 I'm really not a fan of the __ taste of things like Turkish delight or marzipan.
 A perfumed   B glutinous   C hushed

2 If raw meat smells bad and has a __ surface, then it should be disposed of immediately.
 A fine   B slimy   C buzzy

3 Soggy granola is just no good. It should have a satisfying __ to it.
 A clink   B crunch   C sizzle

4 Those with special dietary __ beware. This is not a country that caters well for fussy eaters.
 A requirements B tones   C fits

5 Avoid draining the whole bottle in one go. Instead __ the water slowly over a couple of minutes.
 A sip   B drop   C spoon

/10

29

Sweet, sweet sugar: the bitter truth

Initiated by an American doctor named Robert Lustig, there have recently been calls in the US for laws to restrict sugar as if it were an addictive substance. The more sceptical among us might question whether this isn't just another case of food-related scaremongering*. Obviously, there are products on the market that are toxic, costly for everyone, extremely addictive and that have been proven to cause an array* of diseases. But sugar? OK, we know it rots your teeth if you don't clean them after eating it. Sure, if you eat too much sugar, you put on weight. Admittedly, it can alter your metabolism, so when you eat sugar, you crave* more. And, well, yes there is the 'sugar-high' that anyone who has spent time around 'kids on cola' will certainly acknowledge. But, honestly, sugar is harmless enough, isn't it? Or perhaps it's more accurate to say that most of us are happier not to acknowledge the bitter truth about our apparently sweet friend.

Dr. Lustig is a professor of clinical paediatrics at the University of California, San Francisco, and a respected expert on childhood obesity. His area of expertise is human metabolism – how our bodies break down food and turn it into energy. Some of his lectures are on YouTube and several of them have gone viral. This middle-aged, grey-haired, slightly stocky* doctor, who wears a suit and tie and talks about the metabolism of fructose, has, in fact, had more than two million hits.

According to Lustig, there are now 30 percent more obese people in the world than undernourished people. It is tempting to think that this obesity epidemic and its associated metabolic problems are the result of people eating too much fat, but this, Lustig argues, is not the case. In the seventies, he explains, the medical establishment believed it had discovered a link between dietary fat and heart attacks, and in response, the entire Western world went low-fat. The problem, Lustig tells us, is that 'when you take the fat out, it tastes like cardboard'. The food industry had to do something. What did they do? They added high-fructose corn syrup and sucrose, or in other words sugar. So about thirty-five years ago, the developed world turned its diet upside-down. We stripped away fat, and added sugar; 'invisible' sugar sneaked into everything from steak pie to smoked salmon.

What happens in your liver when you eat too much of this 'invisible' sugar? Well, there's a complicated chain of events, but the upshot* is something called 'leptin resistance'. Leptin is a hormone produced to tell us when we're full. When we eat too much fructose, leptin is sometimes switched off and we lose the ability to tell when we've consumed as much as we need. Interestingly, Lustig offers a hypothesis as to why this happens. He says it might be because there was a time of year, harvest time, when ancestral humans had an abundance* of fruit, followed by a time of year, winter, when they had almost nothing. In crude terms, we evolved to stuff our faces at harvest time. Fructose makes us want to eat more; it tells us not to be satisfied. That was good, then, when food was scarce*, but it's a disaster now, when it's everywhere. Lustig believes this is why so many people are 'off-the-scale' fat these days.

So should sugar consumption be regulated by law? For a substance to be controlled, it must have four characteristics. It must have the potential to be abused, it must be toxic, it must be widespread and it must cause problems for people other than those who abuse it. Sugar, it seems, ticks all these boxes and that's why Lustig thinks it should be ranked alongside alcohol and tobacco. Sugar is everywhere. It's addictive, it's toxic, and, in the end, we all have to pay for it, if not with our health, then at least in our taxes.

There is, of course, a big barrier to any effort to regulate sugar consumption, namely the food industry. 'The food industry,' Lustig believes, 'has no impetus* to change. They're making money hand over fist.' Some industries still have collective influence that somehow allows them to continue selling products that have been proven to kill both users and non-users. Well, it seems there's something even bigger to worry about: 'Big Sugar'. The obesity expert Philip James puts it this way: 'The sugar industry has learnt the tricks of the tobacco industry. Confuse the public. Produce experts who disagree. Try to dilute the message.' Lustig has been accused of irresponsible fear mongering.

What if Lustig is right? What if sugar is the culprit*? What can we do? We can start the long, laborious* process of coming out of denial. We're doing it with other commonly-known addictive substances, and it's working. We made them expensive, harder to buy, and harder to advertise. We kept them away from children. We made them taboo. Can we do this with sugar? Well, perhaps, but sugar is a tougher opponent than other substances. They are only found in a few products, whereas sugar is everywhere. It's in the sausages, it's in the beans and it's in the toast. To radically cut our intake would be to radically shake up the economy.

GLOSSARY

scaremongering/fear mongering (n) = the practice of deliberately making people worried or nervous, especially in order to get an advantage

array (n) = a large or impressive group of people or things

crave (v) = if you crave something (e.g. fame, a cigarette, attention), you desire it strongly

stocky (adj) = short and muscular

the upshot (of sth) (n) = the final result of a situation

abundance (n) = a large quantity of something

scarce (adj) = not widely available; hard to find

impetus (n) = an influence that makes something happen

culprit (n) = the thing or person to blame

laborious (adj) = requiring a lot of time and effort

1 Look quickly through the article. Does the author:

1 criticise the opinions expressed by Dr Robert Lustig? ⬭
2 remain neutral? ⬭
3 agree with Dr Lustig's points of view? ⬭

2 Read the article again. For questions 1–6, choose the best answer A–D.

1 In paragraph 1, what does the writer suggest about the issue of sugar consumption?
   A Consumption of sugar is more harmful than consumption of other addictive substances.
   B Many people are in denial about the negative effects of sugar consumption.
   C Its harmful effects have been exaggerated by the media.
   D The benefits of consuming sugar outweigh the drawbacks.

2 The writer describes Lustig's appearance to emphasise
   A his belief that Lustig is an ordinary person.
   B his claim that Lustig's YouTube lectures are dull.
   C his admiration for Lustig's success.
   D his surprise at Lustig's popularity on YouTube.

3 According to Lustig, extra sugar is added to low-fat foods to
   A increase calories.
   B reduce heart attack risk.
   C improve flavour.
   D tackle diabetes.

4 In paragraph 4 Lustig says he believes a common cause of obesity these days is
   A the insufficient amount of fruit in the modern diet.
   B the overproduction of a certain hormone in the liver.
   C the easy availability of food in modern society.
   D the overconsumption of certain foods at specific times of the year.

5 Phillip James suggests that the sugar industry
   A has copied the tactics of the tobacco industry.
   B is less of a problem than the tobacco industry.
   C has lied about the harmful nature of its products.
   D acknowledges some of Lustig's claims.

6 What is the writer's opinion on the chances of a reduction in sugar consumption in the future?
   A The only challenge lies in changing consumer behaviour.
   B If the consumption of other addictive substances can be reduced, then so can sugar consumption.
   C It would be economically impossible to reduce it enough to be effective.
   D Even acknowledgement of its harmful effects may not lead to a reduction in consumption.

3 Complete the sentences with the words from the box. Use the information in brackets and use the text to help you if necessary.

> ~~acknowledge~~ boxes denial
> face fist upside

Eventually, Pamela had to _acknowledge_ **the bitter truth** (admit that something unpleasant is true) and admitted she was never going to make it as an actress.

1 A few individuals are **making money hand over** _____ (earning large amounts of money) while the rest of the population live in poverty.

2 It's time Shelly **came out of** _____ (stopped lying to herself) and admitted she was partially responsible for the end of the relationship with her fiancé.

3 A new head teacher was appointed and within two months she had **turned the school** _____ **down** (radically changed everything).

4 The trouble with 'all-you-can-eat' places is that I always end up **stuffing my** _____ (overeating) and then regretting it.

5 Being cheap, economical and easy to drive, Ron's new car **ticked all the** _____ (met all the desired criteria).

WORD STORE 3E | Collocations

4 Match the words from boxes A and B to make collocations. Then complete the sentences with the collocations.

> A ~~keen~~ learning processed sensitive
> simple special uncontrollable (x2)

> B binges cravings difficulties ~~sense~~
> food pleasures questions treat

I used to have a _keen sense_ of smell, but after years of smoking it's useless now.

1 Increasing evidence suggests too much _____ in your diet is detrimental to your long-term health.

2 My sister has _____ associated with autism and attends a special school equipped to help her.

3 Occasionally I get these _____ for chocolate and I have to rush out and buy some.

4 People should indulge in _____ such as a walk or a chat with friends, which cost nothing but mean a lot.

5 He was totally creepy and kept asking me all these _____ about my weight or my family.

6 Every so often I have some _____ when I eat everything sweet in the house and then feel guilty.

7 As a _____ to celebrate finishing their exams, Mick is taking his best friends to a posh restaurant.

SHOW WHAT YOU KNOW

1 Match beginnings 1–3 with endings a–c.

Tina is one of those people who constantly cook   (d)

1 In some restaurants, when a waiter sees that
your water glass is almost empty, he will top   ⬜

2 If you consume more calories than you need,
usually they soon pile   ⬜

3 Since embarking on a new diet plan two weeks
ago, my friend has notched   ⬜

a it up without even asking you.

b up her first significant win: a loss of one kilo.

c up and so-called *love handles* appear around your waist.

d up perfect excuses for not going to the gym.

2 ★ Put the words in brackets in the correct places in the sentences.

My nephew, Tommy, loves sugar. He can't do without. (it)
it / V

1 Pete's friends like low-carb snacks so he always makes
a point of stocking up on before every party. (them)

2 After dining at that seaside restaurant the other day,
my friend and I went off completely. (fish)

3 The police officers let off with just a warning and said
she'd be in trouble if she went near the town hall with
a similar banner again. (her)

3 ★ Complete the descriptions with the phrasal verbs from the box.

call for   cheer up   ~~catch up with~~
go down   pays off   plan ahead

⬤⬤◯

MUST-HAVE FOOD APPS

As more and more people are using smartphones as
their cooking resource of choice, we're here to help you
catch up with some of the best apps.

MyFitnessPal for iOS and Android, free

With this calorie-counting app your weight will definitely
¹_____ . It stores over twelve million foods in
its database. The recipe counter makes it really easy to
track the nutrition in homemade meals and helps you
²_____ for things you should avoid. The
exercise tracker lets users see the amount of calories
they've burnt.

Jamie's Recipes for iOS, free

If food preparation makes you frustrated, you will
³_____ when using this Jamie Oliver app – it
doesn't ⁴_____ a master chef. It will inspire you
through fifteen recipes and how-to videos every week.
Subscribers can download seasonal collections and
money-saving meals. Getting this app really ⁵_____ .

4 ★ ★ Correct the mistakes in word order. There is one correct sentence.

When you have to meet a deadline, do you often snack
fast food on to keep you going? *snack on fast food*

1 The takeaway restaurant in the high street was closed
by the town authorities down. _____

2 Do you frequently wolf down whatever you find,
without thinking about what you're eating? _____

3 Do you always plan to eat just what's on your plate or
do you often end having seconds up? _____

4 Do you really think that any self-proclaimed nutritionist
knows how to sort efficiently out our problems? _____

5 ★ ★ ★ Replace the words in bold with phrasal verbs. Use the correct forms of the verbs from the box and add suitable prepositions.

drop   look   ~~put~~   sink   stand

Susan just keeps **postponing** going to the gym.
putting off

1 The authorities are **investigating** the benefits of
withdrawing fizzy drinks from school canteens. _____

2 We **visited** our grandparents on our way home. _____

3 The doctor stopped for a moment to let his words **be
fully understood**. _____

4 You know perfectly well that these animals aren't
capable of **defending** themselves. _____

SHOW WHAT YOU'VE LEARNT

6 Complete the second sentence so that it means the same as the first. Do not change the words in capitals. Use between two and five words in each gap.

That factory has just dismissed half of its workforce. **OFF**
That factory has just *laid off* half of its workforce.

1 The local restaurant was only punished with a fine for
not complying with strict hygiene standards. **OFF**
The local restaurant was _____ for not
complying with strict hygiene standards.

2 Nobody has fully realised the implications of the new
diet yet. **SUNK**
The implications of the new diet _____ yet.

3 Sticking to physical exercise and consuming a variety
of nutrients have finally produced results. **PAID**
Sticking to physical exercise and consuming a variety
of nutrients _____.

4 Maintaining weight requires healthy eating habits. **FOR**
Maintaining weight _____ habits.

5 Whenever I go to a party, I never worry about
overindulging in food and gobble up whatever
passes my way. **DOWN**
Whenever I go to a party, I never worry about
overindulging in food and _____ my way.

6 Sophie stopped liking diet drinks when she found out
they contain sweeteners. **OFF**
Sophie _____ drinks when she found out
they contain sweeteners.

/6

1 Replace the wrongly used prepositions. There is one correct sentence.

What did you say? Could you speak ~~out~~? _up_

1 The lesson dragged up for another half an hour and nobody seemed to be paying attention. ___
2 He poured me out a generous cup of coffee. ___
3 I reminded Emily time and time again, but she refused to pay off. ___
4 Before you cook a beetroot, chop down its leaves. ___
5 Could you start handing off the cutlery, please? ___
6 At the end of the meal, Sebastian broke up a piece of bread and used it to clean the plate. ___

2 Replace the words in bold with the phrasal verbs from the box in the correct form.

> bring up   carry out   ~~come across~~
> cut down   give away   go up
> let down   put away   put forward

A: Derrick, the other day I **found by chance** / _came across_ a TV programme called *Watch What Happens Live*. Do you know it?

D: Sure, they invite celebrities and ask them to ¹**complete** / _____ odd tasks. What did they come up with this time?

A: The host ²**suggested** / _____ the idea that his guest, Salma Hayek, that Hollywood actress, should eat deep-fried frogs' legs, stir-fried silkworms and a jalapeño. And she did! Yuck!

D: Well, Alice, what did you expect? TV stations will do anything to make their ratings ³**increase** / _____ and not to ⁴**disappoint** / _____ their audience.

A: But she swallowed worms! It was amazing how many of them she managed to ⁵**eat** / _____ . And then the host ⁶**introduced** / _____ the topic of diets. She ⁷**revealed** / _____ her big secret to coming back to her pre-baby size: you must ⁸**reduce** / _____ the food you eat and exercise a lot. And drink lots of juice.

D: Wow! That's a shocker!

3 Complete the text with the missing prepositions.

4 Complete each set of sentences with the same word.

a Before the party the girls had to _drag_ the big table from the terrace into the kitchen.
b We're sorry to _drag_ you into this unnecessarily.
c The afternoon lecture seemed to _drag_ on forever and everybody lost interest in the topic.

1 a Health experts say that _____ down on salt lowers the risk of heart disease and stroke.
  b We are against _____ back investments in education.
  c Start by _____ the tops off the carrots from that box.

2 a Visiting that café _____ back many happy memories.
  b When Tim _____ up the issue of eating meat, his wife looked at him angrily.
  c The committee _____ their plans forward by two weeks.

3 a Did you really think _____ your decision to leave Madrid for good?
  b As soon as these changes are put _____ , we will start looking for new staff.
  c Candidates for this post had to go _____ a very challenging process of selection.

4 a The whole family left the country two days before the war _____ out.
  b Somebody _____ in when they were away on holiday.
  c In the past, many visitors to the Acropolis _____ off pieces of ancient buildings and took them home.

5 a All the proposals the tutor _____ forward were rejected by the students.
  b I'd love to stay longer and chat, but I don't want to _____ you out.
  c No snacks before dinner, so _____ the cookies away.

6 a Andy struggled _____ despite the twisted ankle.
  b Even though the man has spent two weeks in hospital, he keeps _____ eating junk food.
  c When the settlers got lost in the desert, they had no choice but to carry _____ walking.

/6

RISKY FISH ROULETTE

Five men from Osaka, Japan, got _together_ at a restaurant last Friday to celebrate their promotion at work. Unfortunately, their celebration was brought to an abrupt end when they got poisoned after dining on a very expensive delicacy: toxic fish called *fugu* (*puffer fish* in English). Although the chef allegedly asked them to think their decision ¹___ , the men insisted on being served banned parts of *fugu*. 'The customer is always right,' as the saying goes, so the waiter meekly handed ²___ plates with *puffer fish* liver. When the gourmets started vomiting and having breathing difficulties, the restaurant staff called an ambulance.

Apart from being very expensive (the sales of *fugu* dishes bring ³___ $200 a piece), it is also one of the world's deadliest fish. The Japanese government has wanted to cut ⁴___ *puffer fish* completely from menus for years, but so far without success. The authorities struggle ⁵___ , but fortunately have managed to put ⁶___ a bill that heavily regulates the delicacy, i.e. chefs who want to serve it are required to train for two years before taking a very demanding test. According to a city health official, the restaurant in question took on a chef with a *fugu-*preparing licence earlier this month and he knew he was supposed to take ⁷___ the banned parts before serving the dish. It is unclear, why he agreed to serve the customers regardless. The restaurant owner claims it will carry ⁸___ serving *fugu*, but the police have closed down the place for investigation.

LISTENING LANGUAGE PRACTICE

3.5

Expressions • phrases • idioms with food • adjectives

---

1 Read the extracts. Put the missing article *the* in gaps a–l if necessary.

> *Extract from Student's Book recording* 🔊 **1.30**
>
> **S1:** I'd never tried oysters before but I was on vacation on *the* East Coast of ª___ US and they're everywhere. You can even pick them up at ᵇ___ street stalls. Anyway, I plucked up the ¹*courage / confidence* and took my first taste and actually I quite liked it […].
>
> **S2:** But ᶜ___ other day a friend recommended this take-away place. I had a feeling ahead of ²*time / game* that it wouldn't be any good, but they still managed to disappoint! ᵈ___ tacos were ³*downcast / downright* unpleasant – ᵉ___ corn tortillas weren't fresh, and ᶠ___ salsa was all sweet and sticky like ᵍ___ tomato ketchup and worst of all it wasn't spicy at all.
>
> **S4:** The other day, I went to my local chippy to get a takeaway and I found that ʰ___ place had changed ⁴*hands / ways*. […] It's disappointing when you're imagining one taste and you get another one, which is nowhere near as nice, but I guess even ⁱ___ best places end up going ⁵*downhill / downward* sometimes.
>
> **S5:** There's this really nice stall where we go to get ʲ___ crepes but it's so popular you usually have to line up right round the ⁶*edge / corner*. […] I asked for mine to be made without ᵏ___ butter and ˡ___ guy who makes them **went nuts** and was really rude about it. He said that he couldn't do it with that number of people waiting.

2 Read the extracts again and choose the correct options to complete the expressions. Use a dictionary if necessary.

3 Use the underlined expressions from the extracts in the correct form to rewrite the parts of the sentences in brackets.

> There's an ice cream shop here and even in midwinter there's a line of people all the way *round the corner* (up to the end of the street and left into the next).

1 Bradley's house looked so fantastic after all the renovation that it _____ (was sold) for twice the original price.

2 Reserving seats _____ (in advance) is always a good thing to do to ensure you don't miss out.

3 With the bad weather and the awful food the picnic was a _____ (far from nice) experience.

4 I'm 100 percent certain that James _____ (isn't brave enough) to ask for a promotion.

5 Have you noticed that the food in the school canteen has _____ (got worse) lately? There must be a new cook.

---

4 Read REMEMBER THIS. Complete the definitions for each of the food idioms using the words from the box. Use a dictionary if necessary.

> cheese   cucumber   eggshells   n̶u̶t̶s̶   pie

go *nuts* – become crazy or extremely angry

1 walk on _____ – behave sensitively around somebody in case you upset them

2 be cool as a _____ – be very calm, not nervous or anxious

3 be _____ in the sky – be a plan, hope or idea that will never happen

4 be like chalk and _____ – be very different or opposites

5 Complete the sentences using the idioms from Exercise 4.

> When I told Jake that I'd eaten the last of the bread, he *went nuts* . What an overreaction!

1 Ever since Ralf failed his driving test, I've been _____ . It's hardly my fault everyone keeps asking me about my new car.

2 I'm so envious of Sarah. She never gets stressed or nervous – she's always _____ .

3 I couldn't believe it when I heard that Sami and Paula were working together on the science project. They're _____ and I thought they'd never get along.

4 Rebecca's dream of being a professional ballet dancer is all _____ . She doesn't practise enough.

WORD STORE 3F | Adjectives

6 Complete the sentences with the correct words. The first letters are given.

> These chips are so **g***reasy* – look how they're dripping!

1 This steak is so **s**_____ I can barely cut it with this knife.

2 Urgh! The milk is **o**_____ . It already smells funny.

3 Don't you find Chinese food rather **b**_____? I prefer much stronger flavours – Indian, for example.

4 I do love Georgian cuisine, but it's incredibly **s**_____ and even a small portion leaves you full.

5 Cherry tomatoes have a lower water content than regular tomatoes, so if you hate **s**_____ sandwiches, you should use them instead.

6 A traditional English breakfast must include **c**_____ toast. Start your day with a crunch!

7 When it comes to pancakes, give me something **s**_____ every time. I don't see the appeal of sweet pancakes with jam or chocolate, for example.

1 Cross out the incorrect option in each phrase.

1 So, I *gather / understand / mention* that …
2 Your father *tells / appreciates / informs* me that …
3 To be *completely / actually / totally* accurate …
4 Well, *I'm afraid / sort of / almost*, though not exactly …
5 That's very *kind / generous / correct*.
6 That sounds *interesting / impressed / intriguing*.

2 Complete the conversation with the words from the box. There are two extra words.

> actually   appreciate   fact   ~~gather~~
> impressed   informs   intriguing
> matter   so   thoughtful   way

Alice: So, Mackenzie, I *gather* you're quite the expert when it comes to food.

Mackenzie: Expert? Well, in a ¹_____ , though not exactly an expert as such, Alice. I er … I know a thing or two, though, yes.

Alice: I'm ²_____ , Mackenzie. You're so worldly!

Mackenzie: Thank you, Alice. Shall we order? Have you decided what you're having?

Alice: Well, ³_____ , not quite. This menu is all so complicated-sounding. I mean, do you know what *quinoa* is?

Mackenzie: *Quinoa*? Er … I … well yes, it's a type of fish, I believe, a freshwater fish, Asian in origin.

Alice: Fish? As a ⁴_____ of fact, I want to start eating more fish.

Mackenzie: Is that ⁵_____ ?

Alice: Oh yes. It's very good for you, you know?

Mackenzie: It's a nice clean food, isn't it? The fish do all that swimming around in water. Fresh water, very clean indeed.

Alice: Clean, yes, and healthy. And, do you know what *silken tofu* is, Mackenzie?

Mackenzie: *Silken tofu*? Let me see. Yes, that's Turkish, I think. If I'm not mistaken, it's a type of chamois, or goat-antelope, Alice, with very smooth hair. Yes, in ⁶_____ as smooth as silk, hence the use of the word 'silken', you see?

Alice: I see, yes. That sounds ⁷_____ , Mackenzie, but I think I'll stick with the fish.

Mackenzie: Well then, why don't I order the boar and then we can try both?

Alice: That's very ⁸_____ of you, but you simply must order whatever you fancy. I insist.

Mackenzie: That's settled then. You have the fish and I'll take the chamois. Waiter!

Waiter: Welcome to Vine Street Vegetarian and Vegan Cuisine, sir, madam. May I take your order?

Mackenzie: Vegetarian and vegan?

Alice: Mackenzie?

3 Complete the conversation. The first letters are given.

Stephen: Ladies and gentlemen, Pierre Blanco Marks, celebrity chef and restaurateur! Hello, Pierre, and welcome to the show.

Pierre: Hello, Stephen. Good evening, ladies and gentlemen.

Stephen: So, I u*nderstand* the new restaurant has opened, Pierre, congratulations!

Pierre: You mean you haven't been yet, Stephen?

Stephen: Well, as a matter of ¹f_____ , I tried but apparently I wasn't rich or famous enough to get a table.

Pierre: You don't ²s_____ ! That's terrible. We'll get you a table, Stephen. I'll have a word with my people immediately after the show.

Stephen: Well, I ³a_____ the offer Pierre, but I couldn't ⁴p_____ accept a free meal.

Pierre: Who said anything about a free meal?

Stephen: Pierre, your former colleague and co-star Johnnie Gulliver was here on the show a couple of weeks ago and he ⁵m_____ that you are famous amongst your fellow chefs for knowing lots of fascinating food facts.

Pierre: Well, that's not quite ⁶t_____ , I'm afraid. To be completely ⁷a_____ , what I have is a head full of useless food-based information.

Stephen: Didn't I ⁸h_____ you say that you have one or two facts to share with us here this evening?

Pierre: Indeed, I do. Did you know that in some Japanese restaurants they have over 200 ways of serving tofu?

Stephen: Oh ⁹r_____ ? Well, I can't say I'm a fan of the product.

Pierre: It's true. I'm planning a field trip, actually. I'm sure it'll give us some ideas about the menu in the new place.

Stephen: Tofu 200 ways … Pierre, I think I might pass on that offer of a table after all!

1 Complete the advice using the words from the box. There are three extra words.

> assist break convince course distinct entire
> formal logically ~~primary~~ show

The _primary_ goal of a proposal is to ¹_____ the reader to follow the ²_____ of action you recommend. You should write in a reasonably ³_____ , impersonal style. To ⁴_____ you in presenting the information clearly, divide the proposal into ⁵_____ parts using appropriate headings. In addition to these headings, remember to give the ⁶_____ proposal a neutral title.

2 Read the notice from a school's website and then the introduction to the proposal. Tick the problem the student has chosen to address.

A large amount of money was recently donated to the school by a former student with the provision that it is used to address a problem and improve the school for all the students. It has been decided that the money will be spent on developing the unused land next to the car park. The following relevant problems have been identified by the student council:

Students would like to learn more about how to grow plants for food, but there are no facilities. ☐

There is a lack of natural habitat for local wildlife in the vicinity of the school. ☐

The school relies on fossil fuels but would like to explore how renewable energy might be used instead. ☐

Students are encouraged to cycle to school, yet there is nowhere secure for them to store their bikes. ☐

Please submit proposals analysing one of these problems and suggesting how the money might be used to develop the land in order to provide a solution.

3 Read the whole proposal and put the following stages in order.

- Include a neutral title. ☐1
- State your recommendations and give reasons and justifications. ☐
- Present the current situation. ☐
- Strongly suggest that the reader takes the recommended action. ☐
- State the aim of the proposal. ☐
- Provide any information needed to explain why you are going to recommend changes. ☐
- Introduce the issue and say why it is important. ☐
- Summarise the benefits of your recommendations. ☐

Proposal for investment in school land

Introduction

Green areas are few and far between nowadays, yet they are **integral** to the **well-being** of all living things. The ¹_reason / purpose_ of this proposal is to discuss the lack of such space near our school and ²_recommend / ask_ how we could use the recent generous donation to address this.

Current situation

The last two years have witnessed the sad disappearance of the natural habitat that once surrounded the school. First, land was sold to housing developers, next the car park was extended, and most recently, a new bus **terminus** was built at the top of the school drive. All this development took place on formerly green land, and has resulted in **drab** views from the classrooms and the virtual **eradication** of wildlife from the area.

Recommendations

In ³_conclusion / response_, I suggest the development of a small nature reserve on the unused land. This would encourage local wildlife back to the area, providing a more pleasant environment and the potential for scientific study. Students could be involved in the establishment of the reserve by planting trees and building and erecting nest boxes for birds. Furthermore, I ⁴_encourage / propose_ that a large pond is dug as part of the reserve so that a wider variety of flora and fauna can set up home. Pathways and benches could also be provided, which would mean staff and students could enjoy the space.

Conclusion

The ongoing nature of the project ⁵_means / results in_ the investment will pay **dividends** long into the future and remind successive generations of students of the value of nature. In this world of concrete and glass, I ⁶_urge / hope_ the school to invest in something more **wholesome**.

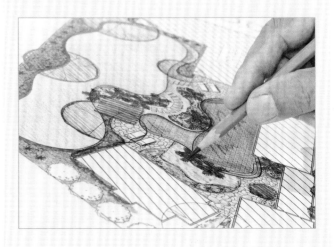

4 Choose the correct words to complete the proposal.

5 Underline examples of the following ways of expressing cause and effect in the text.

- Two linking phrases
- A comment clause to refer back to the whole main clause
- A participle clause to express the result of the main clause

6 Combine the pairs of sentences using the words in bold.

Many students have no experience of growing their own food. This means they have no idea how satisfying it can be. **which**

Many students have no experience of growing their own food, which means they have no idea how satisfying it can be.

1 The school relies entirely on fossil fuels. As a result, energy bills are high. **resulting**

_____

_____

2 The response to our 'Cycle to School' scheme was fantastic. This led to a huge increase in the number of bikes being brought to school. **leading**

_____

_____

3 I recommend the installation of solar panels on the unused land. In this way, the school can save money and students can learn about solar power. **so that**

_____

_____

4 I propose that the students build and maintain a kitchen garden on the unused land. As a result, they will feel closer to nature and gain a better appreciation of the value of fresh food. **with the result that**

_____

_____

5 Four bicycles have been stolen this month alone. This demonstrates how pressing the need for a secure bike park is. **which**

_____

_____

7 Complete the definitions with the correct forms of the words in bold in the proposal.

Something described as being *integral* forms a necessary part of something else.

1 A _____ is the station or stop at the end of a bus route or railway line.
2 If something pays or brings _____ , it is very useful and brings a lot of advantages, especially later, in the future.
3 _____ is the feeling of being comfortable, healthy and happy.
4 If something is described as _____ , it is not bright in colour in a way that stops you from feeling cheerful.
5 _____ is the act of completely getting rid of something such as a species, disease or social problem.
6 If something is described as _____ , it is likely to make you healthy or is considered to have a good moral effect.

8 Complete the sentences with the words from Exercise 7.

Colin had such a tough day at school that he dropped off on the bus and only woke up at the *terminus*.

1 The health and _____ of our patients is this hospital's number one concern.
2 Regular exercise and a healthy diet now will pay _____ in later life.
3 After his wife left, Philip moved into a _____ little apartment, which did nothing to lift his depression.
4 Has the studio's _____ reputation been tarnished after complaints about the violence in its latest film?
5 Thankfully, the _____ of Ebola is now complete and hospital occupancy rates have returned to normal.
6 Chilli is an _____ part of the flavour of a good curry, so if you don't like your food spicy, order something else.

REMEMBER THIS

Use the **passive voice** in proposals to help make them sound more formal and impersonal.

SHOW WHAT YOU'VE LEARNT

9 Read the notice in Exercise 2 again. Then follow the instructions below.

1 Choose one of the remaining problem areas identified by the student council.
2 Brainstorm ways in which the land and donation could be used to provide a solution.
3 Write a proposal analysing the problem and making recommendations.

SHOW THAT YOU'VE CHECKED

Finished? Always check your writing (especially in the exam!) Can you tick ✓ everything on this list?

In my proposal:

• I have begun with a neutral title.	☐
• I have divided the proposal into sections and given each an appropriate heading.	☐
• in the introduction, I have mentioned why the issue or problem is important and stated the aim of the proposal.	☐
• in the main body I have presented the current situation and explained why I am going to recommend changes.	☐
• in the main body I have stated my recommendations and given justifications.	☐
• in the conclusion, I have summarised the benefits of my recommendations and suggested that the reader takes action.	☐
• I have used a formal and impersonal style.	☐
• I have checked my spelling.	☐
• I have checked my handwriting is neat enough for someone else to read.	☐

VOCABULARY

1 Choose the correct option.

Why don't you add a (knob)/ clove / sprig of butter to the salmon before you put it in the oven?

1 What I love on a Sunday morning is the smell of fresh coffee and fried eggs *chinking / sizzling / clinking*.

2 Whenever my sister Sharon was told to share her presents with me, she had a crying *fit / sip / stick* and started throwing things around.

3 Don't eat too much of this pudding. It's quite *bland / slimy / stodgy* and it'll make you feel heavy and sleepy.

4 The aim of *nutritional / occupational / cognitive* therapy is to restore independence to any person suffering from an injury, illness or disability.

5 There's far too much *sensitive / fuzzy / processed* food instead of natural products in our diets nowadays.

/5

2 Complete the sentences with the correct words. The first and last letters are given.

Before you go to see a nutritionist, you have to write down some **b**urning questions you'd like to ask her.

1 It'd be great if you used a pinch of freshly grated **n**_____**g** in this recipe for baked leeks. Not too much though, because it's quite a strong flavour.

2 If you add too much milk to your cereal, it will go **s**_____**y** and won't have any bite.

3 It's not that I'm allergic to seafood, but I've never taken to oysters or other **s**_____**h**.

4 Everybody knows you're eating crisps because of the **c**_____**y** noise they make.

5 My brother and I loved Grandma's rice pudding served hot, but the longer it sat getting cold, the more sticky and **g**_____**s** it became.

/5

3 Complete the text with the correct forms of the words in brackets.

A jockey's diet

For some, food could be one of simple *pleasures* (please) in life. For me – a professional jockey – it's something that I have to watch closely. And although my diet is not too strict, I have to avoid some dishes which I find ¹_____ (tooth), like pizza or heavy chocolate cakes.

First of all, I have to think of the ²_____ (nutrition) value of everything I eat, but luckily I don't have many ³_____ (crave). That said, if there is ice cream in my freezer, it's hard to stop at just one ⁴_____ (spoon). I have been known to wolf down the entire tub!

I am supposed to eat little and often. I tend to pick at something small at lunchtime. However, if I have binged on ice cream, I won't have a meal. I never eat after eight and if sleep is ⁵_____ (elude), I drink chamomile tea.

/5

GRAMMAR

4 Complete the sentences with the appropriate verbs in the correct form.

Since the weather has turned foul, I suggest we *put* off the barbecue until it improves.

1 If I'm not mistaken, we've _____ out three times this week. Can't we cook something at home?

2 Some children have no manners! Little Tom Sanders _____ down his dinner instead of chewing it first.

3 We can't just _____ for a walnut-free cake. We have to check if the whole meal contains no nuts, because Sue is allergic to them.

4 Scientists have always wondered why small children _____ at certain foods or even refuse to eat them.

5 If you don't have enough butter to make this dish, you can _____ without it and use olive oil instead.

/5

5 Match the verbs from box A with suitable words from box B to make phrasal verbs. Then complete the text with the phrasal verbs in the correct form.

A (cut ~~end~~ fill get give snack)

B (back on on rid of up up ~~up~~)

I: Jeff, how did a doctor *end up* in a food business?

J: It actually all began with my grandmother, who would spend hours turning all the fruit from her orchard into marmalade, jams, and juices. As I always loved fruit and kept ¹_____ it, it was great to be around helping and of course ²_____ myself _____ with the finished product until my stomach hurt. After my grandma's death nobody wanted to keep the house and the orchard, so we ³_____ it and I became a student at Medical School. However, after working in a hospital for over twenty years and constantly telling my patients to ⁴_____ fats and carbohydrates, making sure that smokers would finally ⁵_____ their nasty habit, I decided to quit and go back to what I used to love most. I set up a company that produces jams and juices with no artificial additives.

/5

6 Complete the sentences with the correct particle.

It wasn't until Brooke spread *out* the plans of the building that she could visualise her restaurant there.

1 Please be careful when you dish _____ the pudding to ensure that everybody gets some.

2 Did you see how quickly he gobbled _____ the stew? He must have been starving.

3 The waiter picked up a pineapple and sliced the top _____ in front of us. We were truly impressed.

4 In my family, Sunday lunch drags _____ for hours.

5 My nephew has really shot _____ since I saw him last. He must have grown by a foot at least.

/5

Total /30

7 Choose the correct answer A, B, C or D.

The 'fast-casual' phenomenon

In many countries the 'fast-casual' restaurant is currently gaining ground as a popular sector of the food industry, closing the gap between fast food outlets and the opposite extreme: the more traditional '*B* dining' experience, in which **1**__ tablecloths and silver cutlery play a key part in laying the tables.

Although popular fast-casual chains such as Nandos chicken and Shake Shack Burger restaurants may be slightly more expensive than the ever-present '**2**__ food' alternatives, their food is advertised as being made with **3**__ quality ingredients and freshly prepared on the premises. **4**__ of this the restaurants appeal to both **5**__ eaters, who are able to choose exactly what they want to eat, and to the growing number of customers who have **6**__ and can't eat anything which may contain, for example, a trace of nuts.

The **7**__ tones to be found in more formal eateries are a far cry from the buzzy, noisy atmosphere in these new restaurants, many of which are bending over **8**__ to make sure they attract and hold on to their new clientele.

	A good	(B) fine	
	C excellent	D delicious	
1	A fatigued	B stringy	
	C starched	D aesthetic	
2	A junk	B waste	
	C scrap	D trash	
3	A considerable	B high	
	C substantial	D special	
4	A Due	B In addition	
	C Despite	D As a result	
5	A exact	B particular	
	C fussy	D selective	
6	A allergies	B reactions	
	C sensitivities	D aversions	
7	A sizzling	B hummed	
	C hushed	D peaceful	
8	A sideways	B backwards	
	C forwards	D downwards	

/8

8 Complete the text with one word in each gap.

The cost of healthy eating

Visiting my local supermarket to stock *up* on highly expensive soy sausages, almond milk, coconut water, or any other food craze which has recently hit the media, it feels that healthy food is taking **1**_____ our lives completely. The shelves are groaning with a huge variety of food products claiming to make us healthier, which surely **2**_____ be a good thing.

Yet it has not always been like this. In recent years there has been a **3**_____ deal of concern about the amount of obesity, triggered by our high consumption of fat, salt and sugar. Ironically, it is now the turn of so-called 'healthy' food to come under attack for the impact it is having **4**_____ the environment.

Soy sausages, for example, may be responsible for causing even **5**_____ deforestation than real meat does. And the demand for almonds means that water is now running out in California. And so on! So as **6**_____ as costing us a lot of money, our search for new food can have a disastrous effect on the planet too.

/6

9 Complete the second sentence so that it means the same as the first. Do not change the words in capitals. Use between four and six words in each gap.

We'll visit you some other time because of the food poisoning we're suffering from. **OFF**
We need to *put off visiting you/put visiting you off* because of the food poisoning we're suffering from.

1 I know that the syrup tastes disgusting but you need to finish it before you can go and play again. **DRINK**
You can go and play again provided you _____ _____ first however disgusting it is.

2 If you continue to eat crisps with every meal, you'll definitely put on weight. **ON**
You'll definitely put on weight if _____ _____ with every meal.

3 I haven't had a proper look yet at your business plan, but I glanced at it the other day and it looks promising. **FLICKED**
Your business plan looks promising although I _____ so far.

4 Because the food was so much fresher than before, we were pleasantly surprised. **IMPROVEMENT**
There was so _____ of the food that we were pleasantly surprised.

5 My proposal is to let him choose the menu for himself. **RECOMMEND**
I would _____ decision about the menu.

6 If the government invests money in school meals, educational standards will increase dramatically. **RESULT**
Government investment in school meals _____ _____ up dramatically.

/6

Total /20

39

4 The new thing

VOCABULARY

4.1

Music industry • compounds • phrases to describe success and failure • forming nouns from adjectives

SHOW WHAT YOU KNOW

1 Choose the least likely collocation.

1	**attach**	*an app / a file / a photo*
2	**bookmark**	*a website / a page / your profile*
3	**download**	*an attachment / music / your status*
4	**log on to**	*a Wi-Fi network / Facebook / a comment*
5	**post**	*a clip / a link / a homepage*
6	**share**	*a video / music / an app*
7	**stream**	*music / a clip / a link*
8	**update**	*your status / a comment / an app*

2 Choose the correct word to complete each notification.

1 ¹*Update / Bookmark* our page and visit us every day with just one click!

2 Click here to ²*download / log on to* two free sample tracks from Vibert's new album.

3 Your file is too large to ³*attach / share* to this email. Send as link?

4 ⁴*Post / Stream* tonight's episode of *Places Unknown* for free at CNM.com from 7 p.m. onwards.

5 ⁵*Update / Attach* virus definitions before scanning?

6 Enter your ID and password to ⁶*log on to / post* the system.

WORD STORE 4A | Compounds

3 Match the words in boxes A and B to create compounds and then use them to complete the text.

A [~~back~~ brain fan industry
main purpose sound]

B [base built child ~~lash~~
proof standard stream]

Luxurylife .com

Home entertainment

There has been a recent consumer _backlash_ against the poor quality speakers fitted as standard to most laptops and televisions. If you are looking to upgrade and happen to have $300,000 to spare, then perhaps the Goldmund Apologue Speaker System is for you. The ¹_____ of Goldmund, a company synonymous with the very highest end of audio-design for the last thirty years, these speakers are some of the finest money can buy.

Leaving the ²_____ trailing far, far behind, the Apologue system is ³_____ to provide the absolute pinnacle of sound quality. With such a price tag, these are clearly not intended for the ⁴_____ consumer but rather have their ⁵_____ among the bankers and rock stars that can afford such indulgences. The raw power of the speakers may leave neighbours wishing for ⁶_____ walls, although the fact is that those who can afford a pair probably don't have neighbours living anywhere close enough to be disturbed.

WORD STORE 4B | Success and failure

4 Complete the text with the words from the box.

[ascendancy came commercial
downturn herald predominant
~~resurgence~~ started way wayside]

---

businessfocus.com

Fabulous Flops and Famous Failures

We all make mistakes, even big corporations with multi-million dollar budgets. Here's a list of some of the biggest failures of recent years – don't expect any of them to be enjoying a _resurgence_ anytime soon!

* In 1989 Pepsi tried to target the 'breakfast cola drinker' with a colourless version of its cola. The product was a ¹_____ flop and after just a year had fallen by the ²_____ .

* When the DVD ³_____ into prominence in the late 1990s, it was considered the ultimate solution, but barely a decade later the race for an upgrade was on among tech companies. Sony won the contest with its Blu-ray format. Although this remained in the ⁴_____ for some time, it has been overtaken by Ultra HD Blu-ray, which is now the ⁵_____ choice for high-quality viewing - though 'choice' may be misleading as this format is incompatible with regular Blu-ray players.

* In the late 2000s, Google decided it needed to compete with popular virtual world 'Second Life' and so released 'Lively' in July 2008, expecting the general public to ⁶_____ its arrival. Unfortunately, this coincided with a major ⁷_____ in the economy and as global prosperity ⁸_____ to decline and good times gave ⁹_____ to bad, 'Lively' died a death just four months later.

WORD STORE 4C | Nouns from adjectives

5 Complete the sentences with the correct forms of the words in brackets.

This app has clearly been developed with an _awareness_ (aware) of the needs of novice users such as myself.

1 3D cinema is currently in the _____ (ascend) as more and more films are being produced using the very latest cameras.

2 The _____ (popular) of dystopian fiction for young adults has finally begun to wane.

3 What this mini-projector lacks in style, it more than makes up for in _____ (portable).

4 Could this be the product to finally crack Apple's _____ (predominate) in the mobile market?

5 Sam Smith first came to _____ (prominent) in 2012 after appearing on Disclosure's first album.

6 Will cassette tapes see a _____ (resurge) to match that of vinyl?

WORD STORE 4D | EXTRA Nouns from adjectives

6 Complete the sentences with the correct forms of the words in capitals.

AUTHENTIC

a Use _authentic_ ink cartridge replacements and earn discounts on our whole range of products.

b The painting has been withdrawn from auction until its _authenticity_ can be proved beyond doubt.

1 CARELESS

a Carlos read the instructions _____ and failed to notice that the battery needed to be charged for four hours before use.

b There is simply no room for _____ when you are working with highly infectious patients.

2 RELUCTANT

a The shop assistant _____ agreed to refund Sam's money after his multiple complaints.

b Most breeders will admit to a certain _____ when it is time to send the kittens off to their new homes.

3 CONSISTENT

a _____ is key when it comes to training a dog. Decide on the rules and stick to them.

b Esmeralda used to be teased about her name, but now she's older, people _____ say how beautiful it is.

4 SIMPLE

a Don't be fooled by the camera's apparent _____ . It is, in fact, a highly complex piece of equipment.

b Look, I can't make it any _____ . If you don't pay me right now, the next time you see me will be in court.

7 Complete the advert. Some letters are given.

```
○○○
indiajobs.com
```

FortKnox _Se_c_uri_ty seeks full-time security guards in Mumbai, Delhi, Bangalore and Hyderabad

With the growth of [1]a_f_u_n_e in India, there is now an [2]a_u_d_n_e of opportunities for domestic security firms, as safety-conscious families look to invest in their security and [3]p_i_a_y. The [4]e_f_c_i_e_e_s of FortKnox Security Systems depends on the [5]d_l_g_n_e, professionalism and bravery of our quick-response security guards. If you think you have what it takes, contact us at _recruit@fortknox.in_

SHOW WHAT YOU'VE LEARNT

8 Choose the correct answer A–C.

1 Investing in __ walls was the best thing we ever did. We hardly hear the neighbours now.
A watertight   B soundproof   C see through

2 Unfortunately for them, the band's original __ of adolescent girls have all grown up.
A fan base   B supporters   C followers

3 Efforts to develop virtual reality headsets appear to have fallen by the __ in recent years.
A sideline   B sideways   C wayside

4 The gang's preference for leather boots appears to have given __ to colourful trainers.
A out   B way   C up

5 Once mocked as unimaginative, the humble prawn cocktail is currently enjoying a __ .
A reappearance   B remembrance   C resurgence

6 The __ of this mixer should prove very popular with DJs who play at several different clubs each weekend.
A popularity   B portability   C prominence

7 The __ of English as the global language of business stands to change as Mandarin Chinese becomes increasingly important.
A predominance   B authenticity   C effectiveness

8 Until general levels of __ increase, sales of such expensive technology are likely to remain low.
A abundance   B affluence   C ascendancy

9 Consumer groups are demanding greater __ in the quality of electronics sold by supermarkets.
A consistency   B carelessness   C diligence

10 After initial __ , teachers now seem happy enough to receive students' homework by email.
A awareness   B privacy   C reluctance

/10

41

Four writers comment on digital data storage

A If you want to make sure your treasured photographs are available for future generations to enjoy, then the safest option is not to back them up on your hard drive, or store them remotely in the cloud, but to print them out. Recent history has shown that, as technology advances, data storage formats such as audio cassettes, floppy disks or video tapes quickly become **obsolete** making the data they hold **inaccessible**. With this in mind, if we want to preserve our digital lives in the same way we preserve our history in books, we need to make sure that the digital objects we create will be available in centuries to come. One way to do this would be to create a system which will not only store a digital format but hold details of the software and operating system needed to access it, so it can be recreated in the future. Until such a system is in place, printing out your photos and sticking them in the family album remains your best option.

B Storing files remotely rather than on fragile discs or **clunky** hard drives certainly proves helpful for professional as well as home users. One of the biggest advantages of using cloud storage is that it helps to add another layer* of protection for **irreplaceable** and precious files. Secure locations are chosen for the backups that are physically removed from originals. As a result, data kept within the cloud services remains absolutely safe and secure from all types of **unauthorised** use or access. However, there are **potential** pitfalls to storing your data in the cloud and, despite media scaremongering about security issues, perhaps the biggest downside is the likelihood* of technical failure or connectivity issues rendering your files unavailable at just the moment you need to access them.

C Cloud storage removes the need for portable data storage devices and therefore tackles the problem of ageing formats and hardware. However, as recent leaks* of celebrities' private photographs have proved, the cloud may not be a safe place to store personal files. With certain settings, anything you do on your phone is uploaded to the cloud then pulled down by your other devices. Convenient? Yes, but the sacrifice* required is **compromised** security because your data is actually sitting on a server in 'the cloud' on someone else's computer and is therefore **vulnerable** to hackers. There are, of course, ways of encrypting data or stopping it from being uploaded to the cloud but in my opinion, the most effective way of ensuring that sensitive information does not get into the wrong hands is not to record it on a cloud-based device in the first place.

D Research suggests that although some storage devices may last longer than a decade, others may stop working after little more than a year. For this reason, it is vital to regularly create and update copies of your most important data on different storage devices. Even then, considering the rapid evolution of data storage formats, there is no guarantee that your files and photos will be accessible even a few years from now. Cloud storage is being hailed as a solution, but science is looking to nature to find the best way to store data in a manner that will guarantee its availability far into the future. Researchers in Switzerland believe the answer may lie in the data storage system that exists in every living cell: DNA. Fossils* prove that in the right conditions, strands* of DNA can store data for close to a million years. Moreover, its strands are so compact and complex that just one gram of DNA is theoretically capable of containing all the data of Internet giants such as Google and Facebook, with room to spare.

GLOSSARY

layer (n) – one of several levels in a complicated system, organisation or set of ideas

likelihood (n) – the degree to which something can reasonably be expected to happen

leak (n, v) – a situation in which secret information is deliberately given to a newspaper, website, etc.

sacrifice (n, v) – when you decide not to have something valuable in order to get something that is more important

fossil (n) – the shape of an ancient plant or animal preserved in rock

strand (n) – a single thin piece of thread, wire, hair, DNA, etc.

1 **Read the four texts and answer the questions below.**

Which writer

1 refers to a specific media incident to justify a point of view? ⬚

2 reports a biotechnological innovation in storage? ⬚

3 suggests an old-fashioned solution to a modern problem? ⬚

4 questions the validity of an attitude taken by the media? ⬚

2 **Read the four texts again. For questions 1–4, choose from texts A–D. The texts may be chosen more than once.**

Which writer

1 agrees with A about the importance of finding long-term data storage solutions? ⬚

2 is concerned about a different problem with data storage from the other writers? ⬚

3 disagrees with C about the risks involved in data storage? ⬚

4 agrees with B about the importance of backing up data? ⬚

3 **Complete the collocations with verbs from the text. The first letters are given. Use the information in brackets to help you.**

r*ender* (cause something to be – text B) something unavailable/harmless/useless, etc.

1 r_____ (get rid of – text C) the need for something

2 t_____ (try to deal with – text C) a problem

3 l_____ to (depend on for advice/help/a solution, etc. – text D) nature/technology/your parents, etc.

4 h_____ (describe someone or something as being very good – text D) something as a solution/success/masterpiece, etc.

5 p_____ (turn out to be – text B) helpful, useful, impossible, etc.

6 r_____ (need – text C) a sacrifice/patience/concentration, etc.

4 **Complete the sentences with the correct forms of the verbs from Exercise 3.**

The air conditioning *was rendered* useless by the power cut, so they decided to sleep out on the balcony.

1 To complete all seventeen levels and finish the game _____ a level of dedication I just don't have.

2 In certain schools teachers are _____ to the past to try to improve discipline in their classrooms.

3 It _____ impossible to pick the cherries from the highest branches, so they were left for the lucky birds.

4 The band's new album has been _____ as their best yet.

5 The government has appointed a new committee in order to _____ the problem of obesity among the country's children.

6 In the 1990s, the need for aerials on mobile phones _____ by advances in technology.

5 **Match the words in bold in the text to the definitions.**

having the capacity to develop into something in the future *potential*

1 solid, heavy and old-fashioned _____

2 in danger of attack or harm _____

3 unique; incapable of being replaced _____

4 no longer made or used, old-fashioned _____

5 caused to function less effectively _____

6 unable to be reached _____

7 lacking official approval or permission _____

6 **Look at the vocabulary in lesson 4.2 in the Student's Book. Then complete the sentences with the correct form of the words in brackets.**

Fiona went to such *expense* (expend) in preparation for the party and half the guests didn't even turn up.

1 The support of such a high-profile scientist really helps to _____ (legitimate) our project.

2 The crowd's disappointment at the election _____ (manifestation) itself in their distraught faces.

3 The students came up with an _____ (ingenuity) solution to the problem of graffiti at their school.

4 Bradbury was a highly _____ (accomplish) sculptor whose work has been honoured with many awards.

5 Mum's Polish and Dad's English so, at home, we _____ (alternative) randomly between the two languages.

6 Manage your time carefully while revising in order to _____ (optimal) your productivity.

7 As Confucius said, 'Real knowledge is to know the extent of your _____ (ignore).'

WORD STORE 4E | Collocations

7 **Complete the sentences with the correct forms of the words from the box. There are three extra words.**

edge improvement limit ~~line~~
performance picture record time

I don't mind helping you with your homework, but I draw the *line* at letting you simply copy mine.

1 This could be the race in which new _____ are set and personal bests are smashed.

2 Our new foam sole technology enhances both comfort and _____ on the field.

3 European investment has fuelled _____ in public transport and housing provision.

4 The latest concept car from Ferrari pushes the _____ of electric car performance.

GRAMMAR

4.3

Infinitives

SHOW WHAT YOU KNOW

1 Complete the text with one word in each gap.

PRIVACY CONCERNS

Google Glass – a hi-tech device similar to a pair of glasses – was a revolutionary invention that used voice control to allow wearers **1**_____ access a wide range of functions. Its built-in camera **2**_____ users take images and record video of anything around them while also allowing access to a range of Internet tools. Google Glass was created in order **3**_____ provide users with a flexible, convenient, hands-free technology. But while the device **4**_____ to be the answer to all the inconveniences of using a mobile phone, as soon as Google began to sell it **5**_____ the public, it managed **6**_____ arouse a good deal of controversy. Not long after its release, the company took the decision **7**_____ stop producing the device for public use. What caused them to **8**_____ this? Because of privacy concerns, more and more businesses started warning people **9**_____ to use the device on their premises. Cinema managers made customers hand in their devices so as **10**_____ prevent the illegal copying of films, and restaurant patrons wearing Google Glass were reminded that everyone ought **11**_____ have the right to privacy. Faced with these issues, Google realised that the device was not suited to public use, and in 2015 decided **12**_____ focus on commercial uses tailored to specific business needs.

REMEMBER THIS

He **made** me **write** it. vs I **was made to write** it.

---

2 ★ Replace the phrases in bold with *to*-infinitives. Use between two and four words.

We were glad **we could** refer to online dictionaries during the English lesson. *to be able to*

1 Julie ran her slide presentation by me **with the intention of ensuring** that it was correct. _____
2 The tutor must have had a good reason **for punishing** Robbie. _____
3 This is the most useful gadget **that is used** by sportspeople. _____
4 The new student expected **that the school would provide him** with a free tablet. _____
5 All mobile phones **must be** handed in before the lessons. _____
6 **Preparing** PowerPoint presentations for History lessons has become really common. _____
7 I didn't want to switch off my phone, so the examiners insisted on giving it to them. In fact, I was **left no choice**. _____

---

3 ★ ★ ★ Turn the verbs from the box into *to*-infinitives and complete the text. Sometimes you need to make the verb negative.

> become do experience fill
> form live ~~make~~ miss repeat
> save see support turn write

Films Worth Watching Again: *Her*

In one of his most intriguing films, *Her*, director Spike Jonze tries *to make* us believe that it may not be easy **1**_____, or love, in the future. Joaquin Phoenix plays the role of Theodore Twombly, an emotionally bruised man, whose job is **2**_____ beautiful personal letters for customers who choose **3**_____ this themselves. Theodore is anxious **4**_____ over a new leaf after he fails **5**_____ his marriage to Catherine (Rooney Mara). But this time he opts for a highly advanced operating system so as **6**_____ his old mistakes. The system's name is Samantha (voiced by Scarlett Johansson) and, strange as it might seem, their conversations manage **7**_____ a gap in Theodore's life.

Her is a gentle satire on human as opposed to artificial intelligence. The viewer is eager **8**_____ Theodore in his pursuit of happiness. Phoenix is joined on screen by Amy Adams, whose character, Amy, is Theodore's best friend. According to her, connecting with another being is something that everybody is eager **9**_____ , and she wonders why it should be any less normal **10**_____ close to an operating system than to a human being.

Whether the film was correct in its predictions on the nature of future relationships, remains **11**_____ . In the meantime, be sure **12**_____ it on VOD or Blu-ray and see for yourselves if Theodore was lucky **13**_____ his most meaningful bond with an artificial intelligence.

SHOW WHAT YOU'VE LEARNT

4 Complete the sentences with the words in brackets in the correct forms. Do not change the word order. Use between five and six words in each gap.

I'd like to return these light-up trainers because they *fail to flash at night*. (fail/flash/night)

1 This electronic fork is meant _____ (warn/not/eat) too quickly.
2 Please tell others that they _____ (be/not/be/use) any electronic devices right now.
3 Susan was lucky _____ (not/hit) by a car yesterday. I suppose she will never go to the city centre wearing headphones again.
4 Despite the students' wish _____ (allow/use) laptops in lesson, the school refused to agree to it.
5 Before our last school trip, we _____ (make/not/bring) our games consoles with us.
6 This company was _____ (last/start/produce) wearable devices.

/6

1 Choose the odd one out in each group.

1 *Obviously / Curiously / Interestingly*
2 *Honestly / Frankly / Certainly*
3 *In actual fact / In truth / In a way*
4 *Strikingly / Surprisingly / Plainly*
5 *Incidentally / Personally / By the way*
6 *Annoyingly / Hopefully / Potentially*

2 Replace the words in bold with the phrases from the box.

> all things considered   anyway   fortunately
> in fact   sadly   ~~sort of~~   to some extent
> to tell the truth   without doubt

A: You sound **somewhat** / *sort of* downcast, Ellen. Is something wrong?

B: Well, my mum has been to the parent-teacher meeting today, so ¹**actually** / _____ I'm devastated.

A: What did you get up to this time? Is it the report card?

B: ²**Luckily** / _____ , the grades are OK. The tutor complained about my lack of concentration and, ³**admittedly** / _____ , I do find it hard to focus.

A: But why?

B: ⁴**Undeniably** / _____ , my smartphone has something to do with it. I constantly need to look at it. ⁵**Unfortunately** / _____ , I can't help it.

A: I must admit I sympathise with you ⁶**to a certain degree** / _____ . Why don't you just put it in your school bag, though?

B: Chris, ⁷**generally speaking** / _____ , you're right. ⁸**At any rate** / _____ , the problem's solved.

A: How so?

B: My parents decided to take my phone away for a month.

3 Turn the pairs of words in bold into adverbs and then choose the ones that logically complete each sentence.

ᵃ**happy** / *happily*   ᵇ**sure** / *surely*
ᶜ*Happily*, the battery lasted long enough to make one more phone call.

1 ᵃ**regret** / _____   ᵇ**thankful** / _____
Paul has just texted me that, ᶜ_____, he won't be able to join us because of the train strike.

2 ᵃ**evident** / _____   ᵇ**definite** / _____
There was nobody there when we arrived. ᶜ_____, we must have got the times mixed up.

3 ᵃ**crucial** / _____   ᵇ**undoubted** / _____
These electronic devices may affect our brains and, more ᶜ_____, the brains of our children.

4 ᵃ**doubt** / _____   ᵇ**wrong** / _____
The number of adolescents addicted to smartphones will ᶜ_____ rise in the foreseeable future.

5 ᵃ**serious** / _____   ᵇ**presume** / _____
Martha's tablet and mp3 player are still here. ᶜ_____ she's going to come back and get this stuff.

6 ᵃ**understand** / _____   ᵇ**truthful** / _____
I admit I stood her up, so she was ᶜ_____ upset.

4 Choose appropriate modifiers. Then decide if the chosen modifiers indicate attitude (A), soften a message (S) or give emphasis (E).

TWEET LITERATURE

Some wring their hands saying that, ¹*arguably / regrettably* ☐, classical literature is losing popularity among young people. ²*Indeed / Incidentally* ☐, a new survey shows that a shocking 10 percent of young adults (those aged eighteen to twenty-five) have never read a book in their life (³*strikingly / clearly* ☐, however, 75 percent of them, on average, check their mobile device fourteen times a day). ⁴*Curiously / Arguably* ☐ it is because they prefer other forms of experiencing reading, namely social media. Not only do young adults read all kinds of text available online but, ⁵*interestingly / luckily* ☐, more and more of them have a go at creating short stories themselves. Take tweet literature, for example. This latest social networking trend consists of creating narratives in 140 characters. Each story must have believable heroes and a compelling plot. It is ⁶*possibly / plainly* ☐ taking Twitter by storm because hashtags like #VeryShortStory are gaining a few thousand new fans every week. Instead of following celebrities' tweets about what they have for breakfast, those budding writers take to their smartphones to create succinct narratives. If you think it's impossible to tell a meaningful story in 140 characters, just visit Twitter, type in 'veryshortstory' and see for yourself.

SHOW WHAT YOU'VE LEARNT

5 Choose the correct answer A–D.

1 Most students continue to check text messages while in class. ___ , they find it hard to comply with the rules.
   A Incidentally   B Plainly
   C Interestingly   D Potentially

2 My sat-nav has never let me down. ___ , it has helped me out in dire straits.
   A Indeed   B Arguably
   C By the way   D Hopefully

3 With all that talk about the harmful effects of electronic devices on children, ___ , 40 percent of toddlers are reported to have played with their parents' phones.
   A apparently   B surprisingly
   C in truth   D generally speaking

4 Oscar had an accident while texting behind the wheel. ___ , he wasn't seriously injured and will be able to take part in the match – hurrah!
   A Obviously   B Understandably
   C Annoyingly   D Happily

5 I need to say something. ___ , I'm rather upset to hear you've been telling people I'm addicted to Facebook. It's just not true.
   A Curiously   B Presumably
   C Frankly   D Potentially

6 My retired neighbour's just won a big cash prize in a gaming competition. He is ___ living proof that video games are not only for the young.
   A to some extent   B in a way
   C without doubt   D sort of   /6

LISTENING LANGUAGE PRACTICE

Cloze • expressions with *get* • verbs

1 Complete the conversation with an appropriate word in each gap.

Extract from Student's Book recording 🔊 **2.6**

M1: So, the other day I got my new bank card through the mail and it's one of those contactless ones – you just place it on the handset; you don't have to input your pin number or anything. The only thing *is* the maximum transaction is twenty pounds, ¹_____ is a bit of a hassle.

W1: Well, for little stuff, ²_____ if you're in a rush and just grabbing a coffee or whatever, it's great, and people want ³_____ nowadays. But what happens if somebody nicks your card? That'd bother me.

M1: It's bizarre how things have changed over ⁴_____ . Like, you know, you used to swipe your card and then sign ⁵_____ pay for something, and then we had chip and pin, and ⁶_____ we've got to the point where we just tap our cards. It feels like I ⁷_____ have time to get used to one technology before the next one is introduced. […] We're certainly living in a world ⁸_____ we want everything instantly. It's like those travel cards that you can top ⁹_____ on the go. That's what these cards are about – being quick and convenient.

W1: But that means compromising sometimes – and that's not always a good trade-off.

REMEMBER THIS

We use common verbs like ***get***, ***keep*** (see 6.5) or ***come*** (see 9.5) in many informal expressions, e.g. […] ***we've got to the point*** where we just tap our cards.

---

2 Look at sentences 1–8, which all contain expressions with *get*. Read the sentences and match the *get* expressions to definitions a–h.

   to reach a specific stage in the development of something   ⑨

a not to make progress or improvement with a task ◯

b to express the same as 'don't misunderstand me' ◯

c to introduce something which you find annoying ◯

d to say you are confused or do not know or understand something ◯

e to organise or control yourself/something ◯

f to progress or move forward from a current situation ◯

g not to be able to escape from a situation ◯

h to make an effort to deal with something difficult ◯

---

1 Arthur said that **what really gets him** is the fact that it's impossible to have a conversation with anyone anymore without being interrupted by some kind of gadget going off. And he's right, it is incredibly frustrating.

2 Using this instruction manual **isn't getting me anywhere**. I reckon I'd be better off making it up as I go along for all the use it's been!

3 Brody's been a mess since his fiancée dumped him. I tried telling him to **get on with his life** and that it's time he moved on but he didn't want to listen.

4 What's the capital of Latvia? You've **got me there**! Oh, hang on, is it Riga? Or is it Tallinn? No, no it's Riga. I think my brother-in-law went there for a convention once. Tallinn is in Estonia.

5 Listen – **don't get me wrong**. I'm not saying *all* modern technology is bad – it's just that we've become too reliant upon it, that's all.

6 Emma said she was having a nightmare trying to **get to grips with** Javascript. No matter how hard she tries, she can't seem to make it do what she wants it to.

7 Everybody has to do a presentation in front of the whole class. There's **no getting away from it** so you'd better start putting something together.

8 Ethan's presentation was a disaster. First there were problems with the projector and then the sound went. He tried to **get it together** but was so fazed he forgot most of its content.

9 We've finally **got to the point** in development where we need to start looking for serious investors.

WORD STORE 4F | Verbs

3 Complete the sentences with the correct words. The first letters are given.

   What with PayPass technology, soon we'll no longer need to **s**wipe cards to make electronic payments.

1 I really wanted a phone with 4G technology and dual sim capability – but on my budget I had to **c**_____ and choose one over the other.

2 Don't leave your tablet lying around – somebody'll be bound to **n**_____ it if you leave it unguarded.

3 E-magazines will never be able to replace the convenience of being able to quickly **f**_____ through a paper copy in search of an eye-catching headline.

4 I can't read anything on this smartphone when I'm outdoors and the sun is **g**_____ straight on its screen.

5 Breaking up with someone via SMS really **c**_____ relationships, don't you think? Will we value any human contact in the future?

6 Tina's new coffee machine makes an amazing latte. Now she can sit and really **s**_____ her idle Sunday morning coffee and newspaper.

7 My new Bluetooth® speakers really **e**_____ the sound of MP3. I highly recommend them.

1 Put the words in order to make phrases and then mark each as *E* (agreeing enthusiastically), *P* (agreeing in part) or *D* (disagreeing politely).

agree … / I / but …   *I agree …, but …*   ⬭ P

1 right / course / you're / of / but …
_____   ⬭

2 with / have / afraid / to / on / disagree / you / that / I'm / I
_____   ⬭

3 point / got / a / though … / you've
_____   ⬭

4 I / sorry / agree / don't / really / you / there / I'm / with
_____   ⬭

5 got / with / to / you / I've / agree
_____   ⬭

6 not / there / definitely / wrong / you're
_____   ⬭

REMEMBER THIS

English people tend to be very indirect in their interactions, especially when disagreeing. While your language and culture may be more direct, it is a good idea to soften what you say when speaking to an English person.

~~I don't agree!~~ vs I'm not sure I fully agree with you.
~~That's wrong!~~ vs I don't think that's quite right.

---

2 Correct the mistakes.

Leanne: It scares me when people drive and text at the same time.

David: Absolutely! I'm totally ~~on you with~~ that.
with you on that.

1 **Fi:** Even if the story is not true, the damage has already been done.
Polly: You're got that right.
_____

2 **Gustav:** You really should switch off the lights when you leave a room.
Melanie: I know that's truthful, but I always forget.
_____

3 **Harry:** There's nothing but rubbish on the box again tonight.
Diane: I'm agree, but what else are we going to do, talk to each other?
_____

4 **Jude:** Dogs should live outside. They don't belong in the house.
Grace: Sorry, but I don't think that's just right.
_____

3 Complete the conversation. The first letters are given.

Back in 1995 …

Stuart: Have you heard about this new Internet thing?

Olive: Yes, I read about that actually. Sounds like science fiction to me. It'll never catch on.

Stuart: I'm *sorry*, I *really don't agree with you here*. I read that it is going to change the world.

Olive: Well, so did I, but ¹s_____ , I j_____ d_____ t_____ that's r_____ . Apparently, it's just a sea of totally unorganised information and it's impossible to find anything.

Stuart: ²I g_____ you're r_____ , t_____ if someone can find a way to search through all that data quickly, then the potential is incredible. They say we'll be able to listen to music and watch television using it, and also shop and order tickets, book restaurants. All sorts, basically.

Olive: ³Hmm, I'm a_____ I'm n_____ so s_____ . I've got music on my stereo, a television in the corner and shops just down the road. If I want to book tickets or reserve a table, then all I need to do is pick up the phone. Why would I want the Internet if I can already do all these things?

Stuart: ⁴Y_____ r_____ of c_____ , b_____ I still think it would be cool to, for example, press a button and book a train ticket.

Olive: Wouldn't you rather interact with a human being? Plus how would you pay and where would you get the actual ticket from?

Stuart: ⁵Well, you've g_____ a p_____ . I'm not really sure how it would work. Anyway, I think it would be cool to like, be able to send messages to someone on the other side of the world.

Olive: ⁶I'm a_____ I h_____ to d_____ w_____ you on t_____ . How many people do you know on the other side of the world?

Stuart: Er, well … none actually. I mean, I can see there are limitations, of course.

Olive: ⁷Y_____ can s_____ that a_____ !

1 Complete the advice with the words from the box. There are two extra words.

> benefits buyers comparison drawbacks
> list need options ~~purpose~~ service

The _purpose_ of a review of a product is to ¹_____ and comment on the product's features, so potential ²_____ can decide if it is right for them. The introduction should arouse the reader's interest in the product and comment on the ³_____ or problem it offers a solution to. The main body paragraphs should say what the product does and what features it offers, as well as drawing a ⁴_____ with other similar products, if appropriate. Any ⁵_____ or areas for improvement should also be mentioned at this point. Finally, in the conclusion, the ⁶_____ of the product should be summarised.

2 Complete the extracts from product reviews. Some letters are given.

_I_nterested in star-gazing? Want to see more but don't have room for a large telescope?

The bread maker ¹**en**_____ you to bake perfect loaves with very little effort.

The external drive ²**of**_____ excellent features such as one-touch backup.

This ³**op**_____ is particularly useful for anyone who is short of time.

It's the speed at which the data is processed that really ⁴**st**_____ out.

The clear, concise menu makes all the ⁵**di**_____ when it comes to interacting with the device.

The MX5s are some of the most popular desktop computer speakers ⁶**av**_____ in the UK.

The only real ⁷**do**_____ to the phone is the disappointingly short battery life.

It would be a real ⁸**pl**_____ if updates were automatic rather than manual.

3 Read the review. Which type of consumer are drones primarily aimed at?

1 Estate agents ☐
2 Home delivery companies ☐
3 Professional photographers ☐

4 Choose the correct words to complete the review.

THE STAYING-POWER OF DRONES

When drones were first produced in the 1940s, they were strictly ¹_designed / enabled_ for military use, and this remained the case for several decades. Then it became obvious that everyone could find a use for a drone, ²_not / if_ only for practical pursuits, but also to experience the thrill of controlling an object as it flies through the sky.

One of the most prevalent uses for camera-equipped drones is selling houses. Employing a high-quality drone has become the first ³_choice / option_ for estate agents so that they can create **first-rate** advertising. A remote-control drone ⁴_allows / offers_ you to shoot **jaw-dropping** footage, and the ⁵_ease of use / user-friendly_ of the latest models means that **astute** estate agents can do the job themselves, creating **mind-blowing** photos so as to highlight a home's location and other advantages.

⁶_Even / While_ drones are popular amongst estate agents, they have become the **ultimate** necessity in agriculture, forest management and environmental sciences. These specialised drones ⁷_benefit / boast_ features such as monitors to measure soil quality, moisture levels and pest damage, and they offer ⁸_outstanding / expert_ advantages for those who watch over large areas of land. In fact, for keeping the land healthy and productive, the latest specialised drones are **peerless**.

⁹_Some / Others_ might think that using drones for delivering packages to homes would provide a **spectacular** advantage for both customers and the environment, but while it's a **nifty** idea, it has yet to become a reality. Operating a drone above the ground is one thing, but allowing it to land in someone's front garden can be risky, ¹⁰_whether / if_ to playing children or passing drivers. However cool it would be to have your purchases dropped on your doorstep, that feature may have to wait a while so as not to endanger property or innocent bystanders!

5 Match the adjectives in bold from the review to their synonyms. Some words may be chosen more than once.

1 impressive   – *jaw-dropping* / _____ / _____

2 unbeatable   – _____ / _____
3 skilful/agile   – _____
4 perfect   – _____ / _____
5 intelligent   – _____
6 top quality   – _____

6 Choose the correct adjectives to complete the sentences.

1 The site is gorgeous; some of the most *astute* / *ultimate* minds in web design are clearly at work here.
2 The depth of information on DJs and producers is truly *nifty* / *spectacular* and enough to keep even the most ardent fans entertained.
3 This really is the *ultimate* / *first-rate* page for lovers of all things science fiction.
4 Rising way above the competition, this cookery website is *mind-blowing* / *peerless* in its category.
5 Offering plenty of *spectacular* / *nifty* little suggestions, tips and tricks, this site will really help you improve your language skills.

7 Underline the following structures which express purpose in the review.

- Two beginning with *to* + infinitive + noun phrase
- One beginning with *so that*
- Two beginning with *so as (not) to*
- Four beginning with *for*

8 Complete the second sentence so that it means the same as the first. Do not change the words in capitals.

The red button is there to allow you to instantly wipe all data if your privacy is violated. **SO**
The red button is there *so you can instantly wipe* all data if your privacy is violated.

1 It is advisable to limit your workouts to ninety minutes per day to avoid overexerting yourself. **AS NOT**
It is advisable to limit your workouts to ninety minutes per day _____ yourself.

2 The tablet goes to sleep after ten inactive minutes to save battery life. **ORDER**
The tablet goes to sleep after ten inactive minutes _____ battery life.

3 Novice gamers will find this model ideal but it has limited functionality for those who are more experienced. **FOR**
_____ , but has limited functionality for those who are more experienced.

4 Always return your knife safely to its sheath in order to minimise the risk of injury. **AS**
Always return your knife safely to its sheath _____ the risk of injury.

5 Keep a spare ink cartridge in stock so you don't run out in the middle of an important job. **TO AVOID**
Keep a spare ink cartridge in stock _____ _____ in the middle of an important job.

SHOW WHAT YOU'VE LEARNT

9 Read the writing task. Then follow the instructions below.

Reviews Wanted: Most popular websites

You have been asked to write a review for your school's online magazine, in which you evaluate your favourite website. Describe what it is about, who it is for and what the benefits are.

Before you start, follow steps 1–2 below.

1 Brainstorm ideas:
- What kind of website is it? What content is available/service does it provide?
- Who is it aimed at?
- Is it easy to navigate?
- What are its key features? Does it offer anything unique?
- Why do you like it so much?
- Are there any similar websites to which you could compare it?
- Are there any drawbacks or areas in which it could be improved?
2 Make a plan for your review then complete the writing task.

SHOW THAT YOU'VE CHECKED

Finished? Always check your writing (especially in the exam!) Can you tick ✓ everything on this list?

In my review of a product:

• in the introduction, I have aroused the reader's interest in the product.	☐
• I have said what need or problem the product offers a solution to.	☐
• in the main body, I have …	☐
❯ specified what the product does and what it offers.	☐
❯ explained any special benefits or features and used positive adjectives to describe them.	☐
❯ used listing phrases to connect the information.	☐
❯ included a comparison with other similar products if appropriate.	☐
❯ mentioned any drawbacks or areas for improvement.	☐
• in the conclusion, I have summarised the benefits of the product.	☐
• I have used a reasonably formal and impersonal style.	☐
• I have checked my spelling.	☐
• I have checked my handwriting is neat enough for someone else to read.	☐

4.8 SELF-CHECK

VOCABULARY

1 Match words from boxes A and B to form expressions and compounds. Sometimes you need to use a hyphen (-). Then complete the sentences with the expressions and compounds.

A   back   commercial   ~~draw~~
    ever   flick   purpose

B   better   built   flop   lash
    ~~the line~~   through

You can make as much noise as you want, but I _draw the line_ at playing loud music during the rehearsal.

1 Our school will be the first in the region to have a _____ language laboratory.
2 With so much advancement in equipment, sports photographers come up with _____ action shots.
3 After the manager's proposal to work at the weekend, there was a _____ against the idea.
4 Although the band spent months recording their new album, it turned out to be a _____ .
5 Before I decide whether to buy a fashion magazine or not, I first _____ it to see what the contents are like.

/5

2 Choose the correct answer.

The quality of Amy's work started to (decline)/ enhance / compromise so she stopped doing the campaign.

1 Having starred in a few minor plays, George came into _prominence / resurgence / ascendency_ when he got the role of Hamlet.
2 The singer could hardly see the audience because the spotlights _drew / swiped / glared_ straight into her eyes.
3 The first artificial language, Esperanto, was the _brainchild / counterpart / prowess_ of Ludwik Zamenhof.
4 Interviewees should realise that their success in the application process rides _at / in / on_ both their communication skills and being prepared for the interview.
5 Changing the boss of a company doesn't always _enrich / fuel / savour_ improvements in the way it operates.

/5

3 Complete the sentences with the correct forms of the words in brackets.

What struck us most about Pino was his _diligence_ (diligent) in creating the school's webpage.

1 Lowering the prices of smartphones suddenly increased their _____ (popular).
2 Unfortunately, the athlete's misconduct _____ (cheap) his contract with an advertising company.
3 It's hard to put up with his _____ (careless) when it comes to installing new software on his laptop.
4 I'm sure we'll solve the problem of overbooking the concert as a result of our _____ (genius).
5 Our aim is to raise young people's _____ (aware) of the health risks connected with playing video games for too long.

/5

GRAMMAR

4 Complete the sentences with the correct forms of the verbs in brackets. Use at least two words in each gap.

A group of scientists were unable _to identify_ (identify) the problems with the equipment used in space.

1 Maria begged _____ (we/help) her with the research enabling her to write her dissertation.
2 The workers seem _____ (not/do) the demolition work according to the timetable agreed.
3 _____ (find) a cure for cancer is not easy even for the most advanced teams of researchers.
4 Students were made _____ (vacate) the lab while he did some experiments with explosive materials.
5 You are _____ (not/conduct) another survey for a year; all your colleagues have already voted the mobile phone as their favourite invention.

/5

5 Complete the sentences with the correct form of the verbs in the box. Add any other words necessary. The number of words needed is in brackets.

confirm   ~~finish~~   open   play   save   send

Victoria was the first _to finish_ a report about neurosurgery. (2)

1 Your children were seen _____ with the remote controls in the garden. (3)
2 My parents bought a more economical washing machine so _____ money on bills. (3)
3 The PM _____ the Science Centre tomorrow. (3)
4 _____ your booking you should contact us at least a fortnight in advance. (2)
5 Our IT specialist was surprised not _____ any data on the virus. (4)

/5

6 Choose the correct expression.

The rise of e-readers

(Interestingly)/ Annoyingly / To some extent, the first e-readers were not created for ordinary people, but for specialists who wanted to share documents like technical manuals.
[1]_Frankly / Clearly / Fortunately_, these were not for general consumption, but once people realised that electronic books could appeal to a wider readership, more variations of e-readers were produced. [2]_Unfortunately / Likely / Anyway_, each one used a different format. They also differed in the kind of books they made available on their individual platforms. [3]_Thankfully / In fact / Potentially_, some focused on obscure publications, while others on new authors.
In time the commercial market grew, and e-readers can now be seen everywhere. [4]_Strikingly / Without doubt / Personally_, they provide a complete mobile library for avid readers, and their backlit screens mean they can be read anywhere, anytime.
[5]_Apparently / Of course / Incidentally_, sales of paperback books have actually increased despite the popularity of e-readers.

/5

Total   /30

50

7 Choose the correct answer A, B, C or D.

The impact of music

Does music have the same emotional impact as it did in the past? Has technology A a role not only in the way music is composed and recorded but also in its power?

¹__ , current technology allows anyone to stream niche videos and download audio clips, which has created a far wider ²__ base for a greater variety of music than the more traditional ³__ forums of the past. Has this ⁴__ the arrival of a new musical age, though?

As a ⁵__ of fact, it has been suggested that technology has had a negative impact on music. This is because it could make composers reluctant to experiment, relying instead on what has always been popular. This might appear to create a uniformity of sound, which some feel has led to a ⁶__ in musicality.

This opinion is not universally held, ⁷__ there are comments which have been ⁸__ on music websites suggesting that technology has contributed towards reducing music's emotional impact.

	(A) played	B made
	C done	D given
1	A Plainly	B Likely
	C Potentially	D Consequently
2	A enthusiast	B admirer
	C follower	D fan
3	A typical	B average
	C normal	D mainstream
4	A set	B drawn
	C heralded	D pushed
5	A limit	B matter
	C indication	D proof
6	A downturn	B backlash
	C standard	D prominence
7	A conversely	B since
	C potentially	D nevertheless
8	A delivered	B posted
	C informed	D sent

/8

8 Complete the text with the correct forms of the words in brackets.

Is technology good for the sport of motor racing?

The roar of the engines and speed of the cars generate tremendous _excitement_ (excite), as spectators cheer on the top drivers.

Now, as ever more technological advances enhance performance, critics question the modern approach to racing. They say affluent teams have an advantage, as they can ¹_____ (capital) on their financial resources to develop cars that allow them to remain in the ²_____ (ascend), while others fall by the wayside. ³_____ (presume), such critics also feel the complexity of the machinery has replaced simple driving skills, thus depriving the sport of its basic ⁴_____ (authentic).

However, advances in car design bring benefits beyond the racetrack – mechanical ⁵_____ (break) in racing car design filter down to the mass market. For example, rearview mirrors date back to the 1900s, when racing drivers realised their ⁶_____ (effect) for revealing competitors behind them.

Clearly, although the sport remains popular with fans, it's technology that guarantees its continuing commercial success.

/6

9 Complete the text with one word in each gap.

Being a games designer is _the_ best job – ever! I must admit that in a ¹_____ I expected the job to be rather dull and repetitive – at least to a certain extent. When I first saw the designers on my work experience programme, everyone appeared to ²_____ constantly fazed and bleary-eyed from staring at the computer monitor too long. But now I hold their commitment in very ³_____ esteem – in fact, it's a sheer ⁴_____ to see them so focused on their work. Being a designer allows you to ⁵_____ the limits of current technology and even help bring about the next generation of hardware. In order ⁶_____ to go crazy though, you really do need to step away from the screen at regular intervals.

/6

Total /20

5 All in a day's work

VOCABULARY

5.1

Employment and career • phrasal verbs • colloquial phrases • collocations to describe work and money

SHOW WHAT YOU KNOW

1 Complete the text with the correct forms of the words from the box.

> apply   compete   employ   ~~interview~~
> manage   promote   recruit   train

Graduates! Finding it hard to impress _interviewers_ and stand out from other ¹_____ ? At Freshlegs we're here to help you beat the ²_____ and find the office job of your dreams. We are a ³_____ agency specialising in matching graduates with reputable ⁴_____ . We focus on positions that offer on-the-job ⁵_____ and the prospect of ⁶_____ to senior or ⁷_____ positions.

To find out more, visit our website freshlegs.com.

WORD STORE 5A | Phrasal verbs – work

2 Combine words from boxes A and B to make phrasal verbs. Then complete the dialogues with the correct forms of the phrasal verbs.

> A [break   make   ~~order~~   press
>   slave   snow   stand   take]

> A [~~around~~   away   into   on (x2)
>   under   up (x2)]

Conversation 1: Ali and Carol

A: How was your day?

C: Terrible. I was _ordered around_ all day long by my supervisor. I don't mind being told what to do, but she's so rude!

A: Oh Carol, you need to ¹_____ for yourself a bit more! Say something if she's being rude unnecessarily.

C: Well, that's easily said, Ali, but I don't want to make things worse.

A: I know it's difficult. I'll tell you what, why don't we go out for dinner to ²_____ for your bad day. Take your mind off it, you know?

Conversation 2: Fiona and George

F: What do you want to do after university?

G: Actually, I'm hoping to ³_____ acting.

F: Acting? Cool. Are you taking classes?

G: Fiona, acting isn't something you learn. You've either got that special something or you haven't. Actors are ⁴_____ on the strength of a good audition, not because of some course they did.

F: And exactly how do you think actors get good enough to succeed in auditions, George?

Conversation 3: Jean and Geoff

J: I'm constantly being ⁵_____ with more work than one person can reasonably be expected to do. I do my best to keep at it, you know, ⁶_____ , but the pile in the in-tray never seems to get any smaller.

G: You know what they say: 'work to live, not live to work'.

J: Well 'they' can shut up, whoever 'they' are! What am I supposed to do, tell the boss 'OK, I've had enough for today and I'm going home to live my life', while everyone else is still ⁷_____ ?

Jean? I'm afraid she's not available now. She's snowed under with work.

WORD STORE 5B | Colloquial phrases

3 Match the sentence beginnings and endings.

Some graduates are willing to work for nothing to get ☐H

1 Philip dressed far too casually for the interview and so scuppered ☐
2 You can't quit until you find something else, so you'll just have to put on ☐
3 A first class honours degree can really jump ☐
4 If I hadn't had the ☐
5 The chef asked me to keep ☐
6 Although it may be unfair, knowing the right people can help you to get ☐
7 I understand from your supervisor that you've hit ☐

A his chances before he'd even begun.

B guts to change courses after my first year, I might not have got a qualification at all.

C the ground running and surprised everyone in your first month here.

D tabs on the new cook at work and make sure he wasn't messing up the preparation.

E -start your career, especially if it's from a prestigious university.

F a brave face and start looking elsewhere.

G your foot in the door in this business.

H on the first rung of the ladder.

WORD STORE 5C | Collocations – *work*

4 Choose the correct option to complete the sentences.

1 If you ask me, *unpaid* / *plum* internships exploit the young and the inexperienced.

2 Make sure the company covers your *experience* / *expenses* or you won't earn anything from the trip.

3 Every manager should occasionally do *menial* / *minimum* tasks so they don't forget what their subordinates go through on a daily basis.

4 As a freelancer, I don't have a *placement* / *permanent* contract, so I have less job security.

5 With his technical know-how, Peter has made himself *indispensable* / *hands-on* around the office.

6 If you want to be a teacher, working as a classroom assistant is a good way to gain *overtime* / *experience*.

5 Complete the notices. The first letters are given.

Those who have **w**_orked_ **o**_vertime_ this month please submit your time sheets with details of the extra hours by the 31st at 12:00.

Aged between sixteen and eighteen and looking for ¹**h**_____ **e**_____ in the building trade? Contact us now about ²**s**____-**t**____ **p**_____ (two to four weeks) on building sites in the local area.

Sign this petition and support our campaign to increase the ³**m**_____ **w**_____ by 10 percent for all workers.

You'll never ⁴**l**_____ a **p**_____ **j**_____ if your CV is not up to scratch! Click here to find out how we can help you secure the perfect position.

We are now recruiting graduates for ⁵**e**_____-**l**_____ **j**_____ . Start at the beginning and quickly work your way up through our promotional structure.

WORD STORE 5D | EXTRA Collocations

6 Complete the text with the missing words. Use the information in brackets to help you. The first letters are given.

---

whatsnextgraduate.com　　　Home | Search | Contact

Talk to anyone? Full of energy? Why not be a holiday rep?

Among all the short-term jobs available for graduates, being a holiday rep is probably one of the most fun. Of course, it's unlikely to turn into a career and you probably won't **get a p**ension (receive money from employers or the government after you have retired), but you are also not going to have to ¹**work for n**_____ (receive no pay) and reps ²**get p**_____ (receive non-financial bonuses) that are the envy of many a holidaying office worker.

With free accommodation and transport plus cheap food and drinks, it's easy enough to ³**make e**_____ **meet** (earn enough money to survive). Most reps receive a small basic salary then ⁴**work on c**_____ (receive payment according to how much you sell) to top this up. If you sell enough trips and tickets to ⁵**make your t**_____ (sell as much as you have been asked to) or even better go beyond it, it is possible, in relative terms, to ⁶**make a m**_____ (earn a large amount of money). Just one piece of advice. This is a twenty-four-hour job with no early nights or lazy mornings.

---

7 Choose the collocation which is not possible or not likely in each group.

1 **make a** *profit* / *loss* / *rise*
2 **get** *a pension* / *for nothing* / *a rise*
3 **work for** *perks* / *a pittance* / *peanuts*
4 **make** *a mint* / *commission* / *your target*
5 **get** *ends meet* / *a financial incentive* / *perks*

SHOW WHAT YOU'VE LEARNT

8 Complete each pair of sentences with the same answer A–C.

1 a I was so sick of being __ under with paperwork that decided to quit and retrain.
  b It hasn't __ so much since the winter of 1987, when there were drifts of three metres in places.
  A pulled　　B snowed　　C rained

2 a Today's home-baked treat is a delicious seasonal _ and apple crumble.
  b Kit landed a __ job with the BBC and is now filming in the Caribbean.
  A mint　　B top　　C plum

3 a Allergy advice: This product may contain traces of __ or almonds.
  b You know what they say: if you pay __ , you get monkeys.
  A peanuts　　B pittances　　C slave

4 a I've __ everyone who was at the party except Kelly, whose phone is broken.
  b It's almost impossible to get on the first __ of the ladder without a recognised qualification.
  A rung　　B step　　C seen

5 a Are you keeping __ on me? You've been watching me all morning.
  b Warning: You need to close old __ in your browser before you can open new ones.
  A notes　　B tabs　　C eyes

9 Choose the correct answer A–C.

1 We really need to __ on if we are going to have all these orders ready before the holiday rush.
  A work　　B put　　C press

2 Knowing the theory is all well and good but we are looking for someone with hands-on __ .
  A experience　　B commission　　C expenses

3 We recommend an unpaid __ as a way to gain experience.
  A wage　　B contract　　C internship

4 If the company makes a __ again next month, we'll be looking at possible bankruptcy.
  A profit　　B loss　　C target

5 To be honest, without a decent financial __ I can't see any reason to take on a heavier workload.
  A incentive　　B rise　　C pension

/10

The Rebirth of Apprenticeships

Apprenticeships are currently experiencing a renaissance as a hands-on alternative to academic study at a higher education institution. Today, we offer the views of four young people currently enrolled in various apprenticeship programmes in the UK.

A J. Reynard, 18

I'm in my first year of a three-year HR apprenticeship at a well-known British bank and, although it was a shock to be thrown in at the deep end, as I was expected to be on a par with* everyone else, I really feel I made the right decision in taking it on. From day one I was plunged into the HR team and expected to contribute to the real workings of the bank. Through a series of placements in the HR department, I've completed projects in all sorts of things from *change and growth* to *personal development and reward*. Alongside this I'm studying for an industry-recognised, degree-level HR qualification, so by the time I've finished, I'll have the experience and the all-important piece of paper. The academic assignments are all about utilising your day-to-day experience, making observations and linking in the theory, and for me it has proven to be a very efficient way to learn.

Based on my experiences here, I'd say apprenticeships are great for team-players who have a strong drive to learn and are willing to apply themselves to whatever challenges are thrown their way.

B A. Rawlins, 19

When I was a younger teenager, I was in a fairly bad place personally and emotionally. As a result of some less than positive experiences in my personal life, I missed my chance to go to university, and with everything that went on, the last thing I'd thought about was what I actually wanted to do as a career. So, I decided to take things into my own hands and sign up for some training with a view to finding a job. I didn't have high hopes of being accepted on an apprenticeship to be honest, but lo and behold*, here I am two years in and absolutely thriving, I'd say. Working at such a prestigious car company gives me a real sense of pride and people are always intrigued when I say who I work for. There is no denying it's a male-dominated environment, and at first I felt like I had more to prove than the guys who started at the same time as me. However, I showed myself to be capable and competent and quickly earned everyone's respect. If I'm honest, having a sharp tongue helps! I stuck up for myself when I had to and people know not to mess with me now. I think apprenticeships are sometimes overlooked by school leavers, but in my case being an apprentice has provided me with some real direction in life and the added bonus of relative financial stability.

C A. Mendel, 19

My folks are not well off so the only way I could've made it through university would have been to take loans to cover tuition and living. The thought of graduating with tens of thousands of pounds of debt was enough to put me off before I'd even begun. The careers counsellor at my school suggested I try an apprenticeship instead. Frankly speaking, I'd always regarded apprenticeships as being a bit of a lazy option for those who didn't do so well at school, so I was amazed to discover what a wide range of options there actually are out there now. I'm working with my hands, which I love, I've got a stable income, and I'm planning to start my own plumbing business one day. And laziness is strictly out of bounds*, let me tell you*! If something goes wrong, you realise it could be your fault and you have to take responsibility. It's hard work and long hours. I don't remember the last time I went out during the week – I'm too busy and tired.

D Anonymous, 18

I guess most people wouldn't believe me if I told them I was an apprentice spy, but, as I am sworn to anonymity, that's really only a moot point* anyway. The apprenticeship scheme, run by MI5, MI6 and GCHQ (Government Communications Headquarters), has its sights on tackling future threats to national security. There are eighty of us undergoing training in software engineering, telecommunications and mobile phone systems with a view to joining the global fight against cyber crime, terrorism, and espionage. On completion of the two years it takes, we'll have earned a foundation degree in communications, security and engineering, as well as a diploma in IT. Traditionally, security service positions are only open to university graduates, but, as was pointed out to us during the selection procedure, you can't learn what we're covering on any undergraduate course, because we are actually inside the security services, finding out about the systems needed to protect the country from harm. I think this is a prime example of the way apprenticeships are offering a real alternative to university these days, an alternative which equips anyone with industry specific skills and, crucially, doesn't leave them owing a small fortune.

GLOSSARY

on a par with *(phr)* – as good as or equal to
lo and behold *(phr)* – a humorous way to introduce surprising information
out of bounds *(phr)* – forbidden

let me tell you! *(phr)* – used for emphasis
a moot point *(phr)* – an issue that is debatable and open for discussion but of no practical significance

1 Read the article quickly and match each picture to a paragraph.

1 ☐

2 ☐

3 ☐

4 ☐

2 Read the article again. For questions 1–10, choose from sections A–D. The sections may be chosen more than once.

Which apprentice

1 was surprised to be accepted into their apprenticeship programme? ☐

2 compares the usefulness of their apprenticeship with a university degree? ☐

3 chose an apprenticeship for financial reasons? ☐

4 admits that their apprenticeship has had an impact on their social life? ☐

5 felt discriminated against initially in their apprenticeship? ☐

6 praises the way study and work are combined in their apprenticeship? ☐

7 demonstrated their self-confidence to colleagues? ☐

8 was not expecting to take on an employee's responsibilities so early in the apprenticeship? ☐

9 believes their apprenticeship scheme will have far-reaching benefits beyond the personal? ☐

10 acknowledges their early misconceptions about apprenticeships? ☐

3 Complete the definitions with the words from the box. Use the text to help you.

> apply ~~deep~~ hands high sharp small

If you are **thrown in at the** _deep_ **end**, you are made to do something difficult without adequate preparation.

1 If you **have _____ hopes**, you are very optimistic or hopeful that something will happen.

2 If you **owe a _____ fortune**, you have a large amount of debt.

3 If you **_____ yourself to something**, you give it all your focus and attention.

4 If you **take something into your own _____ ,** you stop relying on someone else and take personal responsibility for it.

5 If you **have a _____ tongue**, you speak harshly or critically but in a clever way.

WORD STORE 5E | Collocations

4 Complete the extract from an interview with the words from the box. There are three extra words.

> base business charity ~~dream~~ growth
> insight losses recognition talent

DJ-DIGEST: How did XR records get started?

Damien: Well, I'd always dreamed of starting a record label, so after DJ-ing and producing music for several years, my business partner and I decided to follow our _dream_ and found our ¹_____ . Our first release did really well in the clubs, but we sustained financial ²_____ because of the expense of the start-up. However, the popularity of the record on dance floors helped XR records gain ³_____ among big name DJs and helped us build our customer ⁴_____ . We've just released our twentieth record and are now focusing on recruiting new ⁵_____ to the label.

5 Look at the vocabulary in lesson 5.2 in the Student's Book, then complete the adverts. The first letters are given.

Kickstarter helps you **g**_auge_ **c**_onsumer_ **o**_pinion_ and raise capital for your start-up business.

_____

Vocational training to help you ¹**r**_____ your **p**_____ . Be the best that you can. Now recruiting.

_____

Get your career off to a ²**f**_____ **s**_____ with our CV preparation services: cvservices@cmail.net

_____

³**F**_____ in your **r**_____ ? Rich one minute, broke the next? Sharkey's loans can help your business cope.

_____

Invest with Larkin and Sons financial brokers. Our investments consistently ⁴**s**_____ a healthy **r**_____ within eight weeks.

_____

Are you ⁵**f**_____ **o**_____ of agricultural college and wondering what to do next? Sheffield council is now recruiting summer rangers for its parks and gardens.

_____

If you ⁶**h**_____ a great **r**_____ with children, why not volunteer to help at Blackmore Orphanage?

SHOW WHAT YOU KNOW

1 Complete the sentences with the *-ing* form of the verbs from the box. There are two extra verbs.

> be   call   check   fasciate   ~~have~~
> intern   take   talk   pretend

The two teams were already *having* a brainstorming session when several latecomers arrived.

1 _____ young and single, Jake didn't say no to the relocation to a different city.

2 By mid-spring, he'll have been _____ for us for a year.

3 It's always worth _____ the details of any contract before you sign it.

4 That man _____ to our head teacher is a famous entrepreneur and former student.

5 Many employees admit to _____ to be busy when their boss is looking.

6 It's _____ to imagine where Mark Zuckerberg might be working now if he hadn't dropped out of Harvard.

2 ★ Complete the text with one word in each gap.

THE WEIRDEST JOBS IN THE WORLD

Nancy Rica Schiff, an American photographer, is keen on *bringing* some of the world's oddest professions to people's attention. Would you ever consider ¹_____ such jobs as dog food tester, dinosaur duster or golf ball diver? No? Apparently some people out there have succeeded ²_____ pursuing a career in these strange occupations. ³_____ travelling around the USA for fifteen years, Nancy was tracking down professionals with unique jobs, from the person who dresses Barbie dolls for a living, a gumbuster whose job involves ⁴_____ rid of chewing gum marks from the streets, to a knife-thrower's assistant, to mention just a few. Miss Schiff claims she will never grow tired ⁵_____ spotting occupations with a twist of humour, her favourite ⁶_____ that of a professional mermaid. So next time you fancy ⁷_____ your job, you might want to refer to her art for inspiration.

3 ★ ★ Complete the sentences with the correct forms of the verbs in brackets.

Having studied (study) at the same school as the company owner, Dave hoped to get a better-paid job.

1 _____ (not/have) any kind of formal training before, I seriously doubted they'd give me that job.

2 _____ (dismiss) unfairly, my mum decided to go to court to fight for her rights.

3 Don't tell anyone, but your brother was seen _____ (reprimand) by his boss in the restaurant today.

4 Some students complained about _____ (not/send) any information regarding the scholarship.

4 ★ ★ Complete the sentences with the words in brackets. Do not change the form of the words. Use three words in each gap.

My tutor is concerned *about my working* at the weekends instead of learning. (working)

1 The trainee waiter insisted _____ his weekly wages in advance. (given)

2 My new employer insisted _____ her a reference from my previous boss. (giving)

3 Phil's Maths teacher doesn't approve _____ a 'slave driver' behind his back. (called)

4 Jenny's friends don't approve _____ them only when she needs something. (calling)

5 ★ ★ ★ Complete the second sentence so that it means the same as the first. Do not change the words in capitals. Use between three and six words in each gap.

It's pointless to bring this subject up again. **USE**
It is no use bringing this subject up again.

1 As soon as Bess was given a day off, she went on a shopping spree with her best friend. **ON**
_____ a day off, Bess went on a shopping spree with her best friend.

2 It doesn't make sense to ask him for a pay rise. **POINT**
_____ him for a pay rise.

3 Many entrepreneurs complain that they find it difficult to get enough qualified staff. **DIFFICULTY**
Many entrepreneurs complain that they _____ enough qualified staff.

4 As more and more people leave the country, soon we'll experience a serious shortage of staff. **WITH**
_____ the country, soon we'll experience a serious shortage of staff.

5 It is counterproductive to talk to her about promoting you now. **GOOD**
_____ to her about promoting you now.

SHOW WHAT YOU'VE LEARNT

6 Complete the sentences with the words in brackets in the correct forms. Do not change the word order. Use between four and six words in each gap.

After six months, my brother finally *succeeded in finding a job* (succeed/find/job) as a clerk.

1 _____ (not/be able/find) a job for one year, he was entitled to unemployment benefit.

2 His partner doesn't _____ (approve/he/accept) that new job in the capital.

3 _____ (be/made redundant) so suddenly, Mark's parents hadn't prepared any contingency plan.

4 _____ (on/tell/news), Fiona immediately called her parents for advice.

5 Fifteen years in this profession and Arthur still _____ (have/difficult/get used) to night shifts.

6 _____ (with/she/job/get) too stressful, Ella decided to take a year off and travel.

/6

1 Complete the text with the missing prepositions.

The Young & The Rich

<u>At</u> times we find ourselves drawn to stories of people who become millionaires at a very early age and wish we could swap places with them. **¹___** other words, we all want to be rich. Here are two young entrepreneurs who struck gold:

John Koon – net worth: $80 million

²___ first glance, John looks like an average guy. However, being resourceful **³___** nature, he had already made $1 million by the age of sixteen. His auto parts business was famous **⁴___** co-operating with MTV, but he quickly became more interested in fashion, especially streetwear. The entrepreneur is currently **⁵___** charge of several clothing brands in New York City.

Ashley Qualls – net worth: $8 million

Her passion for self-learning lies **⁶___** the heart of her success. When she was fourteen, Ashley decided to study HTML, which helped her design websites. Having launched Whateverlife.com, she attracted lots of enthusiasm **⁷___** her unique web page designs, and by 2007 had 7 million monthly page hits, which generated a huge income **⁸___** advertising. More recently, Ashley has been battling an autoimmune disease, and is active in projects supporting the chronically ill.

How much money do you get a month?

Erm, about $100,000.

Convention of Young Millionaires

2 Replace the underlined words with the phrases from the box. There are two extra phrases.

> at sea   by chance   by virtue of   in the long run
> in the wrong   ~~to a certain degree~~   to my mind
> to no avail

My parents agree with me <u>to some extent</u> on the subject of my moving out. *to a certain degree*

1 My cousin has sent about 100 applications over the past month, but all <u>in vain</u> as he hasn't received any response yet. _____

2 New workers almost always feel <u>at a loss</u> and they need someone to show them the ropes and answer their questions. _____

3 I put my success down to hard work, but my boss thinks it's just beginner's luck and he claims I found that investor <u>by accident</u>. _____

4 Nepotism means getting the best jobs <u>by means of</u> your family connections. _____

5 The disciplinary committee is investigating the case now and they will decide which one of us was <u>at fault</u>. _____

3 Complete the dialogue with one word in each gap. First letters are given.

B: Dad, can I talk to you about something?

D: By all m*eans*! What is it?

B: There's this girl from Australia who gained popularity on the Internet by posting her photos wearing the latest fashion.

D: And? What about her?

B: Yesterday she surprised her followers, including myself, by announcing that she'd been living a lie. Apparently she had all those clothes at her **¹d_____** because different companies paid her to wear them. Every one of her photos was carefully staged and retouched.

D: Oh, sorry to hear that.

B: I've been so naive. I've read all her messages to **²d____** and honestly believed she looked great. Now she says she wore tons of make-up. True, she admits she was wrong and that now she'll help people understand that social media promote fake images.

D: Well, she definitely should have told her fans in **³a_____** that she was getting paid for the pictures and that she photoshopped them to such an extent. In any **⁴c_____** , she apologised to them and promised to help people.

B: Yes, but maybe it's just another business idea of hers.

D: Could be. Remember, Becky, at the **⁵e_____** of the day everyone has to ask themselves a very important question: do I want to be honest at what I do or risk losing face if I'm not?

B: Quite right. I'm glad we've had this conversation, Dad.

SHOW WHAT YOU'VE LEARNT

4 Choose the correct phrase. Sometimes two are correct.

1 You may think what you want, but ___ it was a rookie mistake and you should've known better than to trust it.
   A by nature   **B** at times
   C to my mind   **D** at first glance

2 Geoff and his two co-workers ought to have notified us well ___ that they were planning on resigning.
   A in advance   **B** in vain
   C by chance   **D** in charge of

3 The trainees had all the company equipment ___ and they could make use of it as they saw fit.
   A in the wrong   **B** at fault
   C in any case   **D** at their disposal

4 I hope I'm mistaken but ___ the whole economy is going to suffer because of the government's decisions.
   A in the long run   **B** by virtue of
   C in other words   **D** by means of

5 56 percent has been the highest unemployment rate among young people in Spain ___ .
   A by all means   **B** at the end of the day
   C to date   **D** at a loss

6 Sheila's parents believe she should seek employment as soon as possible and ___ she agrees with them.
   A to a certain degree   **B** by accident
   C to some extent   **D** at sea

/6

5.5

Synonyms • informal phrases
• word building

1 Read the interview with Jonathan. It contains six examples of the word *important*. Choose the one word in brackets which <u>cannot</u> substitute the word *important* in the context given.

Extract from Student's Book recording 🔊 **2.15**

H: What would you say is the most **important** [1](*crucial* / *essential* / *imperative*) thing people should do to prepare for a job interview?

J: Well, thinking through your answers and doing plenty of research about the business and the position you're applying for ^a<u>go without saying</u> – ultimately there's ^b<u>nothing more you can do about</u> the direction the interview itself might take. I think cultivating self-assurance ^c<u>plays a very big role</u> – this will help you act as if you're confident when answering questions, though clearly without ^d<u>going overboard</u> or pretending you can do things you can't! [...] It's **important** [2](*vital* / *imperative* / *considerable*) not to ^e<u>dwell on your mistakes</u>, but learn from them. And the odd slip is ^f<u>not the end of the world</u>. We're all ^g<u>human after all</u>. That said, willingness to ^h<u>admit your missteps</u> is very **important** [3](*urgent* / *significant* / *influential*) and will be appreciated by the interviewer. And while confidence is **important** [4](*fundamental* / *pivotal* / *essential*), avoid being self-aggrandising or boastful. [...] I think it's **important** [5](*imperative* / *pressing* / *paramount*) to keep things in proportion. Every interview is **important** [6](*extensive* / *critical* / *decisive*) and it's natural to be nervous – indeed I think for most people having no nerves is unrealistic and striving to do so could even be potentially detrimental.

---

2 Match definitions 1–7 to the underlined phrases a–h in the text. Write the letters in the boxes.

Jack, please don't go overboard. This one will be just fine.

	to do too much or try too hard to impress	d
1	to acknowledge the mistakes you make	
2	to be very self-evident or obvious	
3	to concentrate too much on your errors	
4	not as big a problem as you may think	
5	to be naturally prone to errors	
6	to have a significant impact on something	
7	out of your control or ability to influence	

3 Complete the sentences. Use the most suitable underlined phrase from Exercise 1 in an appropriate form.

I know we're a little snowed under right now but there's no need to *go overboard*. Nobody expects you to work 24/7 and the boss won't notice you slaving away.

1 Whilst we all know that Grace was at fault for the error, we all accept that she's _____ and as liable to make mistakes as the rest of us.

2 That small company that Hannah sold became quite prosperous afterwards and she is really kicking herself for selling up so soon. Still, there's _____ it now.

3 Michael said he's having sleepless nights because of the feedback he got. I told him it's _____ .

4 In order to succeed as an actor, perseverance _____ . Take Daniel Craig, for example, he'd been acting for years before he landed the role of James Bond.

5 Well, it _____ that Aiden's self-assurance is the reason behind his success.

6 Although it's crucial to be aware of the things you do wrong, it's not seen as being particularly useful to _____ for any great length of time.

7 How is Jorge ever going to learn if he refuses to _____ ? Surely it's the only way to improve.

WORD STORE 5F | Word building

4 Complete the sentences with the correct form of the word in brackets.

A *willingness* (willing) to work hard and accept criticism is essential in your first post.

1 You really need to be _____ (adaptation) when you work as a journalist – your working conditions can change in the blink of an eye.

2 I know it's good to be enthusiastic but the intern's _____ (keen) is beginning to annoy me.

3 One of the most valued skills in a good teacher is _____ (resourceful).

4 Too much _____ (self-assured) is bound to make you unpopular with colleagues.

5 The *Harry Potter* books were rejected by publishers nine times before finally being printed. You have to admire J.K. Rowling's _____ (persistent).

6 The stamp on the reverse of this painting is proof of its _____ (authentic).

7 Fabio admitted to making the mistake in the payroll. You certainly can't question his _____ (sincere).

8 Most actors aren't known for their _____ (humble) but Keanu Reeves seems to be very down-to-earth.

1 Put the advice in the correct order.

When you respond to questions,	☐ 1
to buy even more time.	☐
which give you time	☐
It is not unusual	☐
you can use expressions	☐
to put several of these phrases together	☐
to think about your answers.	☐

2 Choose the correct words to complete the phrases.

1 Hmm, let me *see* / *think* about it for a second.

2 In actual fact, I've never really been *considered* / *asked* that before.

3 My mind has gone *frank* / *blank*.

4 I mean, to tell you the *honest* / *truth* …

5 Well, all I can *say* / *know* is that …

6 I suppose it *requires* / *depends* what you mean.

3 Complete the extracts from interviews. The first letters are given.

Interview 1: Joel

I: Tell me Joel, if you could have dinner with anyone at all, dead or alive, who would you choose and why?

J: Goodness, **l**et me **s**ee. That **¹r**_____ a **m**_____ **t**_____ .You know, to be **²f**_____ , I don't really fancy the idea of dinner with a dead person, so … er … definitely someone alive … which narrows it down considerably. But … I … er … I don't know really, to be **³h**_____ **w**_____ you, so … maybe … er … Superman?

I: Erm … I see. When I said dead or alive, I didn't actually mean … Actually, you know what, Joel, I think we have everything we need. Thanks for coming and we'll be in touch. Possibly.

Interview 2: Philip

I: OK thank you, Philip. Before we wrap things up, is there anything else important you think we should know about you? Or do you have any questions?

P: Well, I **⁴s**_____ it **d**_____ **w**_____ you **m**_____ by important. Can I ask to what extent criminal background checks are searched?

Interview 3: Hannah

I: You've had four different jobs in the last two years Hannah, could you explain why there have been so many?

H: Well, **⁵a**_____ I **c**_____ **s**_____ is **t**_____ getting a job is something I find easy, but keeping it is sometimes more of a challenge.

Interview 4: Claire

I: Claire, the vacant position requires a good deal of autonomy. Tell us how you set your own personal targets at work.

C: Personal targets? Hmm,**⁶c**_____ you **g**_____ me a **s**_____ ?

I: Of course. Take your time.

C: OK, well, I try not to set my personal goals too high, because I find if you set your targets low, you will rarely be disappointed.

I: Thank you, Claire. No more questions.

Interview 5: Alicia

I: And tell us Alicia, what is it that motivates you more than anything else?

A: **⁷A**_____ , that's a tough **o**_____ . I mean, to **⁸t**_____ you the **t**_____ , my main motivation is money. In fact, I think anyone who says anything different is probably lying.

Interview 6: Bradley

I: And could you tell us about what you consider to be your weaknesses?

B: **⁹In a**_____ **f**_____ , I've never really **¹⁰c**_____ it. I'm not sure I have any.

I: Wouldn't you agree that everyone has weaknesses?

B: Hmm. I suppose so. **¹¹C**_____ to **t**_____ of it, I guess I do have a weakness. I sometimes lie, or let's say I'm economical with the truth. But that should help me in this job, right?

I: Er … that's all we have time for, Bradley. Thanks for coming and please ask the next candidate to come in on your way out.

1 Complete the advice with the correct forms of the words in brackets.

An essay should present a _structured_ (structure) argument. It should be organised into paragraphs, each ¹_____ (deal) with an aspect of the topic.

In the introduction, ²_____ (familiar) the reader with the general topic, then lead into the discussion by ³_____ (acknowledge) different views or stating that a solution or discussion is necessary. In the body of the essay, introduce each main point in a new paragraph ⁴_____ (begin) with a topic sentence. Follow this with examples to support and/or ⁵_____ (clear) your point. You might also choose to introduce an ⁶_____ (oppose) point to show that you take a ⁷_____ (balance) view. In the conclusion, indicate the end of the essay with a summary ⁸_____ (state), then round things off by giving your own point of view.

2 Put the phrases in order.

that … / generally / it / maintained / is
It is generally maintained that …

1 by … / is / illustrated / this _____
2 place … / the / in / first _____
3 everything / into / taking / account … _____
4 main / thing / the / remember / to / is …

_____

5 seems / doubt / there / that … / little

_____

6 a / point … / in / case _____
7 spite / of … / in _____
8 to / say … / this / is _____

3 Complete the essay with the phrases from Exercise 2. There is one extra phrase.

Business has been a truly global affair for several decades now, and this has given rise to the prominence of English as the international language of commerce. While _it is generally maintained that_ this is the status quo, recent shifts in economic prosperity and global trading relationships have led observers and analysts to question the long-term future of the current lingua franca. Can the language of Austen and Shakespeare hang on to the lead indefinitely, or are its days at the top of the pile numbered?

¹_____ , when both native and non-native speakers are factored in, English is far and away the most popular tongue on the planet. ²_____ that in terms of sheer number of users, it is highly likely to remain at the forefront of worldwide trade for the foreseeable future. ³_____ the impressive growth of Mandarin Chinese as a potential challenger, there is still a very long way to go before it can be considered truly global. ⁴_____ the current improbability of a meeting between, for example, Arab, German and Brazilian business people being conducted in Mandarin rather than English.

Perhaps more probable than the toppling of the current language of choice, is the development of certain other **ones** as regional favourites. Mandarin once again is ⁵_____ and may actually be a better option as a second language than English for Japanese or Korean businesses operating in and around the East Asian region.

⁶_____ , English currently maintains a very strong position as a crucial tool for organisations and individuals wishing to operate commercially across borders. Despite the growing popularity of Mandarin, ⁷_____ it will remain the commercial lingua franca for a significant time to come.

4 Complete the extracts. The first letters are given.

Animal testing is undoubtedly a **c**ontroversial **t**opic on which opinions are starkly divided.

1 A **p**_____ **c**_____ is that the welfare system in its current form is open to abuse to those without moral scruples.

2 The **m**_____ **t**_____ to **r**_____ is the importance of tolerance and equality rather than fear and ignorance.

3 **W**_____ **c**_____ be **d**_____ to tackle the persistent problem of youth unemployment and make sure that all young people have the chance to earn a living?

4 **O**_____ the **w**_____ , it would seem that a combination of individual action and government investment are most likely to provide a solution.

5 **I**_____ the **f**_____ **p**_____ , businesses can certainly learn from their customers' comments and complaints.

6 **H**_____ , there are **d**_____ **v**_____ when it comes to the question of exactly what should be done about such human rights abuse.

7 There are, however, still many questions to be answered. **I**_____ **o**_____ **w**_____ , a solution is still a long way off.

8 It is **c**_____ **t**_____ the pluses outweigh the minuses in this particular case.

5 Find the following cohesive features in the model essay.

- Two forms from the same word family as *commerce*
  commercial [1] _____
- Two synonyms for the word *business*
  [2] _____ [3] _____
- A synonym for the word *language*
  [4] _____
- Two synonyms for the word *global*
  [5] _____ [6] _____
- Two forms from the same word family as *probably*
  [7] _____ [8] _____
- A synonym for the word *choice*
  [9] _____
- A linker with a similar meaning as *although*
  [10] _____
- A linker with a similar meaning as *in spite of*
  [11] _____
- The word that *ones* (in bold in the text) is substituting
  [12] _____

REMEMBER THIS

- When substituting a word already mentioned, we <u>do not</u> use **one** to replace <u>uncountable nouns</u>: *Would you prefer chocolate cake or lemon ~~one~~?*
- We <u>do not</u> use **one** immediately after <u>*a/an*</u>. *If you'd like a pear, pick ~~a~~ one from the tree.*

REMEMBER THIS

This and *it* can be used to refer back to previously mentioned situations. *This* is more emphatic than *it* and suggests that an interesting new fact has been mentioned.
*She banged her head on the car door. **It** really hurt.*
*She banged her head on the car door. **This** really hurt and made her dizzy.*

---

6 Read REMEMBER THIS. Correct the mistakes. Sometimes more than one answer may be possible.

Unemployment isn't just a statistic; ~~this~~ is a source of misery. *it*

1 Would you prefer a creative job or an administrative? _____

2 There are several possible solutions, but this essay will examine a one in particular. _____

3 Young people need a solution, a workable ones, and quickly. _____

4 There are some standard subjects I like, but Chemistry is not it. _____

5 Schools can be very traditional places. Some would say that is contributing to youth unemployment. _____

6 Young people lack support while applying for work. It is one reason why so many CVs are substandard. _____

SHOW WHAT YOU'VE LEARNT

7 Read the writing task. Then follow the instructions below.

There are various ways in which the problem of youth unemployment could be solved. Write an essay in which you discuss the following solutions and present your opinion:

- **offering more vocational training at schools.**
- **increasing financial incentives for employers to take on young people.**
- **mentoring young people as they apply for jobs.**

1 Think of examples to illustrate the positive aspects of each solution.
2 Think of any possible negative aspects of each solution.
3 Decide which you think is the most important and why.
4 Decide how you will begin. It is good to use a rhetorical question to start the discussion.
5 Use cohesive devices to make your argument clear and easy to follow.
6 Think of a logical conclusion. What is your point of view?
7 Write your essay.

SHOW THAT YOU'VE CHECKED

Finished? Always check your writing (especially in the exam!) Can you tick ✓ everything on this list?

In my essay:

- in the first paragraph, I have given a general introduction to the topic and included a lead-in to the discussion. ☐
- in the main body, I have … ☐
  › introduced each main point in a new paragraph. ☐
  › begun each main paragraph with a topic sentence. ☐
  › included examples to support and clarify my point. ☐
  › introduced an opposing point to demonstrate a balanced view. ☐
- in the conclusion, I have indicated the end of the essay with a summary statement and given my point of view. ☐
- I have used a reasonably formal and impersonal style. ☐
- I have checked my spelling. ☐
- I have checked my handwriting is neat enough for someone else to read. ☐

VOCABULARY

1 Complete the second sentence so that it means the same as the first. Do not change the words in capitals. Use between two and four words in each gap.

Anne disliked her first job as an assistant secretary because she only fetched coffee and did some photocopying. **TASKS**
Since Anne only did some _menial tasks_ in her first job, she disliked it.

1 Jim travels a lot on business but he doesn't spend any of his money – everything is covered by his company. **COVERS**
Jim's company _____ whenever he goes on a business trip.

2 He remembered I had supported him then. **UP**
He remembered _____ him then.

3 We admired how persistent he was looking for a job. **HIS**
We admired _____ in looking for a job.

4 Soon after Roger started his own business, he earned a lot of money. **MINT**
Roger _____ soon after he started his own business.

5 We all knew Kate was unfairly fired, but no one was courageous enough to say this to the manager. **GUTS**
Nobody _____ to say anything to the manager though we all knew sacking Kate was unfair.

/5

2 Complete the sentences with the correct prepositions.

It should be easy for you to break _into_ the job market since you've got so much experience already.

1 My brother has been singing praises about working _____ commission because he's a really great salesman.

2 Chris seems to be able to establish a great rapport _____ whoever works in the office.

3 It's just a part-time holiday job, so no wonder she works _____ a pittance.

4 Is there anything I can do to make _____ for all the time you spent here last Saturday?

5 I don't know how he can stand being ordered _____ in such a manner! I would quit the job if I were him!

/5

3 Choose the correct word.

Advances in technology have made a lot of people realise the (potential)/ tenacity / start-up of working from home. Some of them are finding a way to turn what was a hobby into paid work despite fluctuations in the [1]tax / revenue / commission at first. I used to enjoy my job as a teacher, even though I didn't have a(n) [2]phony / entry-level / permanent contract. Things changed, however, when we got a new, young and very bossy head teacher. At first I didn't want to [3]enthuse / scupper / strive my chances of getting a full-time post but finally, completely disillusioned, I decided to leave.
Friends warned me that a job with a minimum [4]wage / salary / perk was better than no job at all, but I do not regret turning my love of gardening into a business. Yes, it took time to get my [5]hand / leg / foot in the door, but I would still recommend it highly.

/5

GRAMMAR

4 Complete the sentences with the correct forms of the verbs in brackets.

Despite _having_ (have) a lot of ideas, he still hasn't made up his mind what to do in his life.

1 _____ (Not/know) that she could reach the meeting point from a different street, Sarah missed seeing her friend.

2 _____ (On/see) Jo's commitment to the project, we've decided to make her the leader of it.

3 Most teenagers hate _____ (not/ask) for permission before their parents share some information or photos from their childhood.

4 _____ (find) guilty of stealing some important data from an advertising company, Holly was sacked.

5 The trade unions are opposed to _____ (freeze) employees' wages because of their lack of experience.

/5

5 Complete the sentences with the words in brackets in the correct forms. Do not change the word order. Use no more than six words in each gap.

Having spent hours learning (spend/hour/learn) to operate a new app, Alba decided to ask for help.

1 It was interesting to see how quickly the new coach _____ (succeed/change/relationship) the players.

2 _____ (use/explain/you) absence at the meeting of the team. She won't listen to you anyway.

3 The psychologist _____ (overhear/applicant/talk) problems she had given them to solve when she was waiting for the lift.

4 _____ (not/complete/train) nurses, I can't even think about a job in a care centre for elderly people.

5 With _____ (more/time/use) by apprentices getting to know the trade nowadays, I can see no future for my line of work.

/5

6 Choose the correct expression.

The difference in results from these two groups might have come about (by chance)/ in advance / at a loss.

1 Yes, I've read your analysis but I'm still at fault / in the wrong / at sea as to how to apply it in our company.

2 At times of such deep economic crisis the government cannot solve its financial problems by means of / in any case / to date new taxes.

3 Don't even think that you're training in advance / in the long run / to no avail! I'm sure it'll pay off.

4 I can see your point, but to my mind / at the end of the day / in any case this time your line manager is right.

5 There are far too many accidents that happen at building sites in our country. Who do you think is at a loss / in the wrong / at fault?

/5

Total /30

7 Choose the correct answer A, B, C or D.

Working round the clock

Nearly two million adults attempting to start up a new business in the UK are doing so while at the same time _C_ at their 'day job.' This implies that after being **1**__ under with work all day, these people then have to go home and **2**__ yet more time and energy, not to mention a good deal of money, in their business. It must be tough to hit the **3**__ running like this after a hard day's work, particularly if it is uncertain whether the effort will eventually **4**__ . I suspect that not many of us would feel **5**__ even to contemplate doing this.

Of course the advantage of keeping on a permanent job is to guarantee a stable **6**__ in order to be able to make ends **7**__ and establish some useful contacts at the same time. It also means you have somebody to talk to during the working day. **8**__ as all that, it is useful back-up in case everything goes wrong!

	A enduring		B holding
	C sticking		D clinging
1	A snowed		B rained
	C blown		D flooded
2	A lay		B invest
	C consume		D put
3	A land		B road
	C earth		D ground
4	A pay off		B pay up
	C pay back		D pay out
5	A tenacious		B menial
	C eager		D detrimental
6	A payment		B reward
	C revenue		D income
7	A strap		B meet
	C tie		D link
8	A Moreover		B On top
	C As well		D In addition

/8

8 Complete the text with the correct form of the words in brackets.

For the past several years, the highly profitable company Leveroy Inc. has been ranked among the top five most desirable employers worldwide. Every year, more than a million _applicants_ (apply) hope to be taken on, lured by perks which include subsidised childcare, dog sitting, big bonuses and free meals.

Inevitably, there is a hyper-**1**_____ (compete) atmosphere at Leveroy, and nobody is quite sure of how **2**_____ (recruit) decisions are made apart from the necessity to fit in with the company culture. A large amount of **3**_____ (resource) and an unusually high level of **4**_____ (adapt) is clearly required of every employee. However, there is also a need for **5**_____ (humble), as staff are expected to demonstrate a **6**_____ (willing) to step up and admit their mistakes. As the team includes former Olympians and people of immense intellectual stature, many people would find the concept of working there extremely intimidating. This is just as well, because for every hundred people who are interviewed, ninety-nine are turned away.

/6

9 Complete the second sentence so that it means the same as the first. Do not change the words in capitals. Use between four and six words in each gap.

I suggest becoming an intern during the summer so that you know if nursing is for you or not. **INTERNSHIP**
It'd be a good idea for you _to do an internship_ during the summer so that you know if nursing is for you or not.

1 Don't you think you should do some English revision before going to work abroad? **BRUSH**
Before going to work abroad you should _____ English, don't you think?

2 Despite the introduction of uniforms for his staff without consulting anybody first, there was no apology from the school principal. **APOLOGISE**
The school principal _____ uniforms for his staff despite not consulting anybody first.

3 One of our staff will be available to help you at all times during your visit. **DISPOSAL**
During your visit, one of our staff will _____ at all times.

4 Maria despises working overtime against her will, mainly because she's a single mother. **FORCED**
Maria _____ overtime, mainly because she's a single mother.

5 Stop pretending that nothing's the matter and tell me what's wrong. **BRAVE**
Stop _____ and tell me what's wrong.

6 Did you see Anne being sacked by Betty? **SACKING**
Did _____ ?

/6

Total /20

6 Journeys

VOCABULARY

6.1
Travel and sightseeing • phrasal verbs
• suffixes • colloquial expressions

SHOW WHAT YOU'VE LEARNT

1 Label the pictures. The first letters are given.

b<u>oot</u>   1 b_____   2 g_____   3 o_____
             c_____   s_____   l_____

4 p_____   5 p_____   6 q_____   7 r_____

2 Complete the signs with the words and phrases from the box.

> aisle   bypass   cruise   embarkation
> express   gate   jetlag   ~~sleeper~~

Beds in the _sleeper_ carriages are made up by train staff between 8 and 9 p.m.

Please do not leave luggage in the ¹_____ as access to exits is required at all times.

²_____ for first class passengers (cabin numbers 1-50) via gangways 1-3.

Passengers for Ryanair flight FR65 to Liverpool may now board at ³_____ 17.

Beat ⁴_____ with a fully reclining seat in Emirates business class.

⁵_____ closed for works. For airport access follow signs for E45/City Centre.

Passenger Notice: The Edinburgh to London ⁶_____ has been cancelled due to snow on the tracks.

⁷_____ passengers please note that playing music from mobile phone speakers is strictly prohibited inside the ship.

WORD STORE 6A | Phrasal verbs

3 Add the correct particles to complete the phrasal verbs in the text.

Bikes, bags
and a trip across the country

My father was a competitive long-distance cyclist who took part in races all over the world, and he passed _on_ his love of cycling to me. Not that I could ever pass ¹_____ a professional like my dad, but I do enjoy the sport and ride as often as I can. Last summer, I suggested a long-distance bikepacking trip to some fellow enthusiasts. Although we were all a bit intimidated by the 136 hilly miles of the Sea-to-Sea route in the North of England, we agreed to give it a go. We carried everything in our bags, including the tents, so that we would not be ripped ²_____ by greedy B & B owners, and we were foolish enough to bank ³_____ the weather being fine, which in the UK is always a risk.

As we set off, we were a rather scruffy-looking group, with our older bikes and out-of-date gear, so we didn't exactly fit in ⁴_____ the more professional-looking riders we met on the way. This mattered less and less as we progressed along the route, though, since we were more preoccupied with our aching legs, freezing feet and soggy clothing. We were proud of ourselves for heading ⁵_____ disaster by taking shelter in an old shepherd's hut during a sudden snowstorm, and even prouder that we avoided burning the hut ⁶_____ when we started a fire in the crumbling fireplace. In other words, our expectations were not high, and just the fact that we managed to complete the route in one piece – and to have a good time along the way – was reward enough.

WORD STORE 6B | Suffixes – forming adjectives

4 Complete the text with adjectives made from the words in the box and the correct suffixes.

> bear ~~daunt~~ flap hand
> mind relate respect sweat

---

youcannotbeserious.com

After working hard all year and saving up to be able to afford a fortnight in the sun, it's understandable that holidaymakers complain if things aren't up to standard. However, some complaints tip over into the unreasonable and even the bizarre …

- My wife and I find foreign languages very <u>daunting</u> and were disappointed to discover that all the taxi drivers in Madrid spoke Spanish.
- The ¹_____ towels hung out to dry by the people in the room next to us made so much noise our late afternoon snoozes were all but impossible.
- No one warned us how hot Egypt would be in July and I found myself unpleasantly ²_____ at times.
- Our tour guide was so ugly that we were unable to appreciate the beautiful views. Tour operators should be ³_____ of the fact that ugly tour guides make it difficult for holidaymakers to enjoy sight-seeing tours.
- It would have been ⁴_____ to know that the hot-air balloon rides are not suitable for people who are afraid of heights.
- I thought I had found a perfectly ⁵_____ hostel, although I did wonder about all the uniforms in the website photos. When I arrived, it turned out to be a boarding school.
- Sitting around the pool was just about ⁶_____ but the beach was far too sandy to lie on.
- The flight back from Jamaica to the UK lasted nine hours. ⁷_____ to the Americans, who were home in just three hours, this seems unfair.

WORD STORE 6C | EXTRA Suffixes – forming adjectives

5 Complete the text. The first letters are given. Use the definitions in brackets to help you.

> **D**<u>elightful</u> (charming) mountain chalet for rent in Finkenberg, Austria. Sleeps from six to eight in two bedrooms plus ¹d_____ (able to be split into separate parts) living area with two sofa beds. ²N_____ (located next door) cable car provides direct access to Tyrolean peaks for walking, biking and winter sports. ³S_____ (composing of small pieces of rock) parking area plus ⁴g_____ (turfed) garden for barbecues, etc. ⁵C_____ (similar or better to others in the same area) prices with discounts for longer stays.
>
> Contact vero@chaletveronica.at for more information.

---

6 Complete the sentences with adjectives formed from the words in brackets.

Weather conditions are <u>variable</u> (vary) at this time of year so it's best to pack for all eventualities.

1 The bellboy was actually quite _____ (force) when insisting on carrying our bags up to the room.
2 _____ (dwindle) tourist numbers have forced many bars and restaurants on the seafront to close down.
3 It's easy to forget that behaviour which is acceptable at home may be _____ (offend) in other countries.
4 The projected impact on the coastline was _____ (decide) in the refusal to grant permission for a new hotel.

WORD STORE 6D | Colloquial phrases

7 Complete the tourists' comments. The first letters are given.

> 'It drives me crazy when tourists say 'Oh, we've done Japan already' after they've spent a week in Tokyo. Travel is more than just a t<u>ick</u>-b<u>ox</u> e<u>xercise</u>.'

> 'Make sure you have the address of your hostel and enough money for a taxi. It's a ¹j_____ o_____ t_____ !'

> 'My brother's ²w_____ of w_____ before my trip were limited to "Don't forget your toothbrush."'

> 'I've only planned as far as Buenos Aires and after that I'm just going to see what happens and ³g_____ w_____ the f_____.'

> 'Rather than ⁴s_____ u_____ the l_____ a_____, the torrential rain left us soaking wet in a local café.'

> 'The vaccines are expensive, but they will ⁵s_____ you in g_____ s_____ for at least two years of travelling'.

SHOW WHAT YOU'VE LEARNT

8 Choose the correct words to complete the sentences.

1 The train was cramped but *bearable* / *mindful* in comparison with the bus we'd taken the day before.
2 Don't *check* / *bank* on good visibility if you are visiting the lakes during the winter months.
3 The number of visitors is *decisive* / *dwindling* because of the rumours about scams and rip-offs.
4 Going with the *flow* / *fit* is good until you discover all the accommodation on the island is booked out.
5 Gerry and Philis have been coming to the resort so long that they almost pass *for* / *on* locals.
6 *Respectable* / *Relative* to most European capital cities, eating out in Reykjavik is extremely expensive.
7 The price per night for the cottage is *variable* / *divisible* by the number of guests staying.
8 The idea of having to travel alone was *daunting* / *delightful* enough to give me a sleepless night.
9 Stallholders here can be very *forceful* / *neighbouring* when trying to persuade you to buy their goods.
10 A paper map will stand you in good *head* / *stead* if your phone battery dies or the signal is lost.

/10

1 Look at the blog title and the photo. Which topics do you think are <u>not</u> mentioned in the text? Read quickly and check.

food prices ☐   language problems ☐
local transport ☐   places of interest ☐

My Asian Travel blog

Two weeks after arriving in Cambodia, I've finally found time to update the blog, this time from a **crumbling** but friendly Internet café in Phnom Penh. Though **harrowing** at times – if only because of the somewhat rough travel conditions – Cambodia has proved to be a feast for the senses, and has reminded me of the capacity of travel to make you reassess what is important in life.

1 ☐ After many months as a solo traveller, I appear to have lost my shyness, and confidently strike up conversations with anyone who looks like they might be willing to exchange tips or share a ride. So with newly-recruited travel companions in tow, it's a three-hour journey ahead to Siem Reap, home to the temples of Angkor, spectacular remnants* of the ancient Khmer civilisation.

2 ☐ Such journeys lead to healthy appetites and, as we head out for dinner that night feeling happy to be alive, we are made all the more **ravenous** by the **ubiquitous** smell of burning wood that permeates* the air. The source of these inviting wafts* is actually the hardwood charcoal that burns and smoulders* all day in the population's small clay stoves and beneath its woks and pots of soup.

3 ☐ I make the mistake of being tempted by the traditional after-dinner drink – coffee. Dinner finishes with several hot cups, which back at the hostel keep me awake until the early hours.

4 ☐ It is difficult to describe the feelings you experience while exploring Angkor Wat. Built in the 12th century under the rather **volatile** rule of King Suryavarman II, it covers nearly 400 acres and it is considered the largest religious site in the world. Its sheer size, combined with its artistic extravagance, make it an illustration of how even the greatest achievements of humans can nearly be erased by the forces of nature.

5 ☐ At night, clubs such as 'The Heart of Darkness' draw patrons into their dingy depths, where visitors and locals writhe* to **pulsating** electronic beats. By day, it is the pure energy of the city and its inhabitants that draws visitors into its reverberating, spice-scented streets.

6 ☐ As I pack up my fancy camera and expensive shoes and head for the coast, it is difficult not to contrast the general dissatisfaction of people in my home country, despite their wealth and privilege, with the optimism of the Cambodian people. At least now I have a new perspective, and later this year, when I return home, I will try to recall the positivity of these charming people, and begin every day thinking how truly lucky I am.

GLOSSARY

accost (v) – approach and address someone boldly or aggressively

remnant (n) – a part or quantity left over after the larger part has been removed

permeate (v) – spread throughout

waft (v/n) – a gentle movement of air, or of odour or sound through air

smoulder (v) – burn slowly with smoke but no flame

slurp (v/n) – a loud sucking noise made while drinking or eating

clamber (v/n) – climb with difficulty

writhe (v) – make twisting movements with the body

2 Read the text again. Match paragraphs A–G with gaps 1–6. There is one extra paragraph.

A It is the latter of these delights that my new friends and I opt for that evening. Originating in Vietnam, the Cambodian version of pho we hungrily slurp* is, like much of the country's cuisine, a delicious combination of bitter and sweet, sour and salty, presented simply and accompanied by myriad condiments.

B Here, I am happy to walk randomly through lively markets and pass spirited street vendors pushing rolling woks and grills on wheels, riding motorbikes with stoves attached to the side, and cruising on bicycles with mango-filled baskets attached to the back. The scene is one of hustle and bustle and is frankly a little overwhelming at first, but also gives me a sense of self-assurance which I have rarely felt.

C Having crossed the Thai border into Poipet, I weigh up my options for onward travel. An old public bus rumoured to take around six hours, a tourist mini-bus leaving in two hours, or a taxi offering relative comfort and immediate departure. I decide on the taxi and quickly accost* three strangers, fellow travellers, who are thankfully happy to share the cost and the journey.

D In fact the overwhelming attitude is 'onwards and upwards'. The city is overflowing with life and is a bustling business and cultural hub. I chat to 'Chivy', the owner of a small coffee stall, who tells me her name means 'life', which seems highly appropriate as she is bursting with it. Like many young entrepreneurs, she's working all hours to turn only a small profit, but her optimism is **unshakeable** and her smile as infectious as those worn by the majority of the population.

E Putting such thoughts aside for the moment, it's onwards to the capital which, to be honest, is as scruffy as Angkor is breathtaking. But Phnom Penh has a **tantalising** rawness to it, and a non-stop sense of life that I find truly mesmerising.

F The journey from the city to the temple complex is a long one, but my driver zips along with great confidence, and while daylight lasts the stunning scenery is enough of a distraction that the distance almost doesn't matter. After a staggeringly beautiful sunset, darkness does make the trip stretch out, and I admit to feeling pretty exhausted towards the end of the trip. But I wouldn't have missed it for anything.

G A touch **bleary-eyed**, I clamber* onto the back of a motorbike taxi the next morning and head for the Angkor Wat Temple Complex. I will not even try to put into words the majesty of the place. Suffice to say the countless **hyperbolic** descriptions that decorate the guidebooks and blogs can be taken pretty much at face value. It is a fascinating window onto what used to be a highly-developed civilisation.

3 Match the adjectives in bold in the text to the definitions.

crumbling – disintegrating gradually over time
1 _____ – present, appearing or found everywhere
2 _____ – changing rapidly and unpredictably, especially for the worse
3 _____ – extremely sad or distressing
4 _____ – particularly hungry
5 _____ – deliberately exaggerated
6 _____ – pleasantly inviting
7 _____ – producing a regular beating sensation or sound
8 _____ – having dim or watery eyes because of tiredness

4 Complete the phrases with the words from the box. Use the text to help you. There are two extra words.

> bustle countless ~~feast~~ nature suffice
> unshakeable value weighed word

The floats, music and costumes all make the carnival a true _feast_ **for the senses**.

1 Though I had my doubts about the truth, I decided to **take** the news **at face** _____ .

2 The fact that I grew up in the **hustle and** _____ of a big city means I appreciate the peace and quiet of the countryside more than most people I know.

3 I'll spare you the details, but Jeremy was furious. _____ **to say** we insisted on being moved to a better room.

4 Having _____ **up our options**, we decided on two-hour ski lessons in the mornings.

5 Susie is the most positive person I know. She never gives up, even in the hardest of times. You've got to admire her _____ **optimism**.

6 I cannot believe he didn't pack any waterproof clothing. We should never underestimate the **forces of** _____ , especially in the mountains.

WORD STORE 6E | Descriptive verbs/adjectives

5 Choose the correct words to complete the sentences with the most likely collocations.

1 The temple bell *chugged / clanged* and hundreds of orange-robed monks appeared from nowhere.

2 The Fernsehturm, Berlin's iconic television mast, *towers / staggers* over the city and makes a handy reference point for lost visitors.

3 The spectacular views were sorely missing as the peak was *bounded / shrouded* in cloud on the day of our visit.

4 The reflected city lights *twinkle / flutter* on the water creating a magical view out across the harbour.

5 We continued to wave our goodbyes from the platform as the train *receded / roamed* into the distance.

6 The climbers *trundled / slackened* their pace as they took in the enormity of their task.

GRAMMAR

6.3

Advanced comparative structures

SHOW WHAT YOU KNOW

1 Complete the text messages with the correct comparative forms of the words from the box. There are three extra adjectives.

> ~~bad~~   far   few   high   near
> little   old   pretty   slow

> Bad news ☹ ! I was robbed on the underground! Can my day get any *worse*? Will write soon ...

> Have to cancel our trip ☹ My **1**_____ sister was in a boating accident.

> Should you have any queries, please visit our website for **2**_____ details.

> Disaster ☹! Our holiday resort offers **3**_____ tourist attractions than the one we visited last year. Will keep you posted. Bye!

> Thanks for the tip! The tour guide was an excellent choice ☺! My parents speak **4**_____ of him than the one in Madrid. Luv you!

> I opted for a cheap B & B. It's much **5**_____ the city centre than I thought.

2 ★ Correct the mistakes.

The wind is getting ~~more strong and more strong~~.
stronger and stronger

1 The journey was tougher than dangerous.

_____

2 Lisa and Donald are such a friendly people that I'd love to settle down in their neighbourhood.

_____

3 As steeper the slope, as more difficult it is to ski.

_____

4 On reaching their destination, the tourists weren't so much exhausted than irritated.

_____

5 When Jack and his co-climbers looked at the surrounding peaks, they were overwhelmed rather then thrilled. _____

REMEMBER THIS

Usually adjectives follow articles *a/an*, but in formal writing (with words like **as** and **so**) they precede them:

That hotel has got a nice swimming pool, just like ours.
→*That hotel has got **as** nice a swimming pool **as** ours.*

---

3 ★ ★ Complete the dialogues using the words in capitals. Write between three and four words in each gap.

A: And? Going to Mexico alone wasn't a good idea, was it? **SUCH**

B: Well, it wasn't *such a bad idea*, either. I had a chance to brush up on my Spanish.

1 A: I believe London is a more enchanting city than Edinburgh. **CITY**

B: That's unfair! Edinburgh is _____ as London!

2 A: Our tour guide seems rather distracted, don't you think? **MUCH**

B: I wouldn't say that. She isn't _____ disorganised.

3 A: I reckon the package tour was a fantastic offer. **SO**

B: On the contrary! It wasn't _____ offer as I had previously thought.

4 ★ ★ ★ Correct each sentence by completing it with one missing word. The first letters of the missing words are given in brackets.

                                                   and
Unspoilt beauty spots are becoming rarer ᵛrarer to find. (a)

1 People have easy access to budget flights nowadays that they've forgotten flying used to be a luxury. (s)

2 For adrenalin junkies an active holiday is not much a pleasure as a necessity. (s)

3 That safari in Kenya wasn't as big an adventure the organisers would have us believe. (a)

4 As a general rule, the earlier you book holidays, cheaper they are. (t)

SHOW WHAT YOU'VE LEARNT

5 Complete the text with one word in each gap.

A room with a view, please

More and more hotel managers bend over backwards to make their guests happy, and being offered a room with a breathtaking view is undoubtedly every holidaymaker's top requirement. However, the more we travel, the **1**_____ easily impressed we become and if a hotel aims at making us awe-struck **2**_____ than merely satisfied, it has to go to great lengths these days.

The hotel in the Zoo de La Flèche in France's Loire Valley, for instance, is not **3**_____ typical a place as it seems. It boasts floor-to-ceiling windows through which you can look straight into a polar bear enclosure. Anyone who has stayed there describes the view as not so **4**_____ cute as jaw-dropping.

After spending the night in the next hotel, Skylodge Adventure Suite in Peru, you are guaranteed to be **5**_____ thrilled than rested. To get to your room, first you need to climb a 400ft cliff face. Every suite is a transparent capsule that clings to a mountain peak and offers guests spectacular 300-degree views of the majestic Sacred Valley from £180 a night per person. It is **6**_____ an extreme adventure that only real daredevils have the courage to check in.

Sweet dreams!

/6

1 Put the word *ever* in the appropriate place in each sentence.

>   *ever*
> In our school we hardly ∨ go on field trips.

1 We tried everything, but nothing seems to attract his attention for more than a minute.

2 If you're in Colorado, a visit to the Grand Canyon is a must.

3 Since I can remember, I've steered clear of well-trodden paths.

4 They hoped to settle down somewhere in Tuscany and live happily after.

2 Complete the dialogue with the words from the box. There are two extra words.

> ~~ever~~   however   whatever   whenever
> wherever   whichever   whoever   why ever

Mel: Chloe, now that you've secured your place at the university, it may be worth considering taking a gap year. It's your best *ever* opportunity to travel, earn money and get work experience. What do you say?

Chloe: Mmm, I'm not so sure. ¹_____ I think I'm ready to take the plunge, I come across an article like this and it puts me off going.

Mel: What do you mean?

Chloe: Well, it says here that ²_____ is thinking of taking a gap year should think twice as they can get more than they bargain for. According to this expert, although young people who volunteer to help in orphanages, schools, animal sanctuaries or ³_____ have good intentions, unscrupulous people may take advantage of them.

Mel: How so?

Chloe: ⁴_____ there's money involved, there's bound to be someone who wants to get rich fast. In this case, a girl from Oxford went to an orphanage in Asia only to find out that the children she met weren't orphans at all! They had families who had been persuaded by the orphanage founder to send their children there to make money off gap-year volunteers, who paid for the opportunity to help them!

Mel: That's outrageous! But ⁵_____ depressing this news is, don't give up on the idea of a gap-year adventure. Just do some research beforehand to make sure you choose a legitimate institution.

Chloe: I guess you're right.

3 Replace the underlined phrases with the correct combinations with *ever*.

> Fewer and fewer tourists visit us as the problem of terrorist attacks is <u>always present</u> here. *ever-present*

1 Our travel budget is <u>very</u> tight and we prefer to camp on the outskirts to keep the costs down. _____

2 Italian cafés with views of famous landmarks <u>as always</u> charge exorbitant prices even for an espresso. _____

3 Whenever we make a stopover in Madrid, we stay at a <u>very</u> quaint hotel near Barajas airport. _____

4 Once backpackers were adult travellers, but these days we bump into <u>younger and younger</u> explorers. _____

5 British policemen are <u>very</u> helpful when you need to ask somebody for directions. _____

SHOW WHAT YOU'VE LEARNT

4 Complete each set of sentences with the same word.

  a On landing in Washington, as *ever*, the whole group was interviewed by a customs officer.

  b When we got to Sharm el-Sheikh, there were fewer British holidaymakers than *ever*.

  c On New Year's Eve in Sydney all those looking at the bridge saw the greatest *ever* fireworks display.

1 a I'm planning on going around Europe in my car and I'll take _____ wants to go with me to split the costs.

  b When you're done with that travel magazine, just lend it to Florence or Noah or _____ .

  c _____ could be texting me at such an ungodly hour?

2 a We could study at my house or _____ , I don't mind.

  b _____ did you find that information?

  c Come out, come out, _____ you are!

3 a I'm really fed up because _____ I suggest, my classmates always disagree with me.

  b Before passing through the metal detector gates, you'll have to take out _____ items you have in your pockets.

  c _____ the real reason for his absence is, I still think we should let him know that we're unhappy about this.

4 a It's not fair that my parents blame me _____ my younger brother bursts into tears.

  b _____ is she going to learn that asking people blatantly how much they earn is plain rude?

  c I'm afraid today I have to take a rain check, but we could meet tomorrow or _____ .

5 a Why _____ did you tell our parents that we'd be more than happy to go on holiday with them?

  b To my exasperation, the queue to the check-in moved _____ so slowly.

  c I love sitting in an airport as it is _____ such a good place for making observations concerning passengers.

6 a When you go climbing, you need to follow all safety requirements, _____ experienced you are.

  b Planning your holiday from scratch is exciting, _____ , it's quite time consuming.

  c _____ did they manage to trek across those mountains in just two days?

/6

6.5

Indefinite article *a/an* • prepositions
• informal phrases with *keep*

WORD STORE 6F | Phrases

4 Complete the text with one word in each gap. The first letters are given.

1 **The article *a/an* has been removed from the conversation. The number in brackets indicates how many more are missing in each section. Complete the missing articles.**

Extract from Student's Book recording 🔊 **2.26**

W1: My friends talked *about* taking a̬ cruise, that it was great for seeing places without taking risks – and I'd actually wanted to give it go for while. […] I opted to cruise ¹____ South America, which took me to incredible locations I could only have reached after hours of planning. […] I guess that was the bottom line ²____ me – my job is demanding and I value my leisure time so I need to use what time I have wisely. (2)

M1: I love surfing and last summer my mate and I planned trip where we played it ³____ ear, just rolling ⁴____ at beaches as we chose. […] As we had no particular destination ⁵____ mind, we kept our eye ⁶____ social media to check where the good surf was. (1)

M2: What swung it for me was not that friends who'd done something similar said how good experience it was but that I was able to pay for everything ⁷____ advance. My spa resort happened to be way ⁸____ in the mountains – isolated and stunningly beautiful – so I could disconnect ⁹____ everything that normally gets me down. […] ¹⁰____ chance, I met lovely people, too, and I've kept in touch with them ever since. (1)

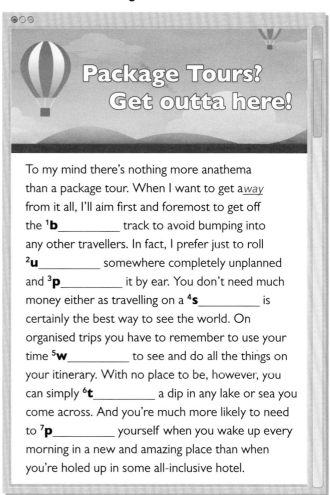

**Package Tours?
Get outta here!**

To my mind there's nothing more anathema than a package tour. When I want to get a*way* from it all, I'll aim first and foremost to get off the ¹**b**_____ track to avoid bumping into any other travellers. In fact, I prefer just to roll ²**u**_____ somewhere completely unplanned and ³**p**_____ it by ear. You don't need much money either as travelling on a ⁴**s**_____ is certainly the best way to see the world. On organised trips you have to remember to use your time ⁵**w**_____ to see and do all the things on your itinerary. With no place to be, however, you can simply ⁶**t**_____ a dip in any lake or sea you come across. And you're much more likely to need to ⁷**p**_____ yourself when you wake up every morning in a new and amazing place than when you're holed up in some all-inclusive hotel.

2 **Complete the conversation with the correct prepositions.**

3 **Look at sentences 1–7, which all contain expressions with *keep*. Read the sentences and match the expressions in bold to definitions a-g.**

1 When travelling alone, you really need to **keep your wits about you** – and especially if you stray off the beaten track.

2 You hear of some dreadful things happening to tourists in some parts of the world. One way to protect yourself is to **keep abreast of** local news and ensure you contact people back home on a regular basis.

3 Vaccinations are a necessity if you are travelling to Africa and want to **keep** yellow fever **at bay**. You'll need to get your injections and beware the nasty side effects of headaches and muscle pains.

4 Many people suffer from homesickness when away from home for a long period of time. The only advice I can give is to **keep your chin up** and make the most of your adventures.

5 We met this really funny French guy while we were backpacking around Australia. He **kept us in stitches** for the whole trip from Alice Springs to Mount Isa.

6 Jetlag can leave people in a really ratty mood. Just make sure that you do your best to **keep a civil tongue** when talking to people and try to get in a few short naps during the day.

7 People that travel on a shoestring often have to make deals with other travellers to keep costs down. Whatever you do, **keep your end of the bargain** and you should avoid any nasty confrontations.

8 My best friend from primary school emigrated to Canada when he was nine and although we haven't seen each other for over ten years, we **keep in touch** regularly.

   to remain in contact with somebody ⑧

a to keep something or somebody away from you to avoid unpleasant situations ⬜

b to do what was promised ⬜

c to remain positive in difficult circumstances ⬜

d to stay up to date with something ⬜

e to stay alert and ready to react quickly ⬜

f to cause somebody to laugh loud and hard ⬜

g to speak politely and without rude words ⬜

1 Match the sentence beginnings and endings. Then mark each phrase as *S* for highlighting similarities or *D* for highlighting differences.

1 Not unlike photo A,   (A) (S)/ D
2 I can see a number of   ☐ S / D
3 On the other hand, photo A   ☐ S / D
4 In this photo, the people look pensive,   ☐ S / D
5 These photos   ☐ S / D
6 Unlike the first image,   ☐ S / D

A photo B shows elderly people engaged in an activity usually associated with youngsters.

B whereas in this photo the atmosphere is clearly more relaxed.

C differs from the other photos in terms of its professional quality.

D the second image conjures up feelings of nostalgia.

E similarities between photos A and B, not least the subject matter.

F resemble each other in that they both show rather cosmopolitan destinations.

2 Choose the correct words to complete the descriptions.

1 Judging by the crowds, the photos are *each / both* taken during some kind of festival or public celebration.

2 It is also *dissimilar / unlike* in that the man pictured here is clearly extremely upset about his predicament.

3 These photos are also *alike / resemble* because they show negative impacts of tourism on the environment.

4 The holidays shown are *common / related* in that they are only suitable for fit, active people who don't mind sleeping outdoors.

5 This mode of transport is only suited to short journeys, as *compared / contrast* to the luxury coach shown in picture B.

6 There are other *various / notable* differences between the two outdoor activities shown here, such as the cost of the equipment required.

3 Read the conversation between two students and choose which two photographs A–D are being compared.

A: These photos have **v**arious **t**hings in **c**ommon, such as the airport setting, of course, and the fact that they show people who are about to set off on a trip of some sort. They ¹e_____ feature two relatively young people who are presumably travelling together and they are ²b_____ taken in modern-looking airports. ³U_____ the f_____ image, the second photo shows people who appear to be travelling for business rather than pleasure, so probably colleagues. Judging by the fact that they seem to be in a hurry, I'd say they are late for their flight. With this in mind, ⁴a_____ c_____ d_____ is the way the people in the photos are likely to be feeling. ⁵I_____ t_____ p_____ , they are probably pretty anxious, you know, concerned that they are late and beginning to think of the consequences of missing the plane, ⁶w_____ here they are only just checking in and both look relaxed and presumably excited about the prospect of the trip they are going on.

B: Yes, the people here are clearly going on a business trip of some sort. They might be going to attend a meeting, give a presentation or even to close a valuable deal. ⁷I_____ c_____ , in this photo the couple are probably going on holiday, or maybe they're students going on an exchange, or to work overseas during the holidays, or something like that.

4 Complete the photo description in Exercise 3. The first letters are given. Sometimes more than one answer is possible.

B ☐

A ☐

C ☐

D ☐

1 Complete the advice with the words from the box.

> each   finish   first (×2)   one   ~~past~~
> penultimate   second (×2)   third

A report is organised similarly to a proposal, except that a report analyses a _past_ or current situation and offers recommendations based on this. It may refer to the results of a survey or to an interview. ¹_____ paragraph, should be given a heading linked to its contents or function according to the requirements of the task. The introduction should summarise the contents of the report followed by the ²_____ main body paragraph, which should set the context. The ³_____ main body paragraph should introduce the ⁴_____ point you wish to present and add supporting details if necessary. The ⁵_____ main body paragraph should state and support a ⁶_____ point and might be used to present some negative aspects. The ⁷_____ paragraph is used to give ⁸_____ or two recommendations based on the evidence that has been presented and the report should ⁹_____ with a short conclusion.

REMEMBER THIS

After verbs **suggest** and **propose** we never use an _object + infinitive_ and after **recommend** we tend to avoid it (especially in everyday contexts) and choose a _that_-clause or an _-ing_ form.

~~I suggest you to avoid the ring road.~~ I **suggest avoiding** the ring road.

~~I propose her to stay longer.~~ I **propose that she stays** longer.

(I recommend him to bring cash.) vs I **recommend bringing** cash. vs I **recommend that he brings** cash.

2 Put the words in order to make phrases.

> to … / report / sets / this / out
> _This report sets out to …_

1 is / aim / to … / report / of / the / this

2 suggest / would / that … / I

3 interviewed … / of / those / all

4 some / only / of / part … / those / taking

5 also / would / recommend … / I

6 preconditions … / given / these

3 Read the report and add headings from the box to each paragraph.

> Conclusion   ~~Introduction~~   Overview
> Potential Problems   Recommendations
> Status as a Great Natural Wonder

Introduction

This report ¹_presents / sets_ an overview of Abisko, Sweden and ²_assigns / outlines_ why it is worthy of inclusion in the World Travel and Tourism Council's campaign to list the greatest natural wonders on each continent. The report will also ³_deter / identify_ potential problems for visitors and make recommendations.

A _____

Abisko is a seventy-seven-km² national park in Swedish Lapland **lauded** for its natural beauty. Situated 250 km north of the Arctic Circle, it is the ideal location from which to see the Aurora Borealis.

B _____

A well-known travel guide recently ⁴_conducted / addressed_ a survey which named the Aurora Sky Station visitor centre, Abisko, the **quintessential** viewing spot from which to experience the Northern Lights. The clear air, the almost permanently cloud-free sky and the lack of manmade light were ⁵_assigned / cited_ as major factors in the choice.

In addition to this ⁶_positive / principal_ attraction, the wider national park is ideal for those seeking outdoor adventure under the area's famous midnight sun.

C _____

While the ⁷_majority / minority_ of visitors encounter **favourable** conditions, it cannot be guaranteed that everyone will see the Aurora Borealis during their visit. As Abisko is a seventeen-hour train journey from Stockholm, it is clear that visitors need to be made ⁸_aware / obvious_ of this **eventuality**.

D _____

Those **undeterred** by the distance must prepare for **isolation** and extreme cold. I would also definitely ⁹_conduct / advocate_ that visitors stick to the principle of leaving nothing (including rubbish) behind them in the national park.

E _____

In the ¹⁰_short / light_ of Abisko's current status as the prime location from which to view what is surely one of the globe's most amazing phenomena, I have no hesitation in recommending that it is added to the ETC's list.

4 Choose the correct words to complete the report.

5 Complete the sentences with the words in bold from the model report. Use the information in brackets to help you.

> Most respondents reported being _undeterred_ (not put off) by the economic situation in the host country.

1 This publisher has been producing the _____ (ultimate) travel guide to Hungary for over a decade.

2 Once _____ (admired) as a design classic, The Grand Hotel now lies empty and crumbling.

3 Visitors to the volcano should be ready for every _____ (possible outcome) as the nearest town is over 400 km away.

4 While some may find the _____ (remoteness) of the islands calming, others will soon begin to miss the comforts of mainland life.

5 Beach bums will undoubtedly find the heatwave _____ (positive) but young children and old people would be well-advised to remain indoors in the afternoon.

6 Complete the extracts with the missing words. The first and last letters are given.

> There was a **d**_ivisio_**n** between the survey respondents into those who enjoyed the resort and those who found it too touristy.

1 The **p**_____**e** of the report is to examine how the increase in tourist numbers has affected the local economy.

2 The former were against the idea of self-catering, while the **l**_____**r** thought it more convenient than staying in a hotel.

3 A key issue that ought to be **a**_____**d** is the erosion caused by so many footsteps on the pathways to the falls.

4 My classmates and I were **a**_____ a street corner and asked to interview as many passersby as possible.

5 The survey was **c**_____**d** using tablet computers rather than traditional questionnaires.

6 A **p**_____**e** step would be the introduction of litter bins in the area immediately surrounding the hot spring.

SHOW WHAT YOU'VE LEARNT

7 Read the writing task. Then follow the instructions below.

The World Travel and Tourism Council has appealed for reports as part of a campaign to promote tourism. The aim of the campaign is to establish a list of the greatest natural wonders on each continent. You have decided to submit a report recommending that a natural wonder you know or have visited is added to the list. In your report, you should give an overview of the chosen natural wonder, explain why you think it deserves to be listed and describe any potential problems visitors might encounter. You should also include some recommendations.

Before you start, follow steps 1–9 below.

1 Decide what you need to include in your report according to the task rubric.

2 Decide what your headings will be. Do they match what you need to include?

3 Decide which natural wonder you will focus on.

4 Think of the main things to include in an overview (location, environment type, etc.).

5 Think why the place deserves to be included in the campaign.

6 Think of potential problems visitors might encounter during a visit.

7 Decide what your recommendations will be.

8 Select the most important information.

9 Plan and write your report.

SHOW THAT YOU'VE CHECKED

Finished? Always check your writing (especially in the exam!) Can you tick ✓ everything on this list?

In my report:

- in the introduction, I have summarised the aim of the report in my own words. ☐

- in the first main body paragraph, I have given any information needed to set the context. ☐

- in the second main body paragraph, I have stated and supported my first point. ☐

- in the third main body paragraph, I have stated and supported my second point and possibly presented some negative aspects or problems. ☐

- in the penultimate main body paragraph, I have given some recommendations based on the evidence I have presented. ☐

- I have used a reasonably formal and impersonal style. ☐

- I have checked my spelling. ☐

- I have checked my handwriting is neat enough for someone else to read. ☐

6.8 SELF-CHECK

VOCABULARY

1 Choose the correct expression.

It was a dramatic spectacle as the boat didn't *recede* / *slacken* speed and crashed into a concrete barrier.

1 We were rather dismayed at having a *stony* / *stone* beach as we had been promised golden sand.

2 When driving through the forest in deep fog, remember to be *mindful* / *divisible* of poor visibility.

3 Josh was woken up at 5 a.m. by the bells *clanging* / *pinching* from nearby steeples.

4 As the train *fluttered* / *chugged* slowly uphill, the Fosters could admire the beauty of the countryside.

5 Because of *dwindling* / *forceful* financial resources the authorities are considering raising taxes.

/5

2 Complete the sentences with the words or phrases from the box. There are two extra words or phrases.

> an eye on   a dip   -beaten   -box
> down   on a shoestring   -ridden   up

The sea is really warm. Why don't we take *a dip*? We won't be able to do this after we leave the coast.

1 My parents highly disapprove of sightseeing as a tick _____ exercise so they make their own itinerary every time they visit new places.

2 Could you keep _____ my bags while I go and buy our train tickets?

3 Although Amanda has managed to save a lot of money, she'll travel _____ because it's such a long trip and she may need it in an emergency.

4 Be careful while camping and remember never to light a fire near the tent because you may burn it _____ .

5 As soon as we saw Steve's weather _____ face, we realised he must have been at sea for a long time.

/5

3 Complete the text with one word in each gap. The first letters are given.

I have always **p**assed for an adventurous person, still every time I embark on a trip abroad, I consider the pros and cons of backpacking because I know there might be something which I will find hard ¹**g**_____ . If I'm going to a foreign country, I always learn a few ²**h**_____ expressions to help me get by.

Travelling through different countries allows you to understand and appreciate their cultures. What's more, you can take your time to ³**s**_____ up the local atmosphere and gain new insights. Besides, you are free to go to local eateries and buy stuff at local markets. You're also often left alone, not chased by ⁴**o**_____ tradesmen who want to sell all their junk and don't take 'no' for an answer.

Backpacking is like rising to new challenges and for me the ⁵**b**_____ line is that it's absolutely never a waste of time or money.

/5

GRAMMAR

4 Choose the correct expression.

On our safari in Africa we saw *so* / *such* an abundance of game that it felt like a dream come true.

1 Be careful in such high mountains because the higher you climb, *the harder* / *harder than* it is to breathe.

2 As they walked in deep snow, it felt that their backpacks were getting *the heaviest* / *heavier and heavier*.

3 The hotel dorm where Sally is going to stay seems to be *as* / *such* popular a place as in the past.

4 Being away from home for over a year, George felt homesick *than* / *rather than* excited about his new job.

5 We weren't *such* / *so* much surprised by the quality of the hotel as impressed by it.

/5

5 Complete the sentences with the words in brackets in the correct forms. Do not change the word order. Use between three and five words in each gap.

The rickshaw rode through *poorer and poorer* (poor/poor) parts of Calcutta.

1 Well, _____ (more/apprehensive/be) about travelling solo, the less likely it is you'll try it.

2 Promoting holidays here wasn't _____ (such/senseless/idea) I had imagined.

3 My parents _____ (terrify/rather/thrill) about my last adventure in Brazil.

4 The prices on the Riviera turned out to be _____ (high/attractive).

5 We realised that Cathy wasn't _____ (experience/traveller) we had thought.

/5

6 Complete the second sentence so that it means the same as the first. Do not change the words in capitals. Use between four and six words in each gap.

When you're travelling in a group, you should accept the wishes of the majority. **FIT**
When you're travelling in a group, you should *fit in with what(ever) most people* want to do.

1 I don't know who came up with the plan first, but it won't work. **WHOEVER**
The plan won't work, _____ first.

2 It doesn't matter if the taxi goes very fast, we still won't get there in time. **HOWEVER**
We won't get there in time, _____ goes.

3 The first guide to arrive in the morning should take the first tour of the castle. **WHICHEVER**
The first tour of the castle _____ guide arrives first in the morning.

4 Finding a cheap hotel here is an incredibly hard task. **EVER**
Finding a cheap hotel here is _____ .

5 Having haggled once in Turkey, I realise that it's very easy to get your price. **EVER**
Having haggled once in Turkey, I realise that it's _____ your price.

/5

Total /30

74

7 Complete the text with the correct form of the words in brackets.

My best trip ever!

It came about quite _unexpectedly_ (expect). I had thought I'd spend the summer as usual, visiting relatives in a ¹_____ (neighbour) town. As a plan, it was perfectly acceptable without being particularly thrilling – after all, I did it every year!

Then, totally out of the blue, I had the chance to join some volunteers going to work with endangered animals in Africa. Although I'm not normally ²_____ (decide), I didn't have to think about it for long – it was an incredible opportunity to do something that would stay with me for ever. I made many ³_____ (delight) friends, especially among the local people, who were eager to show us around their ⁴_____ (settle) and provided us with amazing hospitality. The scenery was spectacular and it happened more than once that its beauty simply took my breath away.

One downside was the ⁵_____ (humid), which made us feel sticky and sweaty, though on the whole it was ⁶_____ (bear). Luckily, the lodge we stayed in was comfortable. We kept in touch with our families through Wi-Fi, though the connection was unreliable and we often couldn't get through.

Would I go again? In a heartbeat!

/6

8 Choose the correct answer A, B, C or D.

Become a travel photographer

Everyone has a _A_ camera on their mobile phone, and imagines they take wonderful holiday photographs. Some even aspire to be professionals! But there's more to travel photography than ¹__ off into the unknown and taking happy snaps. It can feel daunting initially, so here are some ²__ of wisdom to help you decide if it's a career for you.

Buy the best camera you can afford and be prepared to go off the beaten ³__ . It's vital to make your pictures stand out; don't just ⁴__ with the flow – it's a competitive industry, and you must sell your images. Don't let them go too cheaply, though, ⁵__ you might feel you're getting ripped ⁶__ and give up. You should be ⁷__ , and push yourself forward so that your work gets noticed.

Try sending shots to an image library, even though you can't ⁸__ the library accepting them as they may have similar images already.

Whatever happens, you'll get to see the world!

	A	B	C	D
Ⓐ	handy	helpful	fitted	flappy
1	leaving	embarking	departing	heading
2	ideas	words	sayings	thoughts
3	path	road	track	way
4	go	get	put	pull
5	so	as	while	whereas
6	off	in	out	on
7	careful	grateful	peaceful	forceful
8	pick out	set up	bank on	take off

/8

9 Complete the second sentence so that it means the same as the first. Do not change the words in capitals. Use between three and six words in each gap.

You don't have to decide now, so wait and see what happens. **PLAY**

Why don't you _play it by ear because/as/since_ you don't have to decide now.

1 The coach driver went along the winding mountain road very carefully. **EVER**

The coach driver went along the winding mountain road _____ .

2 It doesn't matter what route the cab driver takes, we won't make the train now. **WHATEVER**

We won't make the train now, _____ takes.

3 Of all the art galleries I've been to, I found the Guggenheim Museum in New York incredibly innovative. **AS**

I have never been to as _____ the Guggenheim Museum in New York.

4 Their amazement seeing the wildebeest crossing the Mara River was increasing all the time. **AMAZED**

They were getting _____ seeing the wildebeest crossing the Mara River.

5 You can't have failed to notice that he is obsessed with travel. **HIS**

You must have _____ travel.

6 Reading about the local customs while travelling around foreign countries could be very helpful. **STEAD**

Reading about the local customs while travelling around foreign countries _____ .

/6

Total /20

7 Express yourself

VOCABULARY

7.1

Theatre and musicals
• exaggerated synonyms
• theatre words • compound adjectives

SHOW WHAT YOU KNOW

1 **Complete the names of job titles. The numbers in brackets indicate the number of letters in each word.**

lead singer or musician in a choir or orchestra (7) _soloist_

1 helps musicians record their music in a studio
(2 words – 5,8) _____ _____

2 chooses actors for theatre, film and TV (2 words – 7,5)
_____ _____

3 writes plays (10) _____

4 uses their hands to make three-dimensional pieces of art out of clay, metal, wood, etc. (8) _____

5 leads an orchestra (9) _____

6 is the proprietor of a space in which art is exhibited and sold (2 words – 7,5) _____ _____

7 writes someone else's life story (10) _____

8 is in charge of cameras/lights, etc. when shooting for TV or film (15) _____

9 is responsible for the collections in a gallery or museum, etc. (7) _____

10 writes long fictional stories (8) _____

11 converts written text from one language to another (10) _____

WORD STORE 7A | Exaggerated synonyms

2 **Complete the text. Some letters are given.**

WORD STORE 7B | Theatre words

3 **Match the words from the box to the definitions. There is one extra word.**

aisle ~~choral~~ melodic percussive
props rhythmic stage stilts

of or relating to a choir or chorus _choral_

1 the part of a theatre on which the actors perform _____

2 pleasant to listen to _____

3 leg extenders worn by performers _____

4 relating to percussion instruments such as drums _____

5 articles other than costumes and scenery used by actors during a performance _____

6 with a steady beat or pulse _____

4 **Use the words from Exercise 3 to complete the sentences.**

Percussive instruments include the triangle, tambourine, bongo drums, symbols and many, many others.

1 Heather is taking a circus skills course because she wants to learn how to juggle and walk on _____ .

2 The star of the show fell off the _____ during one of the dance scenes and sprained her ankle.

3 My grandfather has a deep, _____ voice that makes everything he says sound like a beautiful song.

4 The _____ and repetitive sounds of Sheffield's steelworks provided the inspiration for the beats on LFO's early dance records.

5 The only time I ever listen to _____ music is when we listen to songs sung by the national choir on the TV.

6 One of the most recognisable _____ in theatre is the skull of Yorick, the dead jester that Hamlet talks to in the famous graveyard scene.

Reviews ★★★★★

The iconic English spy James Bond has been single-handedly p**acki**ng **o**ut cinemas across the globe since 1962. During that time, audiences have ¹**h_____d their b_____h** as no less than seven different Bonds have dodged ²**fl_____s** of bullets and defeated super-villains in twenty-six films and counting. Throughout his many incarnations, Bond's ³**vi_____l** approach to espionage has led him to bend the rules as he follows his gut instincts and risks his neck to protect his beloved Britain. Despite this and other constants, rather than ⁴**re_____e** the dashing spy slavishly across the films, each time Bond has had a ⁵**re_____t**, successive actors have brought something different to Ian Fleming's original character.

Known for glamorous locations, beautiful people and ⁶**r_____l** stunts that leave viewers with ⁷**g_____g** mouths, the film franchise looks set to continue for many instalments to come. The ⁸**sh_____r se_____e** of occasion that ⁹**sw_____s ar_____d** the opening of a new Bond film means even global news channels report premieres as headline news, an accolade achieved by only a handful of films in recent years.

WORD STORE 7C | Compound adjectives

5 Combine the correct forms of words from boxes A and B to form compound adjectives. Then complete the sentences.

A (~~ill~~ heart long far slack high)

B (gross jaw ~~judge~~ reach run stop)

Sarah's decision to dress up as a recently disgraced celebrity was considered _ill-judged_ by most of the other guests at the fancy dress party.

1 The consequences of his outrageous behaviour at the awards ceremony will be _____ in terms of his image as a wholesome kids movie actor.

2 We went to the cinema hoping for a _____ action movie and what we got was an overly sentimental love story with a couple of car chases.

3 _The Simpsons_ and _Grey's Anatomy_ are examples of _____ animated series, having managed thirty-one and sixteen series respectively.

4 At the time of writing, the _____ movie shot in 3D is _Star Wars: The Force Awakens_, which earned a staggering 936.66 million U.S. dollars at the box office.

5 When Sofia Coppolla walked into the restaurant, all the other diners stopped eating and stared _____ at the famous director.

WORD STORE 7D | EXTRA Compound adjectives

6 Complete the extracts from reviews. Use the information in brackets to help you.

Watch the hilarity unfold as Carrey's **well-**_meaning_ (having good intentions) but incredibly unlucky zoo-keeper attempts to release all the animals from London zoo.

¹Tight-_____ (mean with money) Scrooge is portrayed wonderfully by Murray who gives another of his fine low-key performances.

Cumberbatch is convincing as the **²quick-**_____ (clever) Holmes and Freeman equally so as his trusty sidekick, Dr Watson.

SHOW WHAT YOU'VE LEARNT

7 Choose the best answer A–C to complete the sentences.

1 The __ nature of the portrait exhibition left some visitors in tears and others overwhelmed with joy.
   A sheer   **B** visceral   **C** gaping

2 Viewers are warned not to try to __ these dangerous stunts at home.
   A replicate   **B** reboot   **C** hold

3 There was a __ of activity backstage as the entire cast underwent a costume change.
   A breath   **B** flurry   **C** sense

4 Unrecognisable after __ cosmetic surgery, the former leading man's acting career appears to be all but over.
   A radical   **B** packing   **C** swirling

5 As well as designing the costumes, Florian also organised the many different __ needed for this production.
   A stilts   **B** stages   **C** props

6 The famous drummer's influence has led the band to adopt a more __ style for their second album.
   A choral   **B** rhythmic   **C** melodic

7 The __ sequel to this classic romantic comedy left fans of the original bitterly disappointed.
   A ill-judged   **B** far-reaching   **C** highest-grossing

8 If producers imagined this first series would lead to a __ favourite to rival the ten seasons of _Friends_, then they were sadly mistaken.
   A well-meaning   **B** heart-stopping   **C** long-running

9 The star-studded audience was left __ when a naked man ran onto the stage at the prestigious awards ceremony.
   A action-packed   **B** slack-jawed   **C** tight-fisted

10 The __ script is full of clever observations on teenage life and the stars' performances are entirely convincing.
   A far-fetched   **B** mind-blowing   **C** quick-witted

/10

The **³mind-**_____ (overwhelmingly impressive) cinematography of _Sicario_ peaks with the stunning aerial shots of the US-Mexican border.

What could have been a serious examination of the downsides to the development of artificial intelligence, descends disappointingly into a **⁴far-**_____ (difficult to believe), half-hearted and superficial action movie.

This dialogue-driven period drama is about as far from **⁵action-**_____ (filled with exciting events) as it is possible to get, and yet it is almost impossible to take your eyes off the screen.

1 Read the article. Which section of a newspaper would you <u>least</u> expect it to appear in?

1 Arts and entertainment
2 Teenage matters
3 Home and family
4 Women's supplement

Lorde is many things. Real name Ella Yelich-O'Connor, she's a chart phenomenon who has sold millions of records around the world, a double Grammy-winner, Best International Female Artist at 2014's Brit Awards, and a Billboard chart-topper with her second album, *Melodrama*. On her eighteenth birthday, fellow star Taylor Swift wrote on her Instagram account: 'It's Ella's eighteenth birthday technically but we all know she's really 300 and knows all the secrets of the universe', which does much to capture O'Connor's maturity and wisdom. As is evident in her anti-consumerist lyrics, feminist messaging and thoughtful electronic balladry, Lorde is also entirely her own person, which is no mean feat in a contemporary pop world of pasteurised homogeneity. On the wintry afternoon that we meet, her familiar gothic tumble of hair is scraped and tied back, and she's pale and make-up free, with no attempt to hide the acne troubling her cheeks.

As we settle into her room at a boutique hotel in east London, her mother exiled* to the lobby downstairs, I ask her what she's wearing and her reply is cheerfully vague: 'Some, like, trousers, some boots ... My jumper? I think it's from New Zealand,' she says, referring to her home country. 'I cut the labels out of everything – they scratch me.' Lorde's circumspection* about designer brands, red carpets and celebrity culture was there from the outset, and is articulated in her worldwide smash hit *Royals*. The lyrics spoke to an audience, young and old, hungry for something more real in mainstream music, and when the song brought her some of the trappings she had dismissed in it, it only served to stiffen her resolve.

'I'd just turned sixteen, and people wanted me to do red carpets and I was, like, "I'm still getting used to how I look and I'm still growing." And I don't want to just feel sad because someone said, "Ooh, she's on the worst-dressed list!" So I thought, "I don't have to do this if I don't want to."' The power to say no is not one that many **up-and-coming** artists seem to possess, and on occasion Lorde has been told, 'Everyone else does it, so why wouldn't you?' But she has stood her ground. 'A lot of my audience, they're younger than me or the same age, and a lot of the decisions I make are about trying to portray this whole weird fame-storm that's

happening to me as realistically as possible.'

Ella Marija Lani Yelich-O'Connor has always been a teenager of a different stripe. She grew up in a nice beachside suburb of Auckland, the second of four children. Her mother, a poet, and her father, a civil engineer, created a home environment that was cultured and inquiring, and Ella was a **voracious** and **precocious** reader. Aged thirteen, she signed a record company development deal after a label executive saw a video of her singing Duffy's *Warwick Avenue* at a school talent show. But her goal wasn't to be a singer – she wanted to write, so the label

partnered her with Joel Little, an established musician twice her age, to help develop her compositional skills. Soon her poetry and short stories gave way to lyrics. She wrote about herself, her peers and their suburb, and the suburb beyond it. The claustrophobic bubble of New Zealand was both a stone in her shoe and her inspiration. O'Connor's sound is simple yet cinematic, spinning tales of real teenage dreams – penniless but happy nights out full of longing and loneliness – that reject clichés of mindless fun and hedonistic decadence.

'From the outset, I have written about and for my peers and friends. It is a unifying thing, a call to arms,' she says. 'You never hear people making generalisations about adults, yet everyone will make them about teenagers. People forget that we are human beings and that we think differently from each other.' Her thoughtful take on teenage life is a million miles from the **histrionic** show-off, criticism-drawing tactics of some other teenage singers.

O'Connor is a self-professed* feminist who has attacked the **pernicious** effect of Photoshop culture on young girls' self-esteem, but she insists that she isn't purposefully setting herself up against any particular stars. 'That is definitely an older person's reaction to my songs,' she says.

If teenage stardom can seem like a guaranteed ticket to adult excess, O'Connor, with her concerned mother waiting outside our interview, possesses a maturity that is, for now, inoculating* her from the madness growing around her. 'What I am doing now, I am learning so much that I couldn't learn at any university at any age,' she says. 'Every time I get on stage I learn something new. I'm evolving all the time. My next record could sound completely different.'

GLOSSARY

exiled *(adj)* – separated from country, home, etc.
circumspection *(n)* – caution, wariness

self-professed *(adj)* – acknowledged by oneself
inoculate *(v)* – protect, *literally* vaccinate

2 Read the article again. For questions 1–6, choose the best answer A–D.

1 In the first paragraph, the author mentions modern pop music's 'pasteurised homogeneity' in order to emphasise
   A Lorde's enthusiasm compared to her contemporaries.
   B the non-typical nature of Lorde's lyrics.
   C the difference between Lorde and Taylor Swift's musical styles.
   D how much of Lorde's character is that of a normal teen.

2 According to Lorde, what motivates her rejection of the trappings of fame?
   A Insecurities about her appearance
   B A dislike of mainstream popular music culture
   C Wanting to portray herself as different to other celebrities
   D A desire to communicate the realities of her fame to her fans

3 In the third paragraph, what is implied about most young musicians?
   A They are naive about the pressures that come with fame.
   B They agree to most things in their quest for success.
   C They are uncomfortable with their public image.
   D They strive to stand out from the crowd in any way possible.

4 In the fourth paragraph, it is suggested that while growing up, Lorde found New Zealand
   A limiting yet influential in her compositions.
   B conducive to academic study.
   C too expensive to allow for having fun.
   D old-fashioned in its approach to culture.

5 When Lorde refers to her music as a 'call to arms', she implies that she hopes it will
   A encourage her fans to support feminism.
   B prompt teenagers to rebel against their parents.
   C inspire teenagers to emphasise their individuality.
   D create a backlash against egotistical performers.

6 The writer concludes that Lorde's attitude to fame and success
   A may lead to excessive behaviour in later life.
   B could influence the sound of her next album.
   C provides protection from potential pitfalls.
   D causes her parent's concern.

3 Match the adjectives in bold in the text to the definitions.

pernicious – hurtful, harmful or deadly
1 _____ – engaging in an activity with great enthusiasm
2 _____ – having certain advanced abilities for one's age
3 _____ – excessively dramatic or showy
4 _____ – doing well at a career or occupation and likely to be successful in the future

4 Complete the sentences with the phrases from the box. Use the text and the information in brackets to help you.

> from the outset   no mean feat
> stand your ground   stiffen his resolve
> stone in my shoe   ~~the trappings of fame~~

Reality TV star Lorna is enjoying _the trappings of fame_ (material items that signal success), judging by her latest shopping excursion to Rodeo Drive.

1 My height, or lack of it, has always been a _____ (an annoyance or disadvantage) when it comes to convincing casting agents to hire me.

2 Katharine Hepburn won the Oscar for best actress four times, which is _____ (a great achievement).

3 I felt _____ (since the beginning) that this book was going to be too difficult and after 100 pages I see I was right.

4 Don't let them underpay you. _____ (don't give in) and show them how valuable you are.

5 Rejections only served to _____ (make more determined) and eventually his novel was published to great acclaim.

WORD STORE 7E | Collocations

5 Match the words from boxes A and B to complete the collocations in the sentences. Use the definitions in brackets to help you.

> A ~~immortal~~ epic full-length
>   raw time-worn warring

> B dress materials prejudices
>   proportions tribes ~~words~~

I know you wanted to go first, Danny, but it's Flora's turn, and in the _immortal words_ (special, famous and likely to be used for a long time) of the Rolling Stones, 'You can't always get what you want'.

1 It's time to put away _____ (outdated biases) and acknowledge we are all equal regardless of race, gender or lifestyle choices.

2 _____ (ethnic groups engaged in fighting) in the south agree to cease hostilities in exchange for land deal.

3 The country is rich in _____ , especially minerals, yet almost none of the money generated makes it back to the general population.

4 Johansson looked stunning with her new haircut and a gorgeous _____ (an item of women's clothing, often formal) in emerald green by Versace.

5 With the main run stretching for nearly a kilometre, this is an indoor ski slope of _____ (huge in size or importance).

GRAMMAR

7.3

Advanced conditionals

SHOW WHAT YOU KNOW

1 Read the story about Andy. Then transform the text using conditional sentences. Write in brackets which conditional type each sentence is.

Andy Fields is an art enthusiast who frequents car boot sales in search of real bargains.
If Andy Fields ᵃ*wasn't/weren't* (be) an art enthusiast, he ᵇ*wouldn't frequent* (frequent) car boot sales in search of real bargains. ᶜ(*2nd*)

1 *He went to a jumble sale in Las Vegas a few years ago and bought several paintings for $5.*
If he ᵃ_____ (go) to a jumble sale a few years ago, he ᵇ_____ (buy) several paintings for $5. ᶜ(___)

2 *Mr Fields was convinced one of them was the work of Andy Warhol, so he showed it to an expert from a famous auction house.*
If Mr Fields ᵃ_____ (be) convinced one of them was the work of Andy Warhol, he ᵇ_____ (show) it to an expert from a famous auction house. ᶜ(___)

3 *The expert believes the piece may be original so Mr Fields has put it up for auction on eBay with a starting bid of £1.25 million.*
If the expert ᵃ_____ (believe) the piece may be original, Mr Fields ᵇ_____ (put it up) for auction on eBay with a starting bid of £1.25 million. ᶜ(___)

4 *He is confident the artwork can fetch much more than the asking price and is waiting for serious offers.*
If he ᵃ_____ (be) confident the artwork can fetch much more than the asking price, he ᵇ_____ (wait) for serious offers. ᶜ(___)

5 *He may be lucky and see a great return on his investment.*
If he ᵃ_____ (be) lucky, he ᵇ_____ (see) a great return on his investment. ᶜ(___)

2 ★ Comment on the situations using conditional sentences and beginning with the words given.

You accepted their offer, but I would have advised you against it.
Were *I you, I wouldn't have accepted* their offer.

1 Joe wasn't careful, so he invested his money in shares.
Had ᵃ_____ more careful, he ᵇ_____ his money in shares.

2 It's possible that our plan falls through and perhaps we will face bankruptcy.
Should ᵃ_____ through, we ᵇ_____ face bankruptcy.

3 The band signed the sponsorship deal without consulting a lawyer and they're in trouble now.
Had ᵃ_____ the sponsorship deal without consulting a lawyer, they ᵇ_____ in trouble now.

4 Dylan's track record is not good enough, so he may not get the grant.
Were ᵃ_____ better, he ᵇ_____ the grant.

3 ★ ★ Replace the phrases in bold with the appropriate phrases from the box.

> but for   in the event of   otherwise   say   ~~providing that~~   what if   whether or not   unless I

A: Hey Nick, I've discovered a new way of raising money for your exhibition **on condition that** / *providing that* you're still looking for support.

N: Of course I am! ¹**If I don't** / _____ get it soon, I'll miss my chance to put on a display. So what is it?

A: It's called crowd funding. Well, ²**imagine** / _____ you want to raise capital for your project. First you should choose a platform that provides crowd funding services. You then advertise your project, set the deadline and a minimum funding goal and the rest is up to the people who pledge how much money they are willing to donate. ³**If it hadn't been for** / _____ their donations, many projects wouldn't have come through.

N: But why would anyone want to back me up financially?

A: Usually those who seek help offer some kind of reward.

N: I see, and ⁴**suppose** / _____ I fail to collect the sum I have set?

A: That depends on the platform you sign in with, really. Some of them won't give you any money ⁵**in case of** / _____ failure to meet the goal, others will transfer the resources ⁶**even if** / _____ you miss the target.

N: I think it's worth a try. ⁷**If I don't** / _____ , I'll never know.

4 ★ ★ ★ Use the words in brackets to complete the sentences. Add any other words if necessary.

We will help finance the campaign *on condition that* Sophie takes on the responsibility of Project Leader. (condition)

1 Don't worry! Your father and I will stand by you _____ being admitted to the college of your choice. (event)

2 We won't get mad with Mark _____ promises to do his share of the housework. (long)

3 _____ ask the boss for a day off, do you think she would let me take one? (were)

SHOW WHAT YOU'VE LEARNT

5 Choose the correct answer.

1 *Should* / *If* our company goes bust, guess who's going to be held responsible?

2 We'll give you our financial backing *supposing* / *provided* you show us a feasible business plan.

3 Our charity is bound to help the needy *as long as* / *whether or not* no new law is passed.

4 If that test was as easy as you say, he *should* / *might* have passed it a long time ago.

5 *Were* / *Would* I to take part in the fundraising, you'd have to keep me company.

6 We might never have collected enough funds *providing* / *but for* his hefty contribution.

/6

1 Choose the correct meaning of the underlined phrases.

1 They say that Bruce Springsteen seldom does interviews and is rarely, <u>if ever</u>, troubled by paparazzi.
   A if only   B if at all

2 Taking photos of toddlers isn't a piece of cake. <u>If anything</u>, it may turn out to be quite tricky.
   A If I'm not mistaken   B On the contrary

3 A: Daisy, could you stand right next to Frank and say 'cheese'?
   B: <u>As if</u>!
   A You wish!   B With pleasure!

4 Tell me whether you have any useful tips for me, and <u>if so</u>, I need to make a note of them.
   A if necessary   B if yes

5 When I was taking that photo, her feelings for him, <u>if any</u>, weren't clear.
   A providing there were any   B whether or not

Let me drive, Gran!

As if!

2 Put the verbs in brackets in the correct tenses.

They stared at me as if they <u>knew</u> (know) me.

1 Look at this photo of a model! She looks as if she _____ (not/sleep) for a year!

2 Whenever I hear people speaking Greek, they sound as though they _____ (speak) Spanish.

3 Ethan, Joshua, look at you! You look as if you _____ (just/have) a fight. Who started it this time?

4 After the agility competition, her dog breathed as though it _____ (run) in a marathon.

5 I don't know how to break this to Freddie, but during his presentation yesterday he sweated as if it _____ (be) his first public appearance.

6 Every time I come back home from a long journey, I feel as though I _____ (be) where I belong.

3 Complete the instructions with the phrases from the box. There are three extra phrases.

> as if   if any   if anything   even if
> if in doubt   if necessary   if not   ~~if so~~

Top Tips For Taking Great Photos

Are you the owner of a single-lens reflex camera or a simple point-and-shoot camera? *If so*, **here are some ways to help you take a memorable snap:**

1 Watch the light

It is a rookie mistake to assume that flash is to be used only when it's dark or when you're inside a room. Any good photographer will tell you that prior to taking a photo, you need to know the light source. It may turn out that your subject's face is unevenly lit by the sun so, [1]_____ , you might need to switch on flash even in daylight to dispose of any imperfections.

2 Get close

Before pressing the shutter button, zoom in or take a step or two towards your subject. [2]_____ , you will miss out on all the interesting details such as freckles, smiles or telling gazes. However, if you get too close to them ([3]_____ , see the manual), it will result in blurry photographs.

3 Composition is everything

It's not recommended to place your subject in the middle of the picture but to move it away to either side. Before recomposing the picture, however, don't forget to lock the focus on the subject by pressing and holding the shutter button halfway down. Why? Because [4]_____ you own an auto-focus camera, most of them focus only on the subject that is in the centre of the viewfinder.

SHOW WHAT YOU'VE LEARNT

4 Complete the text with one word in each gap.

THE DANGERS OF TAKING A SELFIE

'How can selfies be dangerous?', you might ask. If <u>in</u> doubt as to the origins of the name, let's just take a quick look at some statistics. A few years ago, a group of seven Indian men drowned after their boat capsized. They thought that standing on one side of the boat would make a nice selfie. If [1]_____ , it led to their untimely demise. A Spanish citizen, aged seventeen, lost his life when he tried to take a photo of himself during the running of the bulls festival. [2]_____ if we make allowances for his young age, he should have known better. Two Russian men had a really outlandish idea of taking a photo with a hand grenade after removing the pin. Seldom, if [3]_____ , do such stories end well. Needless to say, this one didn't. In the following months the death toll continued and, if [4]_____ , you can find the remaining data on our website. It seems that those people have lost their survival instinct and they behaved as if they [5]_____ indestructible. So next time you decide to take a selfie, use your common sense. If [6]_____ , it may cost your life.

/6

Word building • informal expressions • collocations

1 Complete the conversation between a man and a woman. Put the words in brackets into the correct form.

Extract from Student's Book recording 🔊 3.8

W3: So it looks like the decision was to keep the skateboarding park and not do the *development* (develop). That was quick!

M3: I could see it coming. The skateboarders generated lots of ¹_____ (public) – they used social media to whip up a real wave of support. They made a big thing about their own rights and what a ²_____ (history) place the skateboarding park was but they didn't consider the benefits of the ³_____ (develop) for musicians like us who play in the concert halls – or anyone else for that matter. I guess they were too focused on their own ⁴_____ (feel).

W3: Most people didn't understand the ⁵_____ (complex) of the projects that were included in the plans – the new ⁶_____ (rehearse) studios that would have attracted new audiences for us, the pop-up shops that might have been run by young entrepreneurs – it could offer genuine local ⁷_____ (generate) on all fronts, like a real ⁸_____ (create) hub. But that was ⁹_____ (down) by the people involved, which meant it became a real missed opportunity.

M3: The studios would have been good for us and offered local kids a dedicated space where they could develop an interest in culture. The developers just didn't ¹⁰_____ (light) that enough.

W3: It's definitely a case of people not getting the message.

2 Complete the sentences with the underlined expressions from the text. Use the information in brackets to help you. Sometimes you need to change the form.

If only I'd known that there was an Andy Warhol exhibition in town. That was *a real missed opportunity*. (not take advantage of a situation)

1 The local newspaper today is reporting a _____ for the idea of building an amphitheatre in the park. There's talk of putting on not only plays but concerts too and most people seem to be in favour of the idea. (a sudden increase in favour of an idea)

2 Resistance to erecting the new statue is mounting _____ . Local residents, shop owners and the media are against the idea. (from many different angles)

3 They knocked down the old football stadium with public consultation and, like most people, I just didn't _____ . What a shame! (predict an outcome)

4 We told Mia a hundred times that parkour was dangerous, but she never seemed _____ . Still, it's only a broken wrist so I guess she'll recover soon. (understand something that is said or implied)

5 I won't sit through three hours of Verdi – or any other opera _____ . It's just not my thing! (to indicate the equal relevance of a second topic)

3 Complete the phrases and phrasal verbs with the words from the box. Use a dictionary if necessary.

call ~~hot~~ pan rid whip

hot up	– become more lively
1 _____ up	– encourage
2 _____ out	– develop or evolve
3 too close to _____	– impossible to predict
4 get _____ of	– become free of something or somebody

4 Complete the text with the appropriate phrases from Exercise 3. Sometimes you need to change the form.

The finale for the Amateur Band of the Year is really *hotting up* with votes coming in thick and fast from all over the country and at this early stage we really have no idea how things will ¹_____ . A lot of interest has been ²_____ over the last few days thanks to media's speculation who will win this year's coveted prize. Figures so far show that the result is still ³_____ with The Blues Oranges and The Urangabangs pulling away from the other groups with 33 and 34 percent respectively. Wait a minute! News just in! The Urangabangs have decided to ⁴_____ their drummer! Will this affect the voting?

WORD STORE 7F | Collocations

5 Combine the words from boxes A and B to complete the sentences with the most likely collocations.

A creative cultural done ~~legal~~ local pop-up property public redevelopment

B ~~battles~~ consultation deal developers hub institutions plans shops regeneration

Technology companies are constantly involved in *legal battles* over copyright infringements.

1 Property prices are on the up thanks to _____ of the area.

2 The community centre on the corner is becoming a real _____ for musicians and artists owing to the work of local NGOs.

3 _____ are making fortunes nowadays by renovating and selling old buildings.

4 I can't believe there's another row of _____ on the high street. All they sell is cheap junk.

5 The _____ for the stadium have been put on hold because of the change of government.

6 There's no point in protesting to the selling of the park – it's a _____ I hear.

7 There was a _____ and it seems most people are in favour of a new concert hall.

8 Certain _____ like theatres and opera houses may not seem so popular, but they play an essential role in the field of the arts.

1 **Put the words in order to make phrases. Then mark each phrase as *A* for presenting advantages, *D* for presenting disadvantages, or *R* for reaching a decision.**

cons … / pros / and / up / the / weighing
Weighing up the pros and cons …   (R)

1 I / idea / see / one / with / difficulty / that / is …
_____ ◯

2 account … / needs / into / everybody's / taking
_____ ◯

3 in / of … / could / be / that / favour / argument / an
_____ ◯

4 idea, / namely … / against / argument / a / strong / there's / that
_____ ◯

5 you / the / aspects … / consider / if / negative / positive / and / all
_____ ◯

6 main / of / the / one / benefits / of …
_____ ◯

2 **Complete the dialogues with the missing phrases.**

1 Dionne: W*eighing* u*p* the p*ros* and c*ons*, I'd say watching a recording of a play in a cinema is better than not seeing it at all.
   Frederic: I agree. ¹O_____ of the m_____ b_____ is that you get to see close-ups of the actors' faces that you wouldn't see in a theatre.

2 Karen: I'd like to propose that, instead of a play, this year the school holds a disco.
   Phillip: ²O_____ d_____ I see with that is that it isn't really educational, is it?
   Karen: That could be an ³a_____ in f_____ of it though, couldn't it? The kids have worked hard all year. Maybe they deserve something that is for no other reason than fun.

3 Jack: I'd like to see music being taught in all schools as a standard part of the curriculum.
   Helen: There's a ⁴s_____ a_____ a_____ that idea – namely the cost of the equipment required.

3 **Complete the dialogue with the words from the box. There are two extra words.**

> account   advantages   balance
> bearing   drawback   major   negative
> plus   ~~point~~   selling   support   things

K: Lionel, look at this! The city council's going to invest in converting the unused building in the city centre into something useful. There's a range of proposals here on their site. You can vote for the ones you'd like to have.

L: Can you send me the link, Katy?

K: Sure …

L: OK, let's see … public gymnasium and pool – yep, cool, theatre and dance studio – er … nope. Indoor market? Er … well …

K: Wait – theatre and dance studio? That could be fantastic! It could be used for plays and also concerts – get local bands up there on the stage, you know? That's a huge *point* in support of that one, I reckon. You're a big music fan, right?

L: Well, yes, but a ¹_____ downside is that it would probably sit empty most of the time between performances, don't you think?

K: Not necessarily. It could be used for dance or music lessons, or drama classes. I think the fact that it's something educational is a strong ²_____ point.

L: Maybe, but having a gym and pool in the city centre would be a real ³_____ , wouldn't it? The gym at school is rubbish and it's so far to the uni pool.

K: I guess a pool might be OK, but there is one at the university already and there are gyms everywhere. I see that as a ⁴_____ . Not much point in voting for something we've already got.

L: I guess that is somewhat of a ⁵_____ aspect.

K: What about the indoor market?

L: Hmm. Not very exciting, is it? Plus, all ⁶_____ considered, there are enough shops in the city centre already, aren't there?

K: Well, yes, but if it was used to sell locally grown food, an argument in ⁷_____ of it could be that it might actually make it easier for people to eat a bit more healthily.

L: I suppose so, though there are plenty of places to buy fruit and vegetables, for those who can be bothered to cook.

K: True. On ⁸_____ , I'd say the theatre and dance studio wins it. I'm going to vote for that.

L: I guess you're right. ⁹_____ everything in mind, that's probably the best choice on the list. When will the winning project be announced?

K: 17 November, it says here.

L: OK, fingers crossed then.

1 Mark the advice according to the paragraph it most likely relates to: introduction *I*, main body paragraphs *M* and conclusion *C*.

State your overall impression. ⬡ C

1 Give a detailed evaluation. It may be positive, negative or balanced. ⬡

2 If reviewing two things (e.g. book and its film adaptation), start the comparison you will continue throughout the review. ⬡

3 Describe the plot briefly (the main aim is evaluation). ⬡

4 Express a recommendation with reasons. ⬡

5 Catch the reader's attention and indicate the aim and structure of your review. ⬡

2 Match the sentences or sentence halves to form extracts from reviews.

Whereas the book contains scenes of violence, ⬡ G

1 Compare this weak sequel to the first film in the series, ⬡

2 Set in India, the book tells the story of twins Ama and Apu ⬡

3 The first chapter sets the scene and begins with ⬡

4 A possible criticism is that the sub-plot involving the main character's sisters ⬡

5 Not everyone will enjoy the lengthy descriptions of the characters' outfits. ⬡

6 If you like fast-paced, laugh-out-loud, gross-out humour, ⬡

A Even so, there is just enough action to hold the attention of those with no interest in fashion.

B adds little of interest to the ongoing narrative.

C and their childhood on the streets of Mumbai.

D then you have to see Jim Carrey's run of whacky 1990s comedies.

E one of the most memorable opening lines in contemporary fiction.

F which is a classic by anyone's standards.

G the film has been censored to make it suitable for younger audiences.

3 Read the article containing a review and number the paragraphs in the correct order.

4 Complete the article with the correct forms of the words from the box. There are two extra words.

> adapt admit can can't criticise however
> portray profound protagonist story ~~struggle~~

An Amazing Race for Glory: *Ford v Ferrari*

⬡ **A** The entire film is centred around the two men's collaboration and their *struggles* against corporate interference – the head of Ford wanted to remove Miles from the project – and the laws of physics. While most of the film focuses on car design and racing, elements of personal relations and parenthood are brought in to broaden the film's appeal. ¹_____ , the real interest lies in how ²_____ focused the two main characters are on achieving their vision, and what it costs them to reach it.

⬡ **B** All in all, I ³_____ recommend this film to anyone who is interested in cars, engineering, the sixties, or extremely good acting and solid film-making. What I ⁴_____ avoid pointing out is the lack of strong female characters, which – while probably true to the 1960s setting and the car-centric subject matter – seemed to me a flaw in an otherwise praiseworthy film.

⬡ **C** When the Ford Motor Company decided to challenge carmaker Ferrari by attempting to build a race car that was sleeker and faster than anything made by the Italian firm, very few car-savvy people thought it possible. ⁵_____ from a non-fiction book about the famous 1966 '24 Hours of Le Mans' race, *Ford v Ferrari* retells the history of the two main ⁶_____ who led this remarkable mission. Carroll Shelby, the visionary American car designer, is ⁷_____ by Matt Damon, while Christian Bale plays the British driver Ken Miles, famous for his driving skills and fearlessness.

⬡ **D** ⁸_____ , the script plays fast and loose with some of the facts as presented in the book, but real-life events don't always create drama on the big screen, so it's hard to fault writers who have managed to create a gripping drama while staying true to most of the actual history.

★ ★ ★ ★ ☆

5 Replace the adjectives in bold with *very* where possible.

Both the novel and the film are **really** / *very* inspiring for anyone with an interest in snow sports.

1 The final scene is **utterly** / _____ ridiculous and spoils what was otherwise a worthy adaptation.

2 The main character is **deeply** / _____ disturbed and makes a string of appalling decisions which eventually lead to his downfall.

3 As the loving owner of two dogs, I found certain scenes **extremely** / _____ difficult to watch.

4 Ultimately, the fate of the main character is **truly** / _____ heart-breaking and leaves the reader feeling lucky to be alive.

6 Choose the correct adjectives to complete the extracts from reviews.

1 The costumes and the special effects were *absolutely* / *very* amazing considering the budget limitations.

2 While undoubtedly engrossing, there is no denying the story is *profoundly* / *refreshingly* upsetting.

3 In comparison with the film version and all its omissions and flaws, the novel is *rather* / *totally* perfect.

4 As expected, the latest offering from everyone's favourite animation studio is *painfully* / *vastly* entertaining.

5 Whereas the life-affirming novel never ceases to delight, the TV series is *highly* / *surprisingly* dull.

6 Exercise caution before curling up under the covers with this novel, as it is, by any standards, *extremely* / *very* terrifying.

7 Comic fanboys and cosplay enthusiasts will undoubtedly find the film *tediously* / *totally* enthralling, but frankly, I struggled to stay awake past the half-hour mark.

REMEMBER THIS

Very can be used as an intensifier in the structure **definite article/possessive pronoun + very + noun**. It emphasises the significance, appropriateness or relevance of the noun in a particular context.

The very idea that this book could ever be turned into a film has seemed preposterous until now.

His very name conjures glamour, danger and intrigue.

---

7 Tick the sentences where *quite* means *extremely*.

From the very first page to the very last, Saunders' short story collection is quite delightful. ✓

1 Without wishing to include a spoiler, I can report the twist at the end of Herman's novel is quite surprising. ☐

2 There are so many thrills and spills along the way that by the end of the film, the viewer is quite exhausted. ☐

3 The main problem is with the plot, which is so absurd as to be quite unbelievable. ☐

4 After constructing my own image of the hero while reading the novel, I found it quite distracting that such a famous face was cast in the role. ☐

8 Read the writing task. Then follow the instructions below.

Your school website has introduced a 'review' section. Write a review of a book or film you have read or watched for the section. You may compare more than one title or, for example, a book and its adaptation for the screen. You should describe the plot briefly, give a detailed evaluation and make a recommendation to the reader.

Follow steps 1–8 below.

1 Decide on the topic of your review – a book, a film, a book and film adaptation, a film and its sequel/remake.

2 Briefly note down a plot summary.

3 Note down positive and negative points about the item(s) you have chosen to review.

4 If reviewing two things, make notes on how they compare.

5 Decide what your recommendation(s) will be.

6 Select the most important information.

7 Plan and write your review.

8 Add a suitable title.

SHOW THAT YOU'VE CHECKED

Finished? Always check your writing (especially in the exam!) Can you tick ✓ everything on this list?

In my review of a book/film:

• in the introduction, I have	☐
› caught the reader's attention in the opening sentences.	☐
› indicated the aim and structure of my review.	☐
› (if reviewing two things) begun the comparison that will continue throughout the review.	☐
• in the main body paragraphs, I have	☐
› described the plot briefly.	☐
› given a detailed evaluation mentioning positives, negatives, or both.	☐
• in the conclusion I have	☐
› stated my overall impressions.	☐
› expressed a recommendation (for or against) and given reasons.	☐
• I have used a reasonably formal and impersonal style.	☐
• I have checked my spelling.	☐
• I have checked my handwriting is neat enough for someone else to read.	☐

VOCABULARY

1 Match appropriate halves of the sentences.

Maria was determined to learn to walk on ☐ (f)

1 I know that Charles is generally a well- ☐
2 While making a list of the highest- ☐
3 The producer turned out to be a very tight- ☐
4 When Julia got to represent our country at a festival, rumours started to swirl ☐
5 The exhibition of Georgia's photos was quite mind- ☐

a around the way she was nominated to do so.
b blowing as she mainly focused on showing crime scenes.
c meaning person but he can be tactless at times.
d fisted woman economising on props.
e grossing movies of the century, we included all the revenue streams.
f stilts to play very tall clowns in street events.

/5

2 Complete the sentences with the correct words. The first and last letters are given.

During the rehearsal the conductor concentrated on getting the **p**ercussi**ve** rhythms right. He didn't want it to sound as if somebody was just hitting the drums.

1 You wouldn't believe the **s**_____**r** sense of euphoria when they saw Michael performing on stage.
2 When Helen received a standing ovation after the talk, it dawned on her that her experience must have had **f**_____-_____**g** implications.
3 My brother, the owner of a successful online music store, was talked into opening a **p**_____- _____**p** shop for a few days just to get better known in our town.
4 Instead of coming up with **f**_____-_____**d** excuses for not coming to rehearsals, tell us if you want to perform with our troupe or not.
5 The local authorities decided that the disused industrial estate should be turned into a creative **h**_____**b** where local artists could meet and work.

/5

3 Read the text. Complete the gaps with the correct forms of the words in brackets.

On my way through London a few years ago, I watched as thousands of runners took part in the London Marathon. It was a _mesmerising_ (mesmerise) sight. And it was to change my life for ever.
At that time I was struggling to survive as a composer. I was working on an opera about two ¹_____ (war) families that were fighting with each other for dominance, but because I was stuck for ideas as to how to finish it, I took up running to see whether it would inspire me. It was such a success, especially the changes in the ²_____ (choir) arrangements that now I run five or six times a week. I am sure that if I have written anything at all ³_____ (innovation), it is due to my running.
I have a ⁴_____ (suspect) that the current popularity of running is because it gives people some control over their lives. Charity runs, for example, mean that people can make a stand and show both mental and physical ⁵_____ (defy) about what is happening in the world.

/5

GRAMMAR

4 Complete the sentences with one word.

We'll be unable to offer you a discount on the CDs _unless_ you buy at least five of them.

1 _____ it not for the sea walls, the open air theatre would be at risk of flooding.
2 The secretary would have told you what courses were available _____ you had had your ID or not.
3 Say you _____ accused of plagiarism, what then?
4 Always have your passport with you in the _____ of unexpected checks of tourists in the streets.
5 Fortunately, Ann lost some weight before the opening night. _____ , her costume wouldn't have fitted her.

/5

5 Complete the second sentence so that it means the same as the first. Do not change the words in capitals. Use between four and six words in each gap.

Amy is very shy so she was speechless when she eventually met the singer. **NOT**
If she weren't so shy, Amy _would not have been_ speechless when she eventually met the singer.

1 If my sports teacher hadn't encouraged me, I would never have become a successful figure skater. **BUT**
_____ , I would have never become a successful figure skater.
2 Normally, nobody is allowed backstage, but what would you say if we just went there after the play? **WHAT**
_____ after the play, what would you say? I know that normally nobody is allowed there.
3 Helena's membership won't be renewed unless she pays her subscription within the next week. **SHOULD**
_____ within the next week, her membership won't be renewed.
4 If you started learning the drums now, you would soon be able to perform during school events. **WERE**
_____ the drums now, you would soon be able to perform during school events.
5 No tourist may enter unless they wear helmets. **CONDITION**
Tourists may enter _____ helmets.

/5

6 Correct the mistakes in the sentences.

Do you agree there should be more parking places during the festival? If ~~don't~~, why do you think so? _not_

1 Only if the conductor himself asked the audience, I'm sure somebody wouldn't comply with his request. _____
2 Dan's first animated film looked as thought he had made many before. _____
3 If though in doubt, Pete should consult his speech therapist and even practise his talk with her. _____
4 There are very few celebrities, if so, who relish being followed by paparazzi day and night. _____
5 A: Everybody is saying that our team is going to win the championship.
   B: Even if! _____

/5

Total /30

7 Choose the correct answer A, B, C or D.

Lucy Riches was first brought to the public's attention in a _D_ of publicity with the publication of her first novel at the age of thirteen. Only a year later she was the proud ¹___ of the Bookclub Prize, an extremely ²___ award for any writer, let alone a teenager.

The Chosen is a terrifying and action-³___ fantasy novel with an imaginative ⁴___ of characters. Lucy was determined to break away from stereotypical novels aimed at young people and has turned out a ⁵___ different one. She also wanted to create a piece that would have a ⁶___-chilling plot.

Lucy, now a level-headed fifteen-year old, has just finished the second novel in what will be a three-part series, which is to ⁷___ readers' imaginations even more than the first one. She's currently ⁸___ her breath to hear her publisher's verdict on the new book.

	A		B		C		D	
	A stir		B bustle		C tumult		(D) flurry	
1	A recipient		B acquirer		C receiver		D receptor	
2	A top		B major		C prestigious		D peak	
3	A crammed		B packed		C jammed		D loaded	
4	A cast		B team		C family		D crew	
5	A convincingly				B painfully			
	C refreshingly				D considerably			
6	A feet		B spine		C blood		D shoulder	
7	A provoke		B depict		C plead		D fuel	
8	A keeping		B holding		C taking		D saving	

/8

8 Complete the text with one word in each gap.

Is the cinema dead?

For many years now, people have been predicting the end of the cinema. _After_ all, why would you bother to go when films can be accessed on laptops and smartphones? In ¹_____ case, haven't young people rejected film-going in favour ²_____ playing video games instead?

The exception to this, of course, is big budget Hollywood blockbusters, when young people seem to pack cinemas ³_____ . Recently, however, there has been a drive to make films specifically targeting the 'grey market.' It was predicted that if cinemas ⁴_____ to start offering reduced prices mid-week and a more luxurious cinema-going experience, with more comfortable seats and provision of drinks and snacks, older people would be more likely to attend. They were right.

Meanwhile, adventurous young people are being attracted by ⁵_____ known as 'Secret Cinema', ⁶_____ audiences pay upfront to see unnamed films in undisclosed venues such as disused schools and warehouses.

So, against all expectations, the cinema is clearly still alive and kicking more than eighty years after 'talking pictures' first hit the screen.

/6

9 Complete the second sentence so that it means the same as the first. Do not change the words in capitals. Use between three and five words in each gap.

Whatever you do, you should avoid going out in cold weather. With the concert coming up, you shouldn't risk catching a cold. **COSTS**
You should avoid going out in cold _at all costs_. With the concert coming up, you shouldn't risk catching a cold.

1 Jo has recently behaved on stage like she was a prima ballerina, while in reality she's by no means the best. **THOUGH**
While in reality she's by no means the best, Jo has recently behaved on stage _____ a prima ballerina.

2 If somebody had renovated the theatre years ago, it wouldn't be in such a terrible state now. **DONE**
The theatre wouldn't be in such a terrible state now if it _____ years ago.

3 My father only lent me his collection of old LPs provided that I'd be very careful with them. **ON**
My father lent me his collection of old LPs only _____ I'd be very careful with them.

4 It's not very likely that there will be an evacuation but if there is, stay calm and follow the signs to the emergency exit. **UNLIKELY**
In _____ an evacuation, stay calm and follow the signs to the emergency exit.

5 The producer wasn't bold enough to go back on his word after having promised me my own TV programme. **NERVE**
Having promised me my own TV programme, the producer _____ go back on his word.

6 The actress made the director so furious that he could hardly control his anger. **CHECK**
The director was so furious with the actress that he could hardly _____ .

/6

Total /20

8 Text me!

VOCABULARY

8.1

Information and the mind • prefixes
• verb-noun collocations
• phrases with *mind*

SHOW WHAT YOU KNOW

1 Complete the sentences by filling the gap and choosing the correct word.

Silence please! We need your ªunderlined <u>undivided</u> ᵇ(attention) / *information* while we explain what to do in the event of a fire in the building.

1 The court accuses you of ªw_____ ᵇ*attention* / *information* in an attempt to pervert the course of justice.

2 Since I started going to bed earlier, I've noticed that my ª*attention* / *information* ᵇs_____ has improved during lessons.

3 At the very heart of cognitive psychology is the idea of ª*attention* / *information* ᵇp_____ .

4 As a scientist, I am only interested in ªf_____ ᵇ*attention* / *information* and not in unfounded opinions or beliefs.

5 You ªp_____ more ᵇ*attention* / *information* to your phone than you do to your friends.

WORD STORE 8A | Prefixes

2 Complete the sentences with the correct forms of the words from the box and an appropriate prefix.

> existence estimate fact impose
> inform load task ~~trust~~

She has a deep <u>mistrust</u> of dentists and as a result the majority of her teeth are severely decayed.

1 If I open more than a couple of apps at the same time, it totally _____ the processor in my phone and the whole thing freezes.

2 Many claims about the so-called health benefits of herbal remedies are based on _____ rather than solid science.

3 Working mothers are often champion _____ , juggling the responsibilities of motherhood with the pursuit of a career.

4 It emerged that the witness had been paid by the defendants to provide a testimony filled with lies and _____ .

5 Never _____ the power of peaceful protest – join the march and make your voice heard.

6 Doubtful of my own willpower, I decided to enlist the help of a personal trainer after my _____ exercise regime failed miserably.

7 Why can't people simply _____ peacefully instead of hating and fighting each other?

---

3 Complete the text with appropriate prefixes. Use hyphens (-) where necessary.

joystick-magazine.com's game of the week

Black Run for the all home consoles is a <u>multi</u>-disciplinary sports simulation game which includes individual and ¹_____ operative game play modes. To say the graphics are sharp would be an ²_____ statement – the mountain environments are rendered beautifully and the movement of characters is utterly convincing. Game play requires skill and ³_____ composure – it's easy to ⁴_____ estimate your ability to turn at speed in ski and snowboard disciplines, for example, and find yourself launched off the nearest cliff and into thin air. Hours of snowy fun to be had here – highly deserving of the title 'game of the week'.

WORD STORE 8B | Verb-noun collocations

4 Complete the extract from a relaxation CD recording. The first letters are given.

'Welcome to 'A Soul's Search'. To make the most of this relaxation CD, ensure you listen in a comfortable environment where you will not be disturbed. Switch off all your communication devices and when you are ready, lie back, close your eyes and begin to empty your mind of everything that normally **c**<u>lutters</u> your thoughts. Daily life can take its ¹**t**_____ on your mind and body and lead to unnecessary stress and worry. Most of us are aware that taking time out for relaxation is vital for our physical and mental health but the demands of work and family mean we often ²**b**_____ ourselves to this. With the help of this recording, you are going to ³**d**_____ some much-needed attention to yourself. Initially, we will ⁴**p**_____ relaxation tasks and techniques that require minimal practice, so those who are more experienced may ⁵**d**_____ a bias towards the basic. However, we will build steadily towards more advanced techniques, with the ultimate goal of deep and unhurried meditation to heal your mind and body.'

WORD STORE 8C | Phrases with *mind*

5 Complete the extracts from tech reviews with the words from the box. There are two extra words.

> absent ~~blow~~ business clear crossed
> manners out tough two weigh

Extreme sports fans, be prepared to be amazed by the new YesPro helmet cam. The slow-motion video capture will *blow* your mind.

You would have to be ¹_____ of your mind to pay twice as much for a phone that offers half the functionality of the latest model from PlusOne.

If you were in ²_____ minds about which tablet computer to go for, a quick look at the specs of the latest model from Samsung could convince you that this is the one.

Are you the ³_____-minded type? Always forgetting important times and dates? Persoft's Personal Assistant 2.0 could be the personal organiser app you've been waiting for.

The ⁴_____-minded amongst you may not think twice about deleting old photos, but if you are sentimental enough to want to hang on to all your snaps, then what you need is reliable storage.

The anonymity of Internet chat spaces and message boards can lead even those who would normally mind their ⁵_____ to be extremely rude and aggressive while interacting with strangers.

With tech companies' relentless drive to sell us the latest phones and laptops, has it ever ⁶_____ your mind just how many apparently 'obsolete' devices are piling up around the world?

When we asked the software company's CEO to comment on the outcry surrounding their controversial game, we were told bluntly to 'mind our own ⁷_____ '.

WORD STORE 8D | EXTRA Phrases with *mind*

6 Complete the sentences with phrases with *mind* in the correct form. Use the definitions in brackets to help you.

> You can accomplish anything if you *put your mind to it* (decide you are going to do something and give it all your effort).

1 If people could just be a little more _____ (liberal), this would be a much nicer country in which to live.

2 I've stopped watching the news because people are just so awful to each other and it _____ (troubles or worries me) and makes me depressed.

3 I find an early morning swim _____ (helps me forget the things that are troubling me) more effectively than anything else.

---

7 Choose the best answer A–C to complete the sentences.

1 Stereotypically labelled as enemies, dogs and cats can, in actual fact, happily __ .
   A cooperate   B multi-task   C coexist

2 The impact that the Internet would have on daily life was definitely __ in the 1990s.
   A underestimated   B self-composed   C overloaded

3 The troubled president has willingly gone into __ exile in a remote region of Burundi.
   A multi-disciplinary   B self-imposed   C understated

4 It's the air of superiority and the flashy suits that lead me to __ car salesmen.
   A mistrust   B misinform   C overestimate

5 To call Maria's voice exceptional would be a(n) __ – she had the voice of a legendary jazz singer.
   A understatement   B pseudo-fact   C bias

8 Complete each pair of sentences with the same answer A–C.

1 a __ ahead! Slow down and have your ticket and money ready.
   b Years of staring at a computer screen have taken their __ on Anna's eyesight.
   A strain   B toll   C gate

2 a If I __ attention to one dog, the other one barks and whines. It's a no win situation!
   b With this pledge I hereby __ myself to upholding the law and protecting my fellow citizens.
   A show   B promise   C devote

3 a Such tragic news can't help but __ on your mind, I'm sure.
   b A normal-sized matchbox filled with neutron star material would __ approximately 5 trillion tons.
   A hold   B weigh   C prey

4 a I paid the price for __-mindedly leaving my Facebook page open on the school computer.
   b One of the biggest social factors accelerating gang membership is the number of young men with __ or neglectful fathers.
   A short   B tough   C absent

5 a My laptop gets so hot I have to set up the fan to __ cool air on it and stop it switching itself off.
   b Some of the products at this year's tech-innovation exhibition are guaranteed to __ your mind.
   A blow   B push   C open

/10

1 Read the article quickly and choose the best title.

1 Myths and Misconceptions about FOMO
2 FOMO: What It Is and How to Cope
3 How FOMO is Changing Human Relationships

Are you frequently overwhelmed by the feeling that life is leaving you behind, particularly when you browse social media sites and are confronted with all the exciting things your friends are up to? If so, you are not alone.

FOMO, or Fear of Missing Out, is a very real phenomenon which is currently exercising the minds of psychologists and sociologists alike. While it may not be a new manifestation of social unease, the advent of social media has certainly shone a spotlight on the problem, and may very well have exacerbated the problem.

FOMO alludes to the perception that other people's lives are superior to our own, whether this concerns socialising, accomplishing professional goals or generally having a more deeply fulfilling life. It manifests itself as a deep sense of envy, and constant exposure to it can have a debilitating effect on our self-esteem. The feeling that we are always being left out of fundamentally important events, or that our lives are not living up to the image portrayed by others, can have long-term damaging psychological consequences.

While feelings of envy and inadequacy seem to be innately human*, social media seems to have added fuel to the fire in several ways. The reason why social media has such an exaggerated triggering effect is inextricably* tied to the inherent* appeal of social media in the first place: these are platforms which allow us to share only the most glowing* presentations of our accomplishments, while leaving out the more tedious aspects of life. While this kind of misrepresentation could be characterised as dishonest, it is what the polished ambience* of social media seems to demand.

So how do we avoid being lured into the trap of our own insecurities by social media? Firstly, consider your own social media posts. Have you ever chosen photos or quotes which lead others to the rosiest* conclusions about your life? Well, so have others – and what they've left hidden is the inalterable fact that boredom, loneliness and the sheer mundanity of the day-to-day are inexorably* a part of everyone's life, and you're not the only one feeling left out. Secondly, learn to appreciate the positives. You may not be a regular at glamourous parties or a climber of dizzying peaks, but you have your health, a place to live, and real friends who appreciate your presence in their lives. Last of all, learn to shake it off. We are all bombarded daily with images of other people's perfections, but really, what does it matter? They are probably no more real that the most ludicrous reality TV show. And even if you are more susceptible than others to social media envy, all that's needed to put it all into perspective is to look around you and acknowledge that you are doing pretty well after all.

2 **Read the article again. For questions 1–4, choose the correct answer A–D.**

1 According to the second paragraph, frequently experiencing FOMO can lead to
   A less likelihood of professional success.
   B a less satisfying social life.
   C harm to one's feeling of intrinsic value.
   D damage to the opinion others have of a person's worth.

2 In the third paragraph, the author suggests that
   A social media are the only cause of FOMO.
   B the nature of social media encourages the creation of false impressions.
   C our own social media posts help us feel more confident.
   D people who share mundane posts on social media are more confident.

3 In the fourth paragraph, the main reason the author refers to reality TV shows is to
   A point out how artificial what we see on social media can be.
   B emphasise the huge popularity of social media.
   C point out that what we see on social media should never be taken seriously.
   D emphasise how sophisticated social media has become.

4 According to the article, what advice would the author NOT give to FOMO sufferers?
   A Focus on the good things in your life.
   B Post only the most positive things about your life on social media.
   C Remind yourself that much of social media is misleading.
   D Learn to dismiss the negative feelings you get from social media.

3 **Complete the definitions with the words from the box. Use the text to help you.**

> allude bombard characterise exacerbate
> have ~~leave~~ manifest put

leave sth out – not include sth

1 _____ **a problem** – make a problem worse than it was

2 _____ **sth into perspective** – correctly view the importance of sth

3 _____ **sb/sth as** – describe someone or something in a particular way

4 _____ **sb with sth** – make someone face or deal with a lot of sth

5 _____ **to sth** – mention or call attention to sth

6 _____ **itself as** – show itself in a particular form or manner

7 _____ **a debilitating effect** on sth – cause damage to sth

4 **Match the sentence beginnings and endings. Use the text to help you.**

Having been called a child genius, it was difficult for him to live [D]

1 When browsing the Internet, it is easy to get lured ☐

2 I was already angry at him, but it simply added fuel ☐

3 Her brilliant article shone ☐

4 It is often a challenge for young people to accomplish ☐

5 Your problems may seem huge, but talking about them can put ☐

6 Experts agree that the advent ☐

A their professional goals while raising a family.
B into the trap of endless links and comments.
C of social media changed the way people relate to each other.
D up to the image later in life.
E to the fire when he criticised my appearance.
F them into perspective.
G a spotlight on the problem of Internet bullying.

WORD STORE 8E | Phrases

5 **Choose the most suitable answer A–C to complete the sentences.**

1 Many years ago, George's father invested in a small tech company called Apple, and he and the family have been reaping the __ ever since.
   A pluses   B benefits   C advantages

2 Having to replace my broken laptop took a big __ out of my savings.
   A bite   B amount   C bit

3 Something about the defendant's testimony didn't quite ring __ .
   A right   B honest   C true

4 Di is such a talented musician that learning a completely new instrument __ easy to her.
   A will be   B does   C comes

5 The concept of recycling is only just beginning to __ traction in certain parts of the country.
   A gain   B give   C get

6 The key to completing an ultramarathon is just to keep putting one __ in front of the other no matter what.
   A shoe   B foot   C leg

GRAMMAR

8.3
Reporting verb patterns

1 Put the verbs in brackets in the correct form.

Remember _to top up_ (top up) your mobile before going on holiday.

1 Even though Amber told Dylan to stop texting her, he went on _____ (send) her unsolicited messages.

2 If you want to have a successful date, try _____ (switch off) your phone beforehand.

3 I remember _____ (be) told off by my teacher in the first year of primary school.

4 I could tell he was trying _____ (control) his voice during the talk, but his nervousness still came through.

5 Having graduated with honours from university, Elijah went on _____ (become) a successful barrister.

2 ★ Put in the missing prepositions.

R: Zoe, would you object to someone quitting their job by text?

Z: Well, I'm ashamed to admit that I did it once myself.

R: Seriously? I'd never have suspected you ¹____ doing something like that!

Z: Rose, before you accuse me ²____ being selfish, you need to know that I tried to meet my boss several times before sending the text.

R: Well, in that case I can almost understand it. I mean, I won't praise you ³____ the way you handled it, but I'm not going to accuse you ⁴____ being selfish, either.

Z: In my defense, I did apologise to my boss ⁵____ choosing that form of communication, but he just left me no choice. I'd never do it again and I'm definitely not going to boast ⁶____ it to anyone.

R: And I'm sure no one is going to congratulate you ⁷____ having made that choice – certainly not your co-workers! I can almost understand your treating the boss like that, but I'm sure your team had plenty to complain ⁸____ when they discovered you weren't coming back.

Z: I did feel awful about that, but I got in touch with them later and they completely understood. They did say the boss was threatening to go to court and charge me ⁹____ breaking my contract, which was so typical of him! Fortunately, that never happened, and I've insisted ¹⁰____ having short-term contracts with all my subsequent employers.

R: That makes sense. You don't want to have that sort of experience more than once, do you?

3 ★ ★ Choose the best option. Sometimes more than one is correct.

1 Emma claimed _that she was / being / to be_ the one who was unfairly dismissed.

2 Charlie admitted _hacking / that he had hacked / to have hacked_ Phoebe's Facebook account.

3 We advise users _that they create / create / to create_ passwords with numbers and special characters.

4 Harper threatened _exposing / to expose / that she would expose_ her ex-partner as a cheat and a liar.

5 Leo regrets _believing / that he believed / to have believed_ those preposterous conspiracy theories.

6 My neighbour urged me _to get in touch / that I should get in touch / if I could get in touch_ with her immediately.

4 ★ ★ ★ Complete the second sentence so that it means the same as the first. Do not change the words in capitals. Use between four and six words in each gap.

'Let's resolve the matter amicably,' the mediator suggested. **RESOLVING**
The mediator _suggested resolving the matter_ amicably.

1 'I think it would be a good idea if you went there on your own, Jason,' his coach proposed. **GO**
Jason's coach proposed _____ his own.

2 'We must treat the Prime Minister's daughter like other students,' the head teacher recommended. **BE**
The head teacher recommended that the _____ like other students.

3 'Why don't you put us in the picture before you leave, Jacob?' his parents suggested. **SHOULD**
Jacob's parents suggested _____ picture before he left.

4 'We should allow the students to pick the venue for the prom night,' the English teacher insisted. **THAT**
The English teacher insisted _____ to pick the venue for the prom night.

5 Complete the sentences with the words in brackets in the correct forms. Do not change the word order. Use between four and six words in each gap.

When I first met her, she _advised me to buy the latest_ (advise/I/buy/latest) model of smartphone.

1 After the race, everybody _____ _____(congratulate/she/win/place) on the school team.

2 While thanking his voters, the President _____ _____ (claim/he/always/be) a staunch supporter of democracy.

3 Now our cousin _____ (regret/not/be/able) stay longer to celebrate the birthday of our baby son.

4 Last May one student objected _____ (have/he/phone/take) away from him during A-levels.

5 Despite many unsuccessful attempts, he still _____ _____ (try/convince/(one)self) he could fix the broken phone.

6 Yesterday some MPs tentatively _____ _____ (suggest/he/be/oust) from power.

/6

1 **Transform the sentence beginnings into the Passive.**

They say that ... → It *is said* that ...

1 People supposed that ... → It _____ that ...

2 Everybody thinks that ... → It _____ that ...

3 Quite a few people have suggested that ...
→ It _____ that ...

4 All the neighbours knew that ... → It _____ that ...

2 **Complete the second sentence so that it means the same as the first.**

They believe that Facebook has changed their life.
Facebook *is believed to have changed* their life.

1 Newspapers report that some participants of amateur talent shows aren't quite as amateur as TV stations would have us believe.
Some participants of amateur talent shows _____ quite as amateur as TV stations would have us believe.

2 At last month's conference many presenters feared that a large number of teenagers had grown so attached to the reality of social media that it was impossible for them to cut the chord.
At last month's conference a large number of teenagers _____ so attached to the reality of social media that it was impossible for them to cut the chord.

3 Some parents have pointed out that the new school rules weren't discussed with them in any way.
The new rules _____ discussed with parents in any way.

4 Last Friday they alleged that many viral YouTube videos were hoaxes.
Last Friday many viral YouTube videos _____ hoaxes.

5 Specialists agree that seeking validation online in the form of retweets and likes is exacerbating our desire to be accepted.
Seeking validation online in the form of retweets and likes _____ our desire to be accepted.

3 **Read the sentences in bold. Then replace each sentence in the text with two types of the Passive.**

⌣ ◯ ◯

LIFE HACKING

People say that the term 'life hack' was coined in 2004 by technology journalist Danny O'Brien during the O'Reilly Emerging Technology Conference in San Diego, California.

a It *is said that the term 'life hack' was coined* in 2004 by technology journalist Danny O'Brien during the O'Reilly Emerging Technology Conference in San Diego, California.

b The term 'life hack' *is said to have been coined* in 2004 by technology journalist Danny O'Brien during the O'Reilly Emerging Technology Conference in San Diego, California.

---

1 **Back then people understood that the phrase described the shortcuts IT specialists used to complete their work.**

a Back then it _____ the shortcuts IT specialists used to complete their work.

b Back then the phrase _____ the shortcuts IT specialists used to complete their work.

2 **Linguists assume that since then the phrase has spread among the tech and blogging community.**

a It _____ among the tech and blogging community.

b The phrase _____ among the tech and blogging community.

3 **Nowadays everyone widely acknowledges that life hacking refers to any kind of trick, shortcut, skill, or a novelty method that is meant to increase productivity and efficiency.**

a It _____ to any kind of trick, shortcut, skill, or a novelty method that is meant to increase productivity and efficiency.

b Life hacking _____ to any kind of trick, shortcut, skill, or a novelty method that is meant to increase productivity and efficiency.

4 **YouTube users consider that life hack videos have become the solution to a wide array of common problems.**

a It _____ the solution to a wide array of common problems.

b Life hack videos _____ the solution to a wide array of common problems.

5 **People also claim that those short clips are constantly helping them do different things the right way.**

a It _____ people do different things the right way.

b Those short clips _____ people do different things the right way.

SHOW WHAT YOU'VE LEARNT

4 **Complete the sentences with the words in brackets in the correct forms. Do not change the word order. Use between four and six words in each gap.**

It is said that (it/say) she was only after his money.

1 It _____ (final/announce/ Wednesday) online shops would have to comply with the new tax law.

2 Some vloggers _____ (be/ know/become) more popular than some pop bands.

3 It _____ (be/estimate/recent) this phenomenon has taken YouTube by storm.

4 The company was alleged _____ (be/force) tech bloggers into promoting its products for some time now.

5 It _____ (be/assume) all YouTubers are rolling in it, but that's a common misconception.

6 She's been implied _____ (have/get) married only as part of a publicity stunt.

/6

1 Choose the correct answer A–D to complete the conversation between the interviewer, Mark and Paula.

Extract from Student's Book recording 🔊 **3.18**

I: Mark, ªset the scene for us. How would you describe the responsibilities of a professional newspaper journalist?

M: I'd say we inform the public about events and issues and ¹__ their potential impact. We ᵇcomb through public records and ²__ out other sources of information, such as interviewing people or visiting locations where ³__ incidents have taken place. The bottom line is we ⁴__ to present a truthful, well-balanced ⁵__ of things that have happened. Clearly, we ᶜstay within the law and we're careful about things like the privacy of people we write about. And, of course, it goes without saying that we're good writers.

P: [...] Nowadays the prevalence of social media means that news ⁶__ out quickly and often people post or tweet things without ᵈchecking the facts. And ⁷__ their tweet goes viral, it may cause trouble if it's speculative rather than fact-based. But true citizen journalists may want to ᵉtell their side of a story and ⁸__ up a discussion or they may just have happened to ⁹__ something and want to share their experience. Of course, they're unpaid and their views are their own. [...]

M: ᶠFrom the opposing angle though [...] ᵍthere is always the question of whether they ¹⁰__ responsibly, and are backed up by ¹¹__ data. Nevertheless, citizen journalism is regarded positively by many because amateurs provide an ordinary person's view and often ʰa fresh angle.

1	A value	B price	C assess	D praise
2	A look	B search	C watch	D seek
3	A memorable	B noteworthy	C prominent	D noticeable
4	A struggle	B strive	C strain	D scheme
5	A account	B narrative	C homage	D explanation
6	A leaks	B gets	C escapes	D flies
7	A whenever	B how	C however	D if
8	A set	B put	C make	D call
9	A sight	B evidence	C view	D witness
10	A play	B act	C deal	D serve
11	A solid	B heavy	C thick	D rigid

2 Match the underlined phrases in the text to the definitions below.

a new or original viewpoint ⬜ (h)
1 to give your view of an event ⬜
2 to describe a place or situation ⬜
3 from the opposite point of view ⬜
4 used to introduce a problem or doubt ⬜
5 not to do anything illegal ⬜
6 to ensure your information is accurate ⬜
7 to search thoroughly for something ⬜

3 Put the expressions from the text into the dialogue between Pat and Aaron. Change the form if necessary.

P: What's that you're reading? Oh no, that's not a gossip magazine, is it? I can't believe you're reading trash like that. They never *check the/their facts* but make things up and sensationalise everything to sell more copies.

A: Alright, alright – don't go spare. I found it on the bus and started reading this interesting article about gangland crime in the UK. They ¹_____ by showing the current situation in London with some pretty shocking statistics. Then they interview this guy who ²_____ starting with how he first got into gangs and how one thing led to another. It's actually interesting to hear things ³_____ compared to the point of view you normally get on topics like this.

P: Oh, really? And the journalists, if that's what you can call them, actually ⁴_____ to get an illicit interview like that, don't they? Sounds dubious to me. And as I said, ⁵_____ or not you can rely on any of the information or even the sources of information at all. You'd have to ⁶_____ a magazine like that word by word before you find a reliable fact. And that's why, even if they present things from ⁷_____ like you say, you still need to take everything with a pinch of salt.

A: I know, I know. I'm not that gullible, and besides, as I said, I'd never actually buy a magazine like this.

WORD STORE 8F | Collocations

4 Complete the sentences with the words in the box. There is one extra word.

account amateur citizen common
fresh ideological impact media trust

Genuinely unbiased reporters always give a well-balanced *account* of the facts.

1 It's a very _____ misconception that fortune cookies are Chinese – in fact they're from Japan.

2 If you don't trust mainstream _____ , get your news from independent sources on the Internet.

3 Despite plenty of _____ footage, no-one has proved the existence of UFOs.

4 Climate change deniers are those people that refuse to accept the potential _____ of global warming on our future lives.

5 We've recently seen a greatly increased _____ in news reported by the general public.

6 With the use of the Internet, more and more news is based on _____ reports and used by professional journalists to support their stories.

7 Read between the lines of most mass media and you'll see the _____ viewpoint of the editors and writers.

8.6 SPEAKING

Adding emphasis

1 Expand the prompts to complete the experts' views.

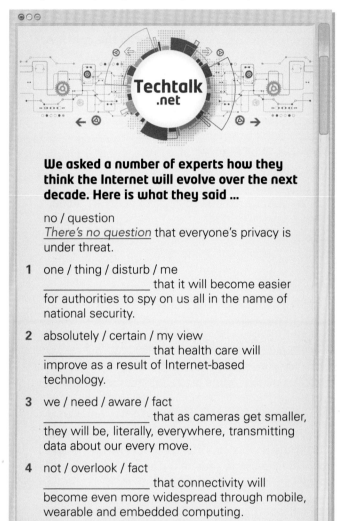

Techtalk.net

We asked a number of experts how they think the Internet will evolve over the next decade. Here is what they said ...

no / question
There's no question that everyone's privacy is under threat.

1 one / thing / disturb / me
_____ that it will become easier for authorities to spy on us all in the name of national security.

2 absolutely / certain / my view
_____ that health care will improve as a result of Internet-based technology.

3 we / need / aware / fact
_____ that as cameras get smaller, they will be, literally, everywhere, transmitting data about our every move.

4 not / overlook / fact
_____ that connectivity will become even more widespread through mobile, wearable and embedded computing.

5 I / not / convince
_____ that the future is all bright and I have serious concerns about the possible breakdown of traditional interpersonal relationships.

2 In each sentence, choose the option which is not possible.

1 And don't *forget / bother / overlook* the fact that this games console is accompanied by two controllers as standard.

2 There's no *point / question / doubt* that rechargeable batteries represent better value for money than disposable ones.

3 The one thing that really *bothers / disturbs / disagrees* me is how easily kids can access adult content on their phones.

4 I think the key *crux / thing / issue* is to encourage people away from screens and into the great outdoors.

5 What's *critical / cognizant / crucial* is to check your privacy settings and change your passwords regularly.

6 I'm absolutely *certain / adamant / decided* in my view that technology has improved our lives.

3 Replace the words in bold in the dialogues with the words from the box so that the meaning is the same.

> adamant   cognizant   disturbs
> doubt   forget   main point   ~~sure~~

Conversation 1: Pauline and Gina

P: I hear that in the US, some supermarket chains, particularly those with stores in affluent areas, get their cashiers to ask every customer whether they'd like to contribute to charity at the checkout. I'm not **convinced** / *sure* that that's fair really. There's no ¹**question** / _____ that asking the public in that way puts pressure on people to contribute, whether they want to or not.

G: Well, to some extent I agree. I mean, we need to be ²**aware** / _____ of the fact that it is morally questionable to shame people into giving, but having said that we shouldn't ³**overlook** / _____ the fact that most people living in such places can probably afford to give a few cents on top of their weekly shop. The ⁴**crux of the issue** / _____ is whether it's more important to raise money for charity or to protect the rights of those who might feel unduly pressured.

Conversation 2: Matthew and Jake

M: Jenny and I had a big argument yesterday.

J: Oh dear. About what?

M: About the fact that she spends so much time on her phone. The one thing that really ⁵**bothers** / _____ me is that she ignores me, you know? I can be telling her a whole story then she looks up from her phone half way through and says 'What?'

J: I know exactly what you mean. I think lots of people are guilty of that these days. I'm absolutely ⁶**certain** / _____ in my view that so-called communication technology is damaging our personal relationships in certain ways.

95

1 Complete the advice with the words from the box. There are two extra words.

> ~~formal~~ organisation persuasive reasons reiterate responding salutation sign support

When writing a _formal_ email or letter, begin with an appropriate **¹**_____ and inform the reader what the letter is **²**_____ to or regarding. Briefly state your **³**_____ for writing and then, in the second paragraph, introduce your first point and **⁴**_____ it with examples. Start another new paragraph to introduce and support your second point and again, another new paragraph to conclude and **⁵**_____ your point of view. At the end of your email or letter, be sure to **⁶**_____ off appropriately.

2 Read the task and the model letter and underline arguments that refer to the three bullet points in the task.

You have read an article about allowing students Internet access during exams in the online edition of a British newspaper. You decide to respond to the article by writing a letter to the editor, giving your own views. Your letter should include responses to these points from the article:

- Allowing Internet access during exams goes against the whole idea of traditional evaluation and would mean a complete redesign of the assessment process.
- Students won't retain core subject knowledge if they can simply copy facts from websites during exams.
- What is the point of, for example, a language exam, if students can just use an online translation tool? Exams are easier than they were these days anyway, without dumbing them down even further by allowing Internet access.

Dear Editor,

I am writing in response to a recent article in your newspaper about whether to allow students to use the Internet during exams. While the author offered several reasons to **maintain the status quo**, she failed to mention any **arguments to the contrary**.

It is **¹**_certainly true / truly certain_ that core knowledge is important and that an exam where students simply copy facts from a website would be pointless. **²**_Truly equal / Equally true_, however, is that in the 21st century, the Internet is used constantly to search for answers to **all manner of** questions that **arise** during our working and private lives. If the role of education is to prepare us for real life, then perhaps traditional assessment methods do need to be **overhauled**. Today's reality is that, rather than regurgitating facts, students need to demonstrate their ability to filter, interpret and apply online data. **³**_We should not / Should we not_ therefore, in addition to encouraging retention of core knowledge, include at least some exam questions that allow the use of the Internet and test these skills?

Taking the author's example of languages, **⁴**_it would / would it_ indeed be difficult to argue that Internet access during exams is appropriate for all subjects. However, **⁵**_were tasks / tasks were_ designed appropriately, some subjects would be more suited to the digital equivalent of open-book assessment. Contrary to your reporter's claims, I do not believe this would necessarily reduce the level of challenge these exams present. As a case in point, many professional exams are open-book, and far from making them easier, the **wealth** of information **to hand** and the limited time available create challenges **akin to** the realities of the world of work.

To conclude, while I agree that allowing students to copy online facts during exams would be **absurd**, and that not all subjects would be suited to exams where Internet access is permitted, **⁶**_above all / all above_ I feel that the realities of modern life should be reflected by the education system and its methods of assessment. If questions were designed to test critical thinking and interpretation of facts, then it is my view that allowing Internet access for certain exams or tasks would be a step in the right direction.

Yours faithfully
G. Benson

3 Choose the correct words to complete the phrases for being persuasive in the model letter.

4 Put the words in order to form more phrases for being persuasive. Add commas where necessary.

> that … / without / goes / saying / it
> *It goes without saying that …*

1 true / it's / of / that … / course

   _____

2 difficult / it / be / to / would / argue / that …

   _____

3 that … / is / it / a given

   _____

4 should / there / all / above / be …

   _____

5 that … / not / it / the / case / is

   _____

6 issues / not … / despite / are / such / this

   _____

5 Match the correct form of the words and phrases in bold from the letter to the definitions below.

> a wide range of   *all manner of*

1 large amount   _____

2 come up   _____

3 leave things as they are   _____

4 examine thoroughly and make necessary
   repairs or improvements   _____

5 similar to   _____

6 opposing points   _____

7 within easy reach   _____

8 pointless or ridiculous   _____

SHOW WHAT YOU'VE LEARNT

6 Read the writing task. Then follow the instructions below.

You have read an article about online lectures as an alternative to live lectures for university students in the online edition of a British newspaper. You decide to respond to the article by writing to the editor, giving your own views. Your letter should include responses to these points from the article:

- Information presented in live lectures may be easier to remember because students are stimulated by circumstances such as the lecturer's presentation style, the lecture venue and other students' reactions.
- Live lectures help students to develop skills such as discerning subtle arguments and making judgements when taking notes, as well as giving them an opportunity to make comments and ask questions.
- Attending lectures is a valuable part of the collective student experience and enough time is spent alone in front of screens already these days.

Before you start, follow steps 1–7 below.

1 Read the task carefully and check who you are writing to and why.

2 Decide whether or not you agree with the three points mentioned in the task.

3 Note down more arguments for and against.

4 Using your notes decide on your overall point of view.

5 Think how you will respond to each point in the task and how you will support your arguments.

6 Decide which language to use to sound persuasive.

7 Write your letter.

VOCABULARY

1 Complete the sentences with the correct words. The first letters are given.

My parents are said to be excellent at **m**ultitasking so cooking, talking on the phone and filling in a tax return at the same time doesn't seem to bother them.

1 We live in a multicultural world so we need to be **b**_____-_____ and open to other cultures.

2 These days a lot of TV stations also use **a**_____ footage when they prepare the news bulletin.

3 The Internet is full of information and it's difficult to filter out **p**_____-_____ and decide what's true.

4 I think we all suffer from information **o**_____ because of so many emails, tweets, etc.

5 When you're struggling for ideas, invite kids to look at the problem from a fresh **a**_____ .

/5

2 Complete the sentences with the verbs from the box in the correct form. There is one extra verb.

~~clear~~ detect mind
prioritise put reap ring

After a heavy day at work I usually take my dog for a long walk to _clear_ my mind and get mentally refreshed.

1 Sue put a lot of time and effort into writing a series of articles about TV and now she is _____ the benefit of it as she was nominated the editor-in-chief.

2 Students should be taught to _____ their tasks so that they learn which things to do first and which later.

3 It was so embarrassing when my sister spilled some juice over an elderly woman. Before we could apologise, we heard ' _____ your manners, young lady!'

4 If you want to win this scholarship, you need to _____ your mind to it and think how to achieve it.

5 Even though as a judge Richard should stay impartial, everybody could _____ bias in his speech.

/5

3 Read the text below and choose the correct verbs.

Picture the situation – you're in a packed restaurant, yet no-one is paying any attention to the person they're with, just (minding) / accomplishing / pursuing their own business. Everyone's on their tablets or mobiles, texting friends not lucky enough to be there. Doesn't it [1]say / ring / tell true to you? For many of us it's a reality, not fiction. However, should we allow ourselves to be [2]disclosed / nurtured / blinkered by the Internet instead of focusing more on the people around us?

Although I am in two [3]thoughts / minds / waves whether mobile phones should be banned in public places, maybe one solution is a 'looks-like' phone, resembling the real thing. It even [4]crossed / moved / came my mind that it could fit in a pocket so that its owner doesn't feel insecure.

If the 'looks-like' phone gained [5]reaction / premise / traction with the public, potentially, this could reduce the toll technology takes on real relationships.

/5

GRAMMAR

4 Correct the mistakes in the sentences.

The chairman demanded ~~us to install~~ anti-virus software on all the computers. _that we install_

1 Maria denied to post any unfavourable messages about her boss on a social networking site. _____

2 Josh reminded to his parents that he had chosen to study IT because they had made him do so. _____

3 The traffic warden urged the tourists to not gather right in front of the museum. _____

4 We all congratulated Kelly in winning a competition for the best webpage. _____

5 After I lost my phone, I proposed my parents to buy me a second-hand one. _____

/5

5 Report the statements using the verbs from the box.

accuse beg explain
~~persuade~~ suggest threaten

'It'd be good to do some research on teenagers.'
My tutor _persuaded me to do_ some research on teenagers.

1 'I'll sack you if you reveal any confidential information'.
My boss _____ if I revealed any confidential information.

2 'Ann, you didn't do a back-up before leaving the office'.
The manager _____ a back-up before leaving the office.

3 'We just don't agree to you using any photos with our child.'
Celia's parents _____ agree to the school using any photos with their child.

4 'Please, don't publish this', the politician asked a journalist.
The politician _____ this.

5 'Jim, why don't you join us for lunch?'
The manager _____ join them for lunch.

/5

6 Complete the second sentence so that it means the same as the first. Do not change the words in capitals. Use between three and five words in each gap.

People think that he is the most watched dancer. **BE**
He _is thought to be_ the most watched dancer.

1 There was a rumour that the video had received a million hits in one day. **SAID**
The video _____ a million hits in one day.

2 People believed that visits to the park had been on the increase for two weeks. **INCREASING**
Visits to the park were _____ for two weeks.

3 People say the popularity of Facebook is not as great as it was. **IS**
The popularity of Facebook _____ its peak.

4 Most people acknowledge his clip is the best. **WIDELY**
His clip _____ the best.

5 Because of services like Spotify®, it is thought we are spending even less money on music. **THOUGHT**
We _____ even less money on music because of services like Spotify.

/5

Total /30

USE OF ENGLISH

7 Choose the correct answer A, B, C or D.

Could I live without it?

Even though friends _B_ the opinion that I was crazy, I chose to cut off my home Internet connection. It was a **1**_____ decision, but one I had been unsure about for some time. What was **2**_____ on my mind was how I would feel without it – I didn't want to cut myself off completely, just not have it permanently to hand. I wasn't trying to prove a point; it **3**_____ to a feeling that my Internet use was controlling my life and in the long **4**_____ , it might ruin it completely.

5_____ I can't pretend it was easy at first, my quality of life has drastically improved. Now I go out to cafés to find a Wi-Fi connection, which means I prioritise things instead of surfing. I can **6**_____ more attention to what's important, so my work has become more efficient and my mind less **7**_____ with random thoughts.

I'm enjoying a social environment chatting to different people, but my friends still think I'm **8**_____ my mind!

	A fringed	(B) raised
	C proved	D embraced
1	A self-imposed	B self-promoting
	C self-aware	D self-indulgent
2	A hanging	B holding
	C pressing	D weighing
3	A get off	B took up
	C came down	D brought forward
4	A view	B run
	C time	D distance
5	A Although	B Even
	C Since	D Given
6	A send	B allow
	C provide	D devote
7	A messy	B untidy
	C cluttered	D scattered
8	A up to	B out of
	C in to	D off with

/8

8 Complete the text with the correct forms of the words in brackets.

To blog or not to blog?

Everyone thinks it's easy to be a blogger, but why should you _personally_ (personal) blog? The idea that blogs tend to focus on trivial things is a **1**_____ (concept), because in fact, it's helpful to share opinions with like-minded people. Anyway, don't **2**_____ (estimate) the fact that you probably have something noteworthy to say. Blogs have a huge potential market and they're interactive, so **3**_____ (told) numbers of readers are able to engage with you by posting comments. These can influence your ideas and possibly cause you to re-evaluate your position and force you to pay more attention to the **4**_____ (objective) of your posts if readers detect bias in your words. What they say can sometimes be a revelation!
If you're thinking of writing a travel blog, you may be able to correct any possible **5**_____ (inform) you spot on other websites. Readers then regard you as an expert, which helps you develop a bigger **6**_____ (reader) and gets your name widely known – invaluable if you plan to self-publish a book on the Internet. Blogging can enrich your life. Why not try it?

/6

9 Complete the second sentence so that it means the same as the first. Do not change the words in capitals. Use between four and six words in each gap.

That most news is biased is completely obvious. **SAYING**
It _goes without saying that_ most news is biased.

1 Apparently the documentary was prepared in collaboration with local charity organisations. **SAID**
_____ the documentary was prepared in collaboration with local charity organisations.

2 The movie star complained to the studio that his image was being used too much by them. **OVERUSING**
The movie star complained that _____ .

3 Everybody knows that the number of Facebook users is decreasing. **KNOWN**
The number of Facebook users _____ decreasing.

4 It's important to make sure that young people go out into the fresh air every day. **BASIS**
It's important to make sure that young people go out into the fresh air _____ .

5 Banks constantly warn customers to access their online accounts only on private networks. **SHOULD**
Banks constantly warn customers _____ their online accounts on networks which are not private.

6 The fine meant that the company's profit last quarter was a lot lower than expected. **BITE**
A very large _____ the company's expected profit for last quarter due to the fine.

/6

Total /20

99

VOCABULARY

9.1

Global warming • synonyms
• environmental problems
• animal idioms

SHOW WHAT YOU KNOW

1 Match the names of meat to the correct animals.

(~~beef~~ mutton poultry veal venison)

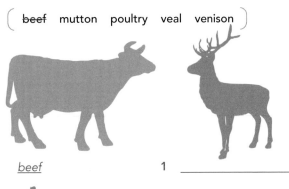

beef

1 _____

2 _____   3 _____

4 _____

2 Solve the puzzle to complete the sentence below.

The average beef cow consumes around twelve kilos of ¹__ ²__ ³__ ⁴__ **per day.**

1 The first letter from the word that means a natural or synthetic substance added to soil to help plants grow.

2 The last letter from the word that means organic matter mostly derived from animal waste and used to help plants grow.

3 The fourth letter from the word that means a substance used to kill cockroaches, flies, wasps, etc.

4 The eighth letter of the word that means a substance used to kill or control certain types of plants and animals that are considered to be a nuisance to agricultural crops.

WORD STORE 9A | Synonyms

3 Complete the text with the correct forms of the words from the box. Use the synonyms in brackets to help you.

(boost catastrophic critical
constitute paramount ~~radical~~
remorseless substantial tackling)

The rise and rise of veganism

Not so long ago, the word 'vegan' conjured up images of anaemic-looking, sandal-wearing hippies with _radical_ (extreme) views on animal rights and the ¹_____ (very harmful) consequences of eating a bacon sandwich on a Sunday morning. But today, thanks to a ²_____ (considerable) number of celebrity followers and super-bloggers, veganism has been given a ³_____ (increase) and is suddenly a ⁴_____ (essential) element in the neo-glamorous lifestyle. Beyoncé and Jay-Z are partners in a vegan food company, while other famous names who wax lyrical about the benefits of their vegan diets include Jared Leto, Joaquin Phoenix, Ellen DeGeneres and Bill Gates. Even sportspeople Venus Williams and Scott Jurek, for whom diet and fitness are ⁵_____ (the most important), have become converts. Proponents claim veganism is effective in ⁶_____ (dealing with) diseases such as diabetes and even cancer, and its ⁷_____ (never ending) rise looks set to continue as the environmental impact of meat production becomes common public knowledge. According to The Vegan Society, the number of vegans in the UK has risen in the last six years from 150,000 to 600,000 which ⁸_____ (makes up) around 1.16% percent of the population.

WORD STORE 9B | Environmental problems

4 Complete the newspaper headlines. The first letters are given. Use the definitions in brackets to help you.

C<u>onsumption</u> (use of a resource) of processed meat linked to increased risk of cancer.

Brazil announces record reduction in tropical **¹d**_____ (the permanent destruction of forests).

²L_____ **s**_____ (the part of the farming industry devoted to raising animals) generates €8.6 billion per year in the Netherlands.

UN **³s**_____ (being able to be maintained) development goals could transform the world by 2030.

Major players discuss **⁴a**_____ (the industry of farming) merger worth $2.3 billion.

Remorseless **⁵a**_____ **i**_____ (the use of machinery to make farming more productive) to blame for huge rise in unemployment in southern states.

Why **⁶b**_____ (the variety of kinds of life in an ecosystem) increase due to global warming is not a good thing.

Beijing to adopt world's strictest **⁷e**_____ (gases sent into the air) control standards.

WORD STORE 9C | Animal idioms

5 Complete the idioms. Some letters are given.

1 l<u>e</u>t s<u>leepin</u>g dogs l<u>i</u>e
2 be l____e w____r o____ a duck's b____k
3 a w____d goose c____e
4 k____l t____o birds w____ o____e s____e
5 s____t f____t____ horse's m____h
6 t____e t____ bull b____ t____ h____s

6 Match idioms from Exercise 5 to the situations below.

Enough talk! It's time to take practical action and actually do something about climate change. ⑥

1 I spent hours trying to find and buy the new model online only to find out it's not even available in Europe until next year. ◯

2 It wasn't until the boss made the announcement that we realised the rumours had been true. ◯

3 My current operating system works just fine so why risk upgrading, even if it's for free? ◯

4 I reduced my consumption of plastic and at the same time managed to save over £50 per month. ◯

5 I would have been really upset if anyone had spoken to me in that tone, but Nick didn't seem to care at all. ◯

WORD STORE 9D | EXTRA Animal idioms

7 Choose the correct words to complete the idioms.

1 let the *rabbit / dog / cat* out of the bag
2 *donkey's / monkey's / elephant's* years
3 a *wolf / tiger / shark* in sheep's clothing
4 hold your *sheep / horses / cows*
5 *pigs / mice / fish* might fly

8 Complete the sentences with the idioms from Exercise 7.

Don't tell Anne any secrets. She can't keep her mouth shut and will almost certainly <u>let the cat out of the bag</u>.

1 Damien may look innocent but, believe me, he can be really nasty. He's a _____ .

2 The brothers have been jokingly sending the very same awful birthday card back and forth to each other for

_____ .

3 Now just _____ for a second. Have you got money and is your phone fully charged?

4 Kerry said she might get an 'A' in the exam and, knowing how little revision she's done, I said 'Yeah, and _____ '. She wasn't very happy.

SHOW WHAT YOU'VE LEARNT

9 Cross out one word that is **not** necessary in each sentence.

Watch out for the boss. At first she seems friendly but she's actually a wolf ~~dressed~~ in sheep's clothing.

1 I firmly believe it's time we took the bull by the two horns and changed the gun control laws.

2 The livestock animal sector has a lot to answer for when it comes to climate change.

3 Yeah, yeah – keep them coming, hater. Your insults are like water running off a duck's back to me.

4 Hold onto your horses for a second my friend; you still owe me €20 from last weekend.

5 It was supposed to be a surprise party, but 'big-mouth' Dan went and let the cat get out of the bag.

10 Choose the best answer A–C to complete the sentences.

1 ___ measures are needed if we are to succeed in eradicating Ebola altogether.
   A Tackling   B Radical   C Paramount

2 The seven individuals now living in captivity ___ the entire remaining population.
   A constitute   B boost   C sustain

3 Melting ice caps have already had the ___ effect of all but destroying the polar bear's hunting grounds.
   A biodiversity B catastrophic C remorseless

4 ___ of timber has already stripped vast swathes of forest from the surface of the Earth.
   A Consumption   B Deforestation
   C Agricultural industrialisation

5 Manufacturer's blamed after ___ reach record levels causing respiratory difficulties for young and old.
   A boosts   B agribusinesses C emissions

   /10

A
B
C
D

Taking Out the Trash*

My name is Lauren Singer. I'm a twenty-three year-old girl living in NYC and I don't make trash. Nada. No garbage bin, no landfill.

1 _____

I didn't always live what's called a 'zero-waste life', but started making the shift about three years ago while working towards an Environmental Studies degree at New York University. At the time, I had become president of a club that hosted weekly talks on environmental topics. As such, I considered myself a true environmentalist, or as my grandma liked to call me, 'a real tree hugger'. Everyone, including myself, thought of me as the 'sustainability' girl, so obviously, I was doing my best to live a green and sustainable lifestyle, wasn't I?

2 _____

One night after a class at the university, I went home and started making that night's dinner. And then it happened. I opened my refrigerator, and I froze. Every item was wrapped or packaged, one way or another, in plastic.

3 _____

In practice, my resolution to do without this ubiquitous substance meant learning to produce all of the products that would have come packaged in it myself. This included everything from toothpaste to cleaning products. I didn't know where to begin, so took to the Internet to search for solutions. While online, I **stumbled across** a blog called *Zero-Waste Home*, which followed the life of Bea Johnson, wife and mother of two children who all live a zero-waste life in California.

4 _____

Inspired by what I'd read, I stopped buying packaged products altogether and began bringing my own bags and jars to fill with bulk products at the supermarket. I also stopped buying new clothing, and shopped only second-hand. On top of this, I downsized my possessions significantly by selling, donating, or giving away superfluous* things such as the ten pairs of jeans that I hadn't worn since high school, and the hordes* of decorative items to which I felt no attachment.

5 _____

Of course, the transition didn't **happen overnight**. The process took more than a year and required lots of small changes, but I'm happy to say it was worth it. Living in a way that aligns with my values has inspired others and improved my life hugely. I spend less time and money shopping, I eat healthy locally-grown produce and I'm proud of what I've achieved, which makes me generally less stressed out and far more content.

6 _____

I didn't adopt this lifestyle to make a statement; I did it because it is the absolute best way I know to live in a way that aligns with everything I believe in.

GLOSSARY

take out the trash *(AmE)* – put the rubbish in the bins outside
superfluous *(adj)* – unnecessary, particularly because there are too many of something
hordes *(n)* – large numbers of something, especially people in crowds

culpable *(adj)* – to blame; guilty
revelatory *(adj)* – revealing something previously unknown

1 Quickly read the article without the missing paragraphs and number pictures A–D in the order they correspond to the text.

2 Read the article again. Match gaps 1–6 with paragraphs A–G. There is one extra paragraph.

A The realisation that I was equally culpable* of generating all this unnecessary waste left me feeling like a total hypocrite, and in that revelatory* moment, feeling like part of the problem, I made the decision to eliminate all plastic from my life.

B In addition to this clearout, a vital step in my journey towards waste-free living was **consciously pre-empting** potentially wasteful situations. This involved saying no to things like single use plastics such as straws in my drinks at cafés, and plastic or paper bags at stores.

C Debatable. In one of my classes at NYU, I had noticed that a fellow student always brought a ton of plastic as part of her meal, and then would throw it all away when finished. This upset me, especially as we were part of an Environmental Studies class. She could have used a paper bag, a reusable box, metal cutlery or a flask to carry her water in.

D I never anticipated that actively choosing not to produce waste would turn into my having a better quality of life in general. It was just a way to align my day to day life with my values. But what was, at first, a lifestyle decision, then became a blog and has now blossomed into what I hope will prove to be a successful eco-friendly business.

E In spite of this, I now make a grocery list when I go shopping, which means being prepared and not grabbing expensive items impulsively. Additionally, buying food in bulk means not **paying a premium**, and when it comes to my wardrobe, I shop second-hand and get my clothes at a heavily discounted price.

F I know what you're thinking, though. This girl must be a total hippie, or a liar, or the **figment of someone's overactive imagination**. Well, I assure you, I'm none of those things; in fact I'm basically just your ordinary New York City girl, who made a decision to change the way she lives 'for the greener'.

G I thought, 'if someone with so many responsibilities can go all the way, then I, as a twenty-one-year-old single girl in NYC, certainly can too.' So, I **braced myself** for the next logical step in my journey and took the leap from zero-plastic to zero-waste.

3 Complete the definitions with the correct form of the phrases in bold from the article and the extra paragraph.

If something *happens overnight*, it occurs very quickly.

1 If something is a _____, it is not real and is created by someone's mind.

2 If you _____ something, you find it by accident.

3 If you _____, you buy something at an unusually high price.

4 If you _____, you prepare yourself mentally or emotionally for something unpleasant.

5 If you _____ something, you knowingly take action to prevent something from happening.

WORD STORE 9E | Collocations

4 Complete each pair of sentences with the same answer A–C.

1 a If we contributed half as much money as we spend on defence to humanitarian __ , much of the world's suffering could be prevented.

  b What __ people to resort to violence rather than negotiation and compromise?

  A affairs   B causes   C aids

2 a Due to a problem with the __ , the rear wall of the house has sunk into the ground by almost ten centimetres.

  b If you ask me, the world needs more philanthropic __ and fewer marketing agencies that waste time promoting things that nobody really needs.

  A materials   B individuals   C foundations

3 a This backward-looking government is determined to build more coal-fired power stations despite the huge environmental __ they have been proved to cause.

  b Should you discover any __ to your product after opening this parcel, please contact our customer services department immediately.

  A problems   B damage   C action

4 a I couldn't get the battery cover off and when I tried to __ it, I dropped my phone and smashed the screen.

  b The soldiers killed were actually part of a peacekeeping __ and were not armed at the time they were attacked.

  A force   B mission   C help

5 a Intergovernmental __ have been strained since the discovery of vast gold deposits on the border between the two countries.

  b Just once I'd like to spend my winter holidays with you in the mountains, instead of trailing round all the __ as usual.

  A relations   B organisations C relatives

SHOW WHAT YOU KNOW

1 Complete the sentences with missing verbs.

A: I never follow long-term weather forecasts as they often prove unreliable. B: Neither _does_ my sister.

1 A: We are busy building shelters along the motorway for the motorists stuck in the traffic jam. B: So _____ the Red Cross volunteers.

2 Her car was blanketed in snow, as _____ all the vehicles in her neighbourhood.

3 _____ I you, I wouldn't hesitate to help with the clear-up operation.

4 _____ it not been for hundreds of volunteers, the roads would have remained impassable even longer.

2 ★ ★ Complete the sentences with the phrases from the box. There are three extra phrases.

~~Never before~~   Not for a moment
Not since   Not until   Only by
Only in this way   Only then   Very rarely

Never before have commuters been faced with such adverse weather conditions.

1 _____ did we think that the road had not been gritted after the heavy snowfall.

2 _____ 1869 has such a massive snowstorm been recorded by American meteorologists.

3 _____ do temperatures surpass 40 degrees Celsius in summer, but when they do, it is always senior citizens that are most likely to be affected.

4 _____ living here for a few years will you ever get accustomed to the vagaries of the English weather.

3 ★ ★ ★ Replace each sentence in the article with inversion. Use the beginnings given.

SHOW WHAT YOU'VE LEARNT

4 Complete the second sentence so that it means the same as the first. Use the words in capitals. Use between five and six words in each gap.

Last week transport services were cancelled and many homes were without power. **BUT**
Last week not _only were transport services cancelled, but_ many homes were also without power.

1 That was the first time so many drivers found themselves stranded on motorways blocked by snow. **BEFORE**
Never _____ themselves stranded on motorways blocked by snow.

2 It wasn't possible for those orangutangs to escape from raging fires in Borneo last month. **COULD**
In no _____ raging fires in Borneo last month.

3 It took New Orleans ten years to recover from the damage caused by Hurricane Katrina. **LATER**
Not _____ New Orleans recover from the damage caused by Hurricane Katrina.

4 In case of a tsunami people should reach higher ground on foot, never by car. **CIRCUMSTANCES**
Under _____ ground by car in case of a tsunami, but on foot.

5 Victims of the earthquake did not have any idea how big the tremors would be. **REALISE**
Little _____ how big the tremors would be.

6 And at that moment we found out that it had been the second highest snowfall on record. **THEN**
Only _____ it had been the second highest snowfall on record.

/6

NOBODY'S SAFE

As soon as the River Thames burst its banks due to heavy rains last Wednesday, floodwater threatened to inundate a local developer's £10 million mansion.

Barely _had the River Thames burst its banks due to heavy rains last Wednesday when_ floodwater threatened to inundate a local developer's £10 million mansion.

1 The developer and his wife bought the 17th century property near Reading, Berkshire only a year ago.

Only _____
the 17th century property near Reading, Berkshire.

2 They were planning to redo its twenty rooms and wanted to redesign the sprawling garden.

Not only _____
redesign the sprawling garden.

3 The Environment Agency has warned that low-lying areas should not be considered safe at all for the next few days.

In no way _____
_____
safe for the next few days.

4 Local residents have been advised that they must not ignore the latest flood alerts.

On no account _____
_____
the latest flood alerts.

5 They should not underestimate the power of the river as even thirty cm of flowing water is sufficient to move a car.

Under no circumstances _____
_____
the power of the river as even thirty cm of flowing water is sufficient to move a car.

6 As of yet the developer has not commented on the situation.

At no time _____
_____
on the situation.

1 Choose the correct option.

1 My mother doesn't like it *that / if / where* some public transport users stand with their rucksacks on their back, especially on overcrowded trams, bashing or leaning on other passengers.

2 I would appreciate it *that / when / if* other passengers didn't plant their bags on the seat next to them on a busy bus.

3 I think it bothersome *to see / if I see / when I see* individuals who stop in front of the ticket gates fishing around in their pockets for their travel cards.

4 The elderly who use public transport *take / owe / find* it frustrating when young passengers don't give up their seat when they see them.

5 When I'm running late and need to catch an underground train quickly, I find it particularly annoying *where / that / if* so many people stand on the left on escalators and block the path.

I find it impossible to slow down.

2 Complete the second sentence so that it means the same as the first. Use the words in capitals. Use between three and six words in each gap.

I would be grateful if you could refrain from looking at your smartphone when you're walking across the street. **APPRECIATE**
I *would appreciate it* if you could refrain from looking at your smartphone when you're walking across the street.

1 We don't think politicians ought to decide on a sensible course of action. **LEAVE**
Let's _____ decide on a sensible course of action.

2 It is considered necessary by the school staff that all students familiarise themselves with the code of conduct before going on any field trip. **NECESSITY**
The school staff _____ all students familiarise themselves with the code of conduct before going on any field trip.

3 I assume you know you are expected to let others get off the tram or a bus before trying to get on. **TAKE**
I _____ you know you are expected to let others get off the tram or a bus before trying to get on.

4 The mayor feels grateful to his voters so he will make sure the new laws contribute to their well-being. **OWES**
The mayor _____ make sure that the new laws contribute to their well-being.

3 Complete the dialogue with the correct form of the words in brackets necessary. Add any words necessary.

T: Just when I thought nothing could surprise me any more, this happens.

A: What is it, Toby? I would *appreciate it if you told* (you/tell) me what shocked you so much.

T: Oh, I'm referring to this revolutionary idea of a shopping centre in Liverpool. You'll love it ¹_____ (they/just/open) Britain's first ever fast lane for pedestrians.

A: They did what?

T: You heard me, Ann. Apparently people find it annoying ²_____ (have to) elbow their way through crowds when they're doing shopping or rushing somewhere.

A: Story of my life! I absolutely hate it ³_____ (dawdlers/stand) in my way when I'm in a hurry, don't you?

T: Well, yeah, they make me late too, but don't you consider it far-fetched ⁴_____ (they/introduce) this solution in a shopping centre where people are supposed to relax? Anyway, how are they going to stop slow walkers from using the fast lane? I'm not so sure it will solve the problem of pavement hoggers.

A: I beg to differ. To be honest, I think it strange ⁵_____ (nobody/come) up with this idea before. I wonder if other cities will follow suit. So when are we heading to Liverpool?

SHOW WHAT YOU'VE LEARNT

4 Complete the text with one word in each gap.

Like many people, I really *hate* it when modern life pushes me to go faster than I feel comfortable going. I would really ¹_____ it if I could take the time to enjoy the natural rhythm of life. I think we ²_____ it to ourselves to take more time and care in our daily lives and, as I believe in the principles of the SLOW movement, I try to let the concepts of Sustainable, Local, Organic and Whole guide me. Why should we ³_____ it to the forces of marketing to decide how we live? Don't you find ⁴_____ annoying that the pressures to make money rule your life? Of course it is hard ⁵_____ accept that everything may not be driven by personal choice, but anybody can make a conscious effort to slow down. I love ⁶_____ when I see people growing their own food, because it reassures me that we can still choose how we affect the planet we live on.

/6

9.5

Verb forms • informal phrases with *come* • verbs

1 Read the recording extract. Put the verbs in brackets into the correct form.

> *Extract from Student's Book recording* 🔊 **3.27**
>
> **K:** Hi everyone – I'm Kathy Thomas and I'm here to tell you about my participation last year in an on-going project monitoring wolves in a US national park. […] First *I'll give* (give) you some background. Years ago, wolves living in the park ¹_____ (simply/see) as predators and a decision ²_____ (make/eradicate) them. I wish scientists ³_____ (understand) then how this would upset the natural balance of the area. […] But lessons ⁴_____ (learn), and in the mid-1990s, wolves ⁵_____ (reintroduce) into the park. As a result, the elk ⁶_____ (leave) the valleys and the trees flourished again. The beavers returned, encouraging new ecosystems – predictably these ⁷_____ (include) fish, otters and ducks in the rivers, and mice and rabbits on the land, which provided food for foxes. I ⁸_____ (not/expect) there ⁹_____ (be) such a large variety of birds, though. So it's clear why the wolves ¹⁰_____ (need/monitor), and that's where we volunteers come in.

2 Look at some common phrases with the verb *come*. Complete the definitions by adding the missing words from the box. Use a dictionary if necessary.

> bridge   head   nowhere
> wall   ~~where~~   worst

> **that's _where_ somebody comes in** – the point that somebody becomes involved
> 1 **cross that _____ when we come to it** – wait for a situation or problem to occur before trying to solve it
> 2 **if the _____ comes to the worst** – if a situation develops in the most negative way
> 3 **come up against a brick _____** – be unable to progress because something or somebody is stopping you
> 4 **come out of _____** – appear unexpectedly
> 5 **come to a _____** – to reach a critical state when a decision or act needs to be taken

3 Complete the sentences with an appropriate *come* phrase from Exercise 2. Sometimes you need to change the form. There may be more than one possibility.

> The threat to the Forest of Dean has become imminent. We need to take a stand and show how much we oppose the proposed changes. And that's *where we/you come in* as we'll need as many bodies as possible for a sit-down protest!

1 The government's attitude seems to be very much one that there's no imminent danger to the ozone layer and if it does become critical, they will simply _____.

2 There's really no point in worrying about that now. We'll have to agree that _____ , we'll take a stand and stick together.

3 The disagreement between landowners and farmers has _____ and the authorities will need to intervene to stop things turning ugly.

4 Due to escalating costs, the threat of legal action and fact that the media have now turned their attention elsewhere, it seems that we have _____ that no one can see a way round.

5 We were walking across this field and then, all of sudden, a herd of buffalo _____ and started charging towards us. I've never been so scared in my life.

WORD STORE 9F | Verbs

4 Use the verbs below in the correct forms to complete the text.

> eradicate   factor in   flourish   monitor
> reintroduce   stagger   ~~upset~~

> It's very *upsetting* to read that the first mammal has been driven to extinction due to human-caused climate change. The Bramble Cay melomys, also known as the mosaic-tailed rat, was only found on a small island off the coast of Queensland, Australia. The existence of the rodent had been ¹_____ since it was first discovered in 1845. Whilst initially found in very high numbers, researchers were ²_____ to find the population had dropped to only several hundred by 1978.
>
> Rising sea levels flooded the island and destroyed the habitat of the animals which were no longer able to ³_____ as they had done in the past. Now, when they are officially classed as 'extinct', it is clearly impossible to ⁴_____ a species that has been forever wiped out. And when the numbers of other species on the edge of survival are ⁵_____ , we have to wonder how many other life forms will be inadvertently ⁶_____ before we can reverse the effects of climate change.

1 Complete the extracts from descriptions of photographs with the words from the box. There are two extra words.

> admittedly   assume   bound   envisage   might
> ~~must~~   potentially   tentatively   wouldn't

The girls look identical in this photo, and it hasn't been airbrushed, so they _must_ be twins. There's no other explanation.

1 I _____ this is a nature reserve of some sort because it's extremely unusual to see so many large animals together in such a relatively small space.

2 I could be wrong, but I _____ think that they are enjoying themselves. They look cold, wet and tired and that's certainly not my idea of a good time.

3 I can _____ how it must feel to be weightless and to float around in space like the astronaut in the picture, but I don't suppose I will ever get the chance to actually experience it for myself.

4 The picture paints an idealistic image of life in the country but in reality, it's _____ to have its downsides and frustrations.

5 _____ , this wouldn't be to everyone's taste, but to me it looks like a great way to spend a holiday.

6 I can't be certain, but _____ , I'd say the woman in the picture is some kind of doctor or veterinarian.

2 Complete the first part of the description. The first letters are given.

These two images show differing visions of the future. Photo A has an almost nightmarish quality to it, and is probably somewhat far-fetched, whereas image B looks more realistic to me. I ¹**p**_____ **t**_____ the planet we see in the sky is Earth, meaning that this place ²**c**_____ be a settlement on a space station, though we can't ³**r**_____ **o**_____ the **p**_____ that the landscape is on Earth itself, in a future where it ⁴**w**_____ **a**_____ nature has died out and only elaborate machines can keep us alive. It's not completely clear what the message of the image might be, but I ⁵**s**_____ that it's a comment on human beings' impact on our planet. Though ⁶**u**_____ to actually happen to this degree, perhaps, the idea is that we have left Earth uninhabitable, and that we might be doomed to repeat the same mistakes on other planets. Judging by how bad we are as a race at learning from our mistakes, I'd say that this is quite ⁷**l**_____ .

3 Choose the correct words to complete the second half of the description. In one case both words are possible.

In comparison to image A, image B presents a rather more coherent and positive view of the future, in my opinion. Clear skies and vegetation ¹*suggest / appear* that environmental problems ²*must / may* well have been brought under control. There's an interesting contrast between the traditional house in the foreground and the futuristic city in the background. There's also a telephone mast, which is ³*tentatively / presumably* obsolete, as I very much ⁴*doubt / envisage* that we'll be using cables to carry communication signals in the future. It would ⁵*seem / imagine* that there are flying vehicles of some sort hovering over the city.
I don't know ⁶*if / whether* this is a realistic vision of the future, but it is ⁷*definitely / likely* more appealing and more believable than the one presented in image A.

1 Complete the second sentence so that it means the same as the first. Use the words in capitals.

1 Nowadays, extreme weather events seem to be happening more frequently. **DAYS**
   These days extreme weather events seem to be happening more frequently.

2 My own stance on the matter is that the billionaire's comments prove he is a serious threat to world peace. **INCLINATION**
   It _____ the billionaire's comments prove he is a serious threat to world peace.

3 While some people insist it is their right to own a weapon, others believe that guns should be banned. **CRITICS**
   Supporters argue _____ believe that guns should be banned.

4 Clearly, what to do about racism in contemporary Europe is a complicated issue. **COMPLEX**
   The _____ one.

5 There is considerable debate as to whether veganism is a healthy lifestyle choice for children. **CONTROVERSY**
   There is a _____ the issue of veganism as a healthy lifestyle choice for children.

6 Most people believe domestic robots are destined to become more numerous in the coming decades. **ACKNOWLEDGED**
   _____ are destined to become more numerous in the coming decades.

2 Complete the tips on writing essay introductions with a word from the box. There are two extra words. Then match the sentences from Exercise 1 to each tip.

> agree approaches controversial
> justify opposing own ~~recent~~

   Summarise the current or _recent_ situation. ①

1 Make a general point that most people would _____ with. ◻

2 State that the issue is complicated, _____ or causes disagreement. ◻ & ◻

3 Summarise _____ views on the issue. ◻

4 Summarise your _____ opinion at the end of the introduction (opinion essay). ◻

3 Complete the introduction to an essay. The first letters are given.

> It is widely **a**_cknowledged_ that businesses have been reducing their number of employees for decades. In ¹**r**_____ **y**_____ , automation has made it increasingly possible to perform tasks with machines. Not ²**e**_____ **a**_____ that automation is a positive step, and there is no ³**s**_____ **a**_____ when it comes to preserving jobs. ⁴**W**_____ some people argue that this change is unavoidable, ⁵**o**_____ **c**_____ that retraining workers could keep everyone employed. My ⁶**o**_____ **v**_____ of the matter is that governments and businesses must cooperate to find a solution.

4 Choose the correct words and phrases to complete the rest of the essay.

> Without _a_ / no doubt, there are substantial arguments both for and against self-service shopping. ¹_To begin with / In the beginning_, it would seem that most of the advantages are on the side of the **retailers**, and that customers and job-seekers pay the price for the store's savings. At the other ²_end / side_ of the spectrum, **proponents** argue that cost savings are passed on to customers, and that many shoppers love the speed and convenience of self-service.
>
> Looking at the advantages, there are several which apply to both businesses and customers. ³_Firstly / Then_, businesses can reduce labour costs while offering less waiting time for customers. ⁴_However / Furthermore_, customers who are comfortable with the technology enjoy the independence and speed of self-service. ⁵_On the other hand / Moreover_, if service jobs in stores were eliminated, everyone would be freer, ⁶_meaning / due to_ customers could shop at their own pace, and young people could pursue meaningful careers instead of being **stuck** at a cash register.
>
> ⁷_Never mind / On the flipside_, there are arguments against self-service shopping both for retailers and customers. ⁸_Then / Firstly_, the substantial expense of installing and maintaining the technology is a huge **hurdle** for businesses. ⁹_Additionally / Unless_, there is an increase in complaints from shoppers who dislike having to serve themselves, not to mention an increase in (sometimes accidental) thefts. ¹⁰_However / Furthermore_, considering that many shoppers are confused and **intimidated** by new technology, and that young people already have trouble finding entry-level jobs, the arguments against self-service shopping have a lot of weight behind them.
>
> ¹¹_All things considered / No matter_, there are persuasive arguments on both sides. And while it seems **inevitable** that increasing numbers of machines will replace humans, I believe that every chance to provide personal service to customers should be **seized upon**, since personal interactions are a part of what keeps us truly human.

5 Complete the definitions with the words in bold from the model.

retailers – businesses which sell directly to customers

1 _____ – made to feel afraid or not capable of doing sth

2 _____ – unable to be stopped or avoided

3 _____ – unable to escape from a bad or boring situation

4 _____ – supporters

5 _____ – a problem or difficulty to be overcome; also, the frames over which athletes jump during a race

6 _____ – take advantage of

6 Complete the text with the words and phrases from the box.

> another step   ~~as well as~~   even so
> first   no matter   on balance
> this means   unless   whether

Home | Search | Contact   www.haveyoursay.org

Have your say – this week's topic: environment

Gavin404 writes …

World Environment Day is celebrated globally to remind us of our impact on the environment _as well as_ the things we can do to protect it. How can individuals most effectively contribute to solving environmental problems? **1**_____ what age we are, there are various ways in which we can all contribute.

2_____ , we need to respect life and renew our bond with nature. **3**_____ recognising that all living things have a right to live on this planet. **4**_____ there is respect for nature, there will be no desire to protect it. **5**_____ we can take is to influence the organisation we belong to, **6**_____ it is a school or a company, to be more environmentally friendly.

7_____ , I believe the best way for individuals to help protect the environment is by spreading the environmental message. Of course, it can be difficult to persuade others of the importance of environmental issues. **8**_____ it is important to make that effort.

SHOW WHAT YOU'VE LEARNT

7 Read the writing task. Then follow the instructions below.

As artificial intelligence advances, the prospect of machines that can think, feel and operate independently is becoming more of a reality. Though they would be designed to make our lives easier, such machines may also present a danger to the human race. Write an essay in which you present your opinion on the topic. In your essay discuss the following aspects:
- the ways in which AI machines might make life easier.
- the dangers that AI machines could present.
- potential solutions to these dangers.

1   Read the task carefully. Have you read any books, seen any films or played any games that deal with this topic? What viewpoints were presented there?

2   Make notes under each of the three bullet points in the task.

3   Decide what your overall opinion on the topic is. To what extent do you agree that AI machines pose a threat to the human race?

4   Write your introduction using a selection of the techniques mentioned in Exercise 2.

5   Look at your notes and organise the points into two or three main body paragraphs.

6   Consider the linkers you will use to join your ideas.

7   Write your essay.

SHOW THAT YOU'VE CHECKED

Finished? Always check your writing (especially in the exam!) Can you tick ✓ everything on this list?

In my essay:

- in the introduction, I have used two or three of the techniques mentioned in Exercise 2 p. 108 (see also Writing Focus in Student's Book p. 109 for more details). ☐

- in the main body paragraphs, I have presented points relating to all three bullet points from the task. ☐

- I have used linkers to join my ideas in a logical way. ☐

- in the conclusion I have summarised my main points, stated my overall opinion and finished with a point for the reader to think about. ☐

- I have used a formal and impersonal style. ☐

- I have checked my spelling. ☐

- I have checked my handwriting is neat enough for someone else to read. ☐

9.8 SELF-CHECK

VOCABULARY

1 Complete the sentences with the verbs from the box in the correct form. There is one extra verb.

> boost   cheapen   ~~eradicate~~
> put   tackle   take   upset

The government's goal is to _eradicate_ poverty in the next five years with international help.

1 Nutritionists are trying to _____ the amount of fresh fruit and vegetables consumed in school canteens.
2 The good food which is served here will really _____ this vegan restaurant on the map in no time.
3 If illegal fishing is not _____ soon, there'll be no fish left in our ponds.
4 It needs to be assessed whether the new fish species will _____ the natural balance of the region or not.
5 Poor marketing of organic products made in our company can seriously _____ the brand.

/5

2 Complete the sentences with the correct words. First letters are given.

It is said more needs to be done to **r**aise the profile of organisations fighting against poachers.

1 It seems that **d**_____ occurs all over the world but tropical rainforests are particularly targeted.
2 A: I think very soon cars will run on water.
  B: Yeah, and **p**_____ might fly!
3 The need to combat global warming is **p**_____ since increasing temperatures make sea levels rise.
4 Looking for the woman you saved during the tsunami is a wild **g**_____ chase when you don't know her name.
5 Instead of supporting large-scale international **a**_____ companies, why not involve local farms into the production and distribution of their produce?

/5

3 Choose the correct answer.

When considering whether to become a vegetarian, everybody should first (factor) / account / hinder in such things as their general health and the availability of fresh produce. My family have been into vegetarianism for [1]donkey's / sheep's / dog's years and we've never had any problems or side effects.

Some vegetarians, including my mother, choose to eat fish because they believe fishing doesn't impact on land use. My sister is so committed she doesn't even drink milk, but my father eats a(n) [2]staggered / essential / substantial number of eggs, which provide enough protein. With a high level of agricultural [3]awareness / consumption / industrialisation, the only option for me is to become a fruitarian and buy local produce.

Generally, it is [4]consecutive / critical / sustainable to pay attention to the benefits and risks of any diet before deciding to follow it. I believe it is wiser to hear about the choice someone has made straight from the [5]cat's / horse's / duck's mouth rather than criticise such options straight away.

/5

GRAMMAR

4 Correct the mistakes in the sentences.

~~Little we realise~~ the full extent of the forest fire until a survey of it had been completed. _Little did we realise_

1 Not there was only a flower display but the organisers had also presented a large grass collection. _____
2 No sooner had the baby elephant been trapped in a bog when it started raining heavily. _____
3 Under any circumstances the zookeeper is allowed to enter a lion's cage without a tranquiliser gun. _____
4 Only after did they examine the soil did they find out the possible source of contamination. _____
5 At any point you're to leave the jeep when we're driving through the game park. _____

/5

5 Complete the second sentence so that it means the same as the first.

Marion didn't seek any medical help for her injuries at any time as she was living in the wild then.
At _no time did Marion seek any medical help for her injuries as she was living in the wild then._

1 Mandy did a course in aromatherapy and also became qualified in the therapeutic uses of essential oils.
  Not only _____
2 My family didn't know that it would be so hard to clear the debris after a tornado went through our village.
  Little _____
3 Tom only began to relax once he left the farm as he couldn't stand the conditions the animals were kept in.
  Only once _____
4 The children finished building the sandcastle moments before it was washed away by a wave.
  Hardly _____
5 After Julian's parents noticed the benefits of having a cat at home, they let their son finally have one.
  Not until _____

/5

6 Complete the sentences with the words in brackets in the correct form. Do not change the word order. Use between five and six words in each gap.

We _all like it when children treat_ (like/children/treat) animals with respect and consideration.

1 I'm sure my sister _____ (not/find/easy) to be a vegetarian as she's never liked vegetables.
2 Environmentalists in our town_____ (appreciate/they/receive) new premises, but apparently there are no available ones at the moment.
3 Most people _____ (leave/local/authority) to decide how often to collect rubbish.
4 Colin really _____ (hate/I/keep/criticise) his attitude towards saving water.
5 My grandparents love nature and _____ (consider/advantage/live) in the country.

/5

Total   /30

110

7 Complete the text with the correct form of the words in brackets.

Deforestation

Forests are complex ecosystems with a _connection_ (connect) to almost every species. Deforestation means the permanent ¹_____ (destroy) of forests, which is done to create land for agriculture or to provide energy. Methods used include burning or cutting down trees, but these techniques are ²_____ (controversy) because of the damage they cause. Both have been practised for centuries, but recently there has been a rapid acceleration in their use to unprecedented levels. What deforestation does is set off a ³_____ (remorse) chain of events not only locally but globally. It's considered a major factor in climate change, and it affects the growth of vegetation. The rapid disappearance of natural habitats leads to the extinction of some species and creates unbalanced ecosystems, which contributes to general loss of ⁴_____ (biodiverse) of living organisms. With allegedly roughly 75,000 square kilometres lost annually through deforestation, we need to act now, engaging ⁵_____ (government) organisations, so that we tackle this problem on a global level. We have to think about future generations and ⁶_____ (sustain) development which does not cause severe ecological damage.

/6

8 Choose the correct answer A, B, C or D.

When it comes to environmental issues, a lot of people are willing to support good _C_, especially those that involve cutting down on the use of ¹__ fuels. People also seek out lifestyle changes that are both cheap and environmentally friendly. Luckily, it needn't be a hard grind nor does it have to ²__ such serious problems. Consider our use of cars – apart from any financial advantages, choosing to walk or cycle instead offers ³__ increased health benefits.

I feel strongly about being a green consumer. This means before I buy anything, I evaluate the potential ⁴__ done by its packaging, production or transport, then choose the product with the lowest environmental impact and definitely give items with excessive carbon footprint a wide ⁵__ . If enough people did this, manufacturers would ⁶__ action to remedy the situation. Only if more is done to shine a ⁷__ on such issues, will anything change.

Maybe it's a ⁸__ of highlighting the implications of _not_ looking after our environment.

	A		B		C		D	
	A beliefs		B purposes		Ⓒ causes		D objects	
1	A fossil		B prey		C insecticide		D flock	
2	A slash		B flee		C threat		D pose	
3	A considerably				B absolutely			
	C totally				D completely			
4	A hurt		B injury		C damage		D loss	
5	A miss		B berth		C break		D hand	
6	A have		B make		C do		D take	
7	A lamp		B spotlight		C torch		D indicator	
8	A question		B reason		C motive		D task	

/8

9 Complete the second sentence so that it means the same as the first. Use the words in capitals. Use between three and six words in each gap.

If you think you could combat the problem of rats in the houses by the river, I'd be most obliged. **APPRECIATE**

I _would appreciate it if you could_ combat the problem of rats in the houses by the river.

1 They had no idea how bad the weather was going to get. **KNOW**
Little _____ the weather was going to get so much worse.

2 Knowing Jeremy, he will not leave the issue alone and investigate the accident fully, which may cause him much more trouble. **SLEEPING**
Jeremy _____ but instead will want to investigate the accident in full.

3 It was pure luck that they missed the worst of the volcanic eruption. **CHANCE**
Only _____ the worst of the volcanic eruption.

4 The authorities believe a dam on the river should be built to protect the Old City from flooding. It's crucial and should be done as soon as possible. **CONSIDER**
The authorities _____ a dam on the river as soon as possible to protect the Old City from flooding.

5 We weren't able to devote more time to their project until we finished ours. **UNTIL**
Not _____ we able to devote more time to theirs.

6 When the vet comes, ask him to check the cattle and also vaccinate our dogs against rabies. It'll save us a separate trip to the surgery. **KILL**
Why don't we _____ and get the vet to check the cattle and also vaccinate our dogs against rabies.

/6

Total /20

Read the texts and decide which answer A, B, C, D best fits each gap.

TASK 1

Social networking

Social networking has grown rapidly over the past few years. Just under half of the eight-to-seventeen age group and over 20 percent of adults have _D_ up their own profile on a social networking site. A profile is a personal webpage through which the user **1**__ up a list of contacts or 'friends'. These may be relatives and real friends, or people the user has never actually met. Once you're someone's friend, you can browse their profile and **2**__ with them directly or by **3**__ comments for others to see. Social networkers tend to be one of five **4**__ types. First, there are those who use sites intensively for a short period to **5**__ people up. Then there are the **6**__ people who love lots of attention from others and post numerous photos and make their profiles very personal. Some people join in order to **7**__ up with what their peers are doing, whilst others look for people they've lost contact with to find out about **8**__ friends. Finally, there are functional users, who use social networking for a specific purpose.

Most people's **9**__ of social networking is positive and enjoyable, but sharing **10**__ information with strangers can **11**__ a risk. Indeed, some governments have commissioned research to investigate whether social networking is just **12**__ entertainment or not.

	A		B
	A turned		B done
	C made		(D) set
1	A uses		B builds
	C comes		D writes
2	A contact		B email
	C communicate		D exchange
3	A post		B posts
	C posted		D posting
4	A distinct		B separate
	C apparent		D dissimilar
5	A charm		B chat
	C talk		D tell
6	A gullible		B notorious
	C trivial		D superficial
7	A keep		B make
	C put		D come
8	A common		B known
	C mutual		D trusted
9	A feeling		B understanding
	C experience		D interest
10	A personal		B particular
	C individual		D character
11	A take		B pose
	C source		D bring
12	A meaningless		B inoffensive
	C undamaging		D harmless

TASK 2

Preparing for a job interview

Most of us _B_ job interviews as much as we fear a visit to the dentist, but with preparation, you can **1**__ a good impression.

Go to the employer's website and get hold of any documents or reports so that you can **2**__ up on exactly what they do. Check out relevant publications to see if they've been in the **3**__ . Doing this is a good way of demonstrating that you can **4**__ your initiative. Try to anticipate the questions you'll be asked so that you can have some answers ready. Then you won't dry up as you rack your **5**__ for an intelligent response. Be confident about your abilities but don't exaggerate your skills. You can say you have a **6**__ knowledge of something but are keen to develop in this area. If you feel you have to admit that something's not your strong **7**__ , immediately offer another relevant skill you excel at. Keep the conversation positive and try to **8**__ a good rapport with the interviewer. Think carefully about your **9**__ beforehand. Most situations call for something smart so choose items which don't **10**__ badly. Don't forget to polish your shoes – they're often forgotten and can make you look very **11**__ . Once you're in the interview, your body language says almost as much as your words, so smile, appear confident and try to keep a **12**__ head.

	A		B
	A object		(B) dread
	C neglect		D admit
1	A find		B make
	C do		D take
2	A dig		B look
	C mug		D keep
3	A reviews		B articles
	C listings		D headlines
4	A exercise		B use
	C work		D apply
5	A brains		B head
	C mind		D skull
6	A temporary		B starting
	C working		D limiting
7	A mark		B point
	C item		D note
8	A do		B achieve
	C make		D establish
9	A suit		B costume
	C outfit		D garment
10	A crease		B fold
	C wrinkle		D pleat
11	A messy		B disorderly
	C scruffy		D unruly
12	A calm		B quiet
	C still		D cool

TASK 3

Eat breakfast and lose weight

Eating breakfast helps teenagers lose weight, a survey of eating _A_ in the United States has found. The study showed that those who have a **1**___ meal at breakfast time – and therefore end up with a higher **2**___ intake – are more likely to be within a healthy weight range than those who **3**___ the first meal of the day.

Although it may seem **4**___ to swallow, the people who ate more did more **5**___ activity during the day, and that may be because they didn't feel so **6**___ . Dr Pereira, who led the research, said that even cooked breakfasts were better than missing out on food altogether. 'While it's best to **7**___ for a healthy option – a wholegrain cereal for instance – the evidence does **8**___ that eating anything is better than eating nothing.'

Other studies have also shown that those who eat breakfast are less likely to feel **9**___ mid-morning and snack on high-fat foods before lunch. They therefore have a more **10**___ diet.

Dr Pereira said: 'This study clearly supports what other studies have shown: kids who don't eat breakfast tend to **11**___ on more weight.' This obviously has a **12**___ effect on their long-term health. Missing breakfast is a common approach to dieting, particularly among teenage girls, but they would do well to heed advice and develop a taste for breakfast.

	A habits	B routine
	C behaviour	D practice
1	A whole	B round
	C square	D main
2	A nutrients	B calorie
	C ingredient	D nourishment
3	A jump	B leap
	C step	D skip
4	A hard	B bad
	C difficult	D tough
5	A vitalising	B invigorating
	C brisk	D refreshing
6	A immobile	B inoperative
	C lethargic	D redundant
7	A go	B eat
	C nibble	D pick
8	A offer	B propose
	C persuade	D suggest
9	A parched	B allergic
	C peckish	D fussy
10	A beneficial	B nutritious
	C healthful	D energetic
11	A take	B get
	C carry	D put
12	A hurtful	B detrimental
	C unfavourable	D disadvantageous

TASK 4

Restorative justice in schools

Restorative justice is a relatively recent innovation in the judicial _C_. It is now gaining ground in schools as a more appropriate way of **1**___ with unacceptable behaviour than **2**___ to retribution. The traditional approach asks what happened and then **3**___ to identify who is to blame and what response will be the best **4**___ to prevent repetition. It assumes that punishment can change behaviour, but what it often **5**___ about is anger and **6**___ . Moreover, it encourages troublemakers to be more aware of what will happen to them if they misbehave again, rather than **7**___ how their behaviour has affected others.

A restorative approach to conflict focuses on how relationships have been damaged and what **8**___ can be taken to repair them. It encourages people to think about the **9**___ of their behaviour on other people and what harm their **10**___ behaviour has done. The 'restorative conference' is a process which offers an opportunity for everyone involved in the conflict to explain, listen and **11**___ sense of what happened. Apologies can be given and accepted. A sense of closure is achieved and young people understand how and why they can take **12**___ for their behaviour in the future.

	A scheme	B department
	C system	D organisation
1	A solving	B handling
	C tackling	D dealing
2	A responding	B resorting
	C retreating	D relating
3	A tries	B try
	C trying	D tried
4	A restraint	B deterrent
	C limit	D restriction
5	A leads	B puts
	C brings	D gets
6	A opposition	B annoyance
	C objection	D resentment
7	A considering	B allowing
	C concerning	D relating
8	A paces	B stages
	C steps	D strides
9	A products	B consequences
	C outcomes	D results
10	A unsociable	B offending
	C ineffective	D antisocial
11	A take	B find
	C make	D bring
12	A responsibility	B care
	C advantage	D advice

Read the texts and think of one word which best fits each gap.

TASK 1

Space 'smells like fried steak'

NASA has commissioned Steven Pearce, <u>a</u> chemist and managing director of a fragrance manufacturing company, to recreate the smell [1]_____ space in a laboratory. His research [2]_____ be used to help astronauts prepare [3]_____ the conditions they will encounter in space. Mr Pearce began working for NASA in August and hopes to [4]_____ recreated the smell of space [5]_____ the end of the year.

He had done some work for an art exhibition in July [6]_____ was based entirely on smell, and [7]_____ of the things he created was the smell of the inside of [8]_____ Mir space station. NASA heard about it and contacted Mr Pearce to see if he could help them recreate the smell of space [9]_____ order to help their astronauts.

Interviews with astronauts after they had been outside and then returned to the space station reveal a few clues [10]_____ to what space smells like. [11]_____ the time they were taking off their space suits and helmets, they all reported quite particular odours.

Apparently, [12]_____ comes across is a smell of fried steak, hot metal and even welding a motorbike. So the purpose of Mr Pearce's task is [13]_____ create realism for the astronauts, who are trained in their suits by [14]_____ put in big water tanks to simulate the loss of gravity.

'We have already produced the smell of fried steak, [15]_____ hot metal is proving more difficult,' said Mr Pearce.

TASK 2

New York City wildlife research

Join our project to help lead the <u>way</u> in urban ecosystem research and show how the environment can be protected in and near the places most of [1]_____ live. At research sites in and around New York City, as [2]_____ as in some rural areas, you'll study a range of wildlife species and the quality of their varied habitats. [3]_____ on the time of year, you may track and camera-trap mammals, catch frogs and salamanders in nets or pitfall traps, identify birds, or survey native and invasive plant species. Each day you'll also [4]_____ able to learn about the 'big picture' of the research, gain skills in a variety [5]_____ field research methods, or hear about other research topics [6]_____ guest speakers.

[7]_____ surprising number and diversity of birds, amphibians, small mammals and other wildlife live alongside the 8.2 million human residents of New York City. In the greater metropolitan area, extending roughly 100 miles from Manhattan [8]_____ every direction, the diversity of plants and animals is [9]_____ more extensive. The research team will guide you as you investigate the plants and animals in the metropolitan region's protected areas, and learn [10]_____ conditions they need to survive. With [11]_____ than half of the world's population living in cities, understanding the health of the environment in urban areas has [12]_____ been more important. The data you help gather [13]_____ assist regional planners [14]_____ protecting urban nature and wildlife, and will help scientists to better understand how and [15]_____ urbanisation affects animals and plants.

TASK 3

Behind the scenes at the Royal Shakespeare Company

In collaboration <u>with</u> the Costume Department, the costume supervisor and designer decide [1]_____ the best way to create the costumes for a new production. [2]_____ may include the shoes, hats, armour, underwear, jewellery, buying the fabrics, booking the costume makers and setting [3]_____ the costume fittings.

To create [4]_____ particular period feel, neutral fabrics often arrive direct [5]_____ the factory to be treated by the Dyeing Department. Fifty percent of costumes are broken down in [6]_____ way to look worn or to show general wear and tear. Common tools of the trade for the department include a cheese grater, sandpaper, Stanley knives, a blowtorch, emulsion-based paints and fabric paints.

[7]_____ the beginning of rehearsals all the actors' measurements [8]_____ taken. The Armoury and Boot Department make, recycle or adapt boots and shoes for a production. The Hats and Millinery team create a particular look using a wide variety [9]_____ materials.

Hairdressing, wigs and make-up complete [10]_____ final look. An actor often uses their own hair in a production. The Wigs team may [11]_____ to cut, curl, dye or add extensions or hairpieces to an actor's hair.

[12]_____ specialist make-up is required, most actors apply their own make-up. The team creates blood effects for daggers, blood bags or smearing using glucose and fruit colouring. Black treacle is used [13]_____ darken the blood.

The team may [14]_____ be required to make artificial parts of the body [15]_____ as the nose in *Cyrano de Bergerac*.

TASK 4

Slow Food

The Slow Food movement began in the mid-1980s years ago _when_ farmers and foodies got together to promote and support traditional local production methods and to introduce ¹_____ to an audience who wanted ²_____ same, pure, natural products. No growth stimulants, no steroids, no impurities, just old-style food, produced at the speed of Mother Nature. ³_____ the support of Slow Food, many artisan producers, growers and fishermen would ⁴_____ had to cease production and amazing flavour sensations would have been lost. Isn't this ⁵_____ many people say they want in Britain? Fewer miles, more local produce?

The movement has grown worldwide – slowly, obviously – and has become a huge, complex organisation – 100,000 members in 160 countries according ⁶_____ their website – but even ⁷_____ it very much represents the interests of the new generation of quality farmers and producers, it hasn't caught ⁸_____ so well in the UK.

Is it seen ⁹_____ too specialist or elitist? Is it because we have ¹⁰_____ many food-based TV programmes that ¹¹_____ is already plenty of exposure for artisan producers without Slow Food?

Personally, I think this devotion ¹²_____ quality in food and wine could reach ¹³_____ bigger audience in the UK. It's not ¹⁴_____ the Slow Food movement isn't spreading but perhaps it needs to be a bit ¹⁵_____ dynamic in the UK to capture the public imagination.

TASK 5

The temperature of feelings

Holding a hot drink makes you feel more positive towards a stranger _than_ if you were holding an ice-cold drink, according to a study that has found a link ¹_____ physical and emotional warmth.

Scientists tested the idea ²_____ giving volunteers either hot or cold drinks to hold before interviewing them about their feelings. The volunteers consistently displayed warmer emotions ³_____ holding the hot drink.

The researchers then went ⁴_____ to study the effects of warm and cold objects and found similar results, indicating that ⁵_____ was not the drink as such ⁶_____ the physical temperature of the object ⁷_____ held.

'It appears that the effect ⁸_____ physical temperature is not just on ⁹_____ we see others, it affects our own behaviour as well. Physical warmth can make us see others as warmer people, but also causes us to be warmer, more generous and trusting ¹⁰_____ well,' said John Bargh, Professor of Psychology at Yale University.

Volunteers in the study, published in the journal _Science_, did not know why they ¹¹_____ given a hot or cold drink to hold – they were simply asked to do it – and ¹²_____ the findings indicate that there is a deep psychological reason why physical temperature is linked to emotional feelings.

The findings suggest ¹³_____ warm drinks or snacks could make someone more trusting ¹⁴_____ others, which could be exploited by companies on the lookout for new marketing tools. So beware the sales person who gives you a warm cookie ¹⁵_____ a cold day.

TASK 6

Shedding light on dark matter

It is _one_ of the biggest mysteries in science which has baffled scholars for ¹_____ than seventy-five years, but now a team of cosmologists believes it has found a way of discovering ²_____ the universe is made ³_____ .

About 85 percent is neither stars ⁴_____ planets but some form of mysterious matter. It cannot be seen or detected by conventional scientific instruments, which is ⁵_____ the precise nature of this 'dark matter' has eluded the finest minds in science.

Now cosmologists believe the problem will ⁶_____ solved within two years, thanks to the results of a vast computer simulation of the Milky Way galaxy that has provided the first cosmic map of where dark matter ⁷_____ be found and how to find it.

The simulation predicts ⁸_____ there are regions near the centre of the Milky Way ⁹_____ dark matter will emit a glow of powerful gamma radiation, which could be detected ¹⁰_____ a NASA satellite launched this year specifically to search for this type of cosmic ray.

Powerful supercomputers ¹¹_____ have modelled all known aspects of dark matter predict that a set of hitherto undiscovered sub-atomic particles must account ¹²_____ the 85 percent of the matter in the universe that is missing ¹³_____ view.

The simulation predicts that in regions near the centre of our galaxy ¹⁴_____ sub-atomic particles become tightly packed so they collide, and ¹⁵_____ the process emit a gamma ray glow that should be detectable by the Fermi telescope, the latest satellite observatory to be launched by NASA.

Complete the texts with the correct forms of the words in brackets.

TASK 1

The history of film music

The history of music to go alongside visual _entertainment_ (ENTERTAIN) is surely a long one. Without going back to
¹_____ (ANTIQUE), there is all manner of musical theatre, variety shows and various forms of opera. In all of
this, music can adopt a range of roles, from being background atmosphere enhancing the ²_____ (EMOTION)
reaction to being an intrinsic part of the spectacle.

When it comes to film as a ³_____ (PROJECT) through celluloid, the earliest examples consisted of
⁴_____ (MOVE) pictures only and no sound. But a silent movie without music seems totally empty, so music was
⁵_____ (TYPICAL) provided in the theatre by a pianist or organist (or a group of players) to give emphasis to the
story.

At first it was up to these theatre ⁶_____ (MUSIC) to choose or improvise the music, but there were music
publishers who specialised in producing music ⁷_____ (SUIT) for film. It wasn't long before film-makers exerted
greater control over the musical ⁸_____ (ACCOMPANY), by specifying the music to be played, and even in some
cases having it ⁹_____ (SPECIAL) written for the occasion.

It is interesting to note at this point that one of the great ¹⁰_____ (PERFORM) of the silent era, Charlie Chaplin,
also composed the music for some of his own films, such as _City Lights_.

TASK 2

500 places to see before they die

The first guidebook of 'last chance saloon' holidays will be published tomorrow for travellers who want to visit the most
endangered (DANGER) tourist destinations across the world. Frommer's _500 Places To See Before They Disappear_ provides
a list of sites where it is still possible to see rare and vulnerable animal species, ¹_____ (STAND) landscapes and
unique cultural sights in their ²_____ (SPOIL) glory.

Co-author Holly Hughes said: 'The ³_____ (DEVASTATE) caused by climate change and direct man-made
⁴_____ (INTERFERE) is familiar to all of us. This book is a carefully chosen list of destinations that the eco-conscious
traveller can enjoy for possibly the last time.'

With 500 ⁵_____ (THREAT) destinations to choose from, she suggests heading to the Everglades in southern
Florida. Filled with rare species, this ecosystem is degenerating with alarming ⁶_____ (RAPID). Already half has
been lost to agricultural and urban development. Dwindling water levels and pollution have ⁷_____ (SEVERE)
compromised what remains. 'There has been a ⁸_____ (SUBSTANCE) decrease in the number of bird species and
many of the fish and even the alligators who remain show high mercury levels,' said Hughes.

The Nazca lines in Peru, one of the world's most intriguing ancient sites, face ⁹_____ (DESTROY) as roads are built
and global warming and ¹⁰_____ (FOREST) cause widespread floods and mudslides.

TASK 3

Ways of looking at art

One way to look at a painting is _simply_ (SIMPLE) to enter a gallery and spend some time deciding which painting most
strikes you. Following this you can develop ¹_____ (JUSTIFY) for your choice: are you drawn to the colour, the
tone, the ²_____ (THEME) material? It is a good idea to carry out this exercise with other people, each of you
choosing a painting to discuss. This can help you to develop your critical ³_____ (AWARE), and ability to reason
your ⁴_____ (JUDGE).

Another way of looking at art in a gallery, and one quite ⁵_____ (SIMILAR) from that mentioned above,
is to simply enter a room and make a beeline for the piece you most like. Don't read the literature, just make an
⁶_____ (INSTINCT) choice. In doing this you may notice a pattern ⁷_____ (EMERGE) in those
pieces you gravitate to. You may wish to do this occasionally to break away from rational ⁸_____ (OBSERVE) of
artworks, and to experience a more direct 'communication' with them. In conjunction with more ⁹_____ (LOGIC)
ways of viewing works, this will help to give you a fully rounded ¹⁰_____ (APPRECIATE) of art.

Complete the sentences with the correct forms of the words in capitals.

TASK 4

Dan wasn't very _receptive_ to Carly's idea of getting a dog. **RECEIVE**

1   The judge said that such a heinous crime deserved a long term of _____ . **PRISON**

2   Sally told me a great joke this morning, but I'm afraid it's _____ . **REPEAT**

3   Please state your seat _____ – window or aisle. **PREFER**

4   Eva likes everything to be planned and organised. There's no _____ about her. **SPONTANEOUS**

5   This soup is great in the winter because it's so _____ . **NOURISH**

6   There was a very _____ scene at the restaurant, when a man threw his food at the waiter. **DRAMA**

7   It was very _____ of Jeff to miss his mother's birthday celebrations. **CONSIDER**

8   Is Beth OK? She was behaving rather _____ yesterday. **RATIONAL**

9   A skilled politician can slip _____ into different modes of behaviour, depending on who they're talking to. **SELF-CONSCIOUS**

10 I love the colour you've painted the living room. It's very _____ . **REST**

11 Jan took a deep breath, summoned up her _____ and stepped up to the microphone. **CONFIDENT**

12 It was _____ of Tom to stand up to his boss. **COURAGE**

13 It's becoming _____ obvious that Rick dislikes his brother-in-law. **INCREASE**

14 If you need extra grammar practice, you can find plenty of _____ worksheets on the Internet. **DOWNLOAD**

15 Kate thought working for a charity would be rewarding, but it turned out to be badly run and she became pretty _____ very quickly. **ILLUSION**

16 Victor was _____ when he heard he'd won the Science prize – it was so unexpected. **SPEECH**

17 Although her patients don't really understand what's happening, she always treats them with great _____ . **TENDER**

18 Lottie's worried about whether she's really up to the job. She's very _____ about her abilities. **SECURE**

19 Kit's not coming skiing with us this year. He says it's too _____ for him. **ENERGY**

20 I can't see what the critics find to praise in her work. It always looks _____ to me. **REMARK**

21 Guy was _____ by all the setbacks and was determined to carry on with the trip. **DETER**

22 We're looking for someone with excellent _____ skills. **ORGANISE**

23 You sound dreadful! Here, have one of these throat lozenges. They're very _____ . **SOOTHE**

24 The management has made it very clear that they're looking for a _____ in costs. **REDUCE**

25 It was almost impossible to choose a winner because all three finalists were _____ good. **EQUAL**

26 Subcontracting the deliveries was an _____ solution to the problem. **INVENT**

27 Michael attended one of the most _____ universities in his country, so it's no surprise he went on to do great things. **PRESTIGE**

28 Please note that there is no _____ to the theatre after the performance has started. **ADMIT**

29 Each student has a weekly _____ with a member of staff so that individual issues can be tackled. **TUTOR**

30 She was very _____ about people and always recruited good people onto her team. **PERCEPTION**

31 It's not an easy piece to listen to, but there is a lovely _____ passage towards the end. **MELODY**

32 Most people find constructing flat-pack furniture difficult. The instructions are extremely _____ . **LEAD**

33 Their final position in the league was _____ because the team had been playing badly for weeks. **PREDICT**

34 Economic growth has been unprecedented and it's now a booming, _____ country. **PROSPER**

35 Ray greeted his sister _____ despite their recent disagreements. **AFFECTION**

36 The role requires someone who is utterly reliable and completely _____ . **TRUST**

37 The flats on the south side of the river tend to be smaller, but are more _____ . **AFFORD**

38 The audience showed their _____ with a sustained round of applause. **APPRECIATE**

39 Many people find dieting difficult because some of the recommended foods are _____ and bland. **APPETITE**

40 If temperatures rise by only one degree in certain places, it will be a _____ for local communities. **CATASTROPHIC**

41 It is believed that Schmidt and his fellow _____ operated from a flat in the downtown district. **CONSPIRE**

42 Some people find him intriguing, but I find his _____ tedious and rather egotistic. **ECCENTRIC**

43 It's hardly a career job, as the work is repetitive and _____ , but it'll help pay towards my costs at college. **DEMAND**

44 The new boss can seem a bit _____ , but she's actually very approachable. **INTIMIDATE**

45 Until there were fewer _____ in the test results, the ethics committee felt they couldn't approve the new drug. **CONSISTENT**

46 When I arrived, my uncle was searching _____ for his car keys. **FRANTIC**

47 If there's a leak, you may detect a slight odour, but the gas is absolutely _____ . **HARM**

48 About fifty years ago, there was quite a bit of _____ development, but the area has since gone into decline. **INDUSTRY**

49 At £199.99 the new video game is considerably _____ , but if you've got money to spare, it's well worth it. **PRICE**

50 With _____ energies being developed, it is thought a global energy shortage can be averted. **NEW**

51 I've asked you _____ not to play loud music when Gran is here, but you just don't take any notice. **REPEAT**

52 That's a very _____ coat! Where did you get it? **STYLE**

53 The earthquake occurred in the most _____ region of the country and it is proving very difficult for the rescue teams to get through. **MOUNTAIN**

54 Bob glowered _____ as his sister won her race easily. **RESENT**

55 Why does the media have to be so _____ about celebrity stories? **SENSATION**

56 It's important that traditions are passed on to the next _____ . **GENERATE**

57 Allowing people to vary their working hours seems to have had a _____ effect on the company. **BENEFIT**

58 _____ is something many young business entrepreneurs aspire to, but it's not guaranteed. **AFFLUENT**

59 We don't know where Emma gets her _____ from. It certainly isn't from us! **CREATIVE**

60 The theme for the party was _____ , and the decorations were rather drab, but we had a good time. **IMAGINE**

USE OF ENGLISH: KEY WORD TRANSFORMATION

Complete the second sentence so that it means the same as the first. Do not change the words in capitals. Use between three and five words.

Jake promised to do anything she wanted to make her happy. **WHATEVER**
'I'll do _whatever makes you_ happy,' Jake promised her.

1 I have been working at IBM for just over a year. **STARTED**
This time last _____ my job at IBM.

2 It is only possible to buy tickets from authorised agents. **CAN**
Tickets _____ from authorised agents.

3 The sales reps are doing all they can to compensate for the poor results last month. **MAKE**
The sales reps are doing all they can _____ the poor results last month.

4 They met when they were at university. **EACH**
They have _____ were at university together.

5 Walking briskly is supposed to be better for you than running. **THOUGHT**
It _____ is better for you than running.

6 Nina has always respected her father. **UP**
Nina has always _____ her father.

7 Scientists experimented with genetically modified crops. **EXPERIMENT**
What _____ with genetically modified crops.

8 Car manufacturers are tempting customers with huge discounts. **OFFERED**
Huge discounts on cars _____ customers at the moment.

9 The waiter brought the bill immediately after we started eating. **THAN**
No sooner _____ the waiter brought the bill.

10 We're not on speaking terms with my mother because of our plan to move to the country. **FALLEN**
We _____ my mother over our plan to move to the country.

11 Cracow has won the Cultural City of the Year award. **NAMED**
Cracow _____ Cultural City of the Year.

12 I managed to leave the meeting quietly when the director's mobile phone rang. **POINT**
The director's mobile phone rang, _____ quietly left the meeting.

13 Ben was unaware that Gina and Harry are related. **REALISE**
What Ben _____ Gina and Harry are related.

14 The school management has announced an end to tests for eight-year-olds. **GET**
The school management says it will _____ tests for eight-year-olds.

15 You ought not to have screamed. **BETTER**
It would have been _____ screamed.

16 Despite seeing him every day, Helen didn't recognise Jim without a beard. **EVEN**
Helen didn't recognise Jim without a beard _____ every day.

17 The manager put Brendan in charge of the weekly sales report from his first day. **TAKE**
On his first day, Brendan was asked _____ the weekly sales report.

18 The manufacturers had to supply parts for 2,000 new cars. **BE**
Parts _____ for 2,000 new cars.

19 As Laura didn't arrive until 4 p.m., it was too late to eat lunch. **BY**
Laura didn't arrive until 4 p.m., _____ too late to eat lunch.

20 They are training more teachers as a result of a big recruitment drive. **LED**
A big recruitment drive has _____ trained.

21 I couldn't tolerate Nadia's complaining any longer. **UP**
I really couldn't _____ Nadia's complaining any longer.

22 My brother and I were twelve years old when we first saw snow. **BEFORE**
Neither my brother nor I _____ we were twelve years old.

23 You could have told me you were a vegetarian. **WISH**
I _____ you were a vegetarian.

24 The mayor says he's thought of a brilliant solution for solving the traffic problems. **COME**
The mayor says he _____ a brilliant solution for solving the traffic problems.

25 Only later did I remember who the stranger was. **UNTIL**
It _____ I remembered who the stranger was.

USE OF ENGLISH: KEY WORD TRANSFORMATION

26 The Picasso painting had been sold to my grandmother, who hid it in her cellar. **WHO**
My grandmother, _____ , hid it in her cellar.

27 We missed the flight because we didn't set out early enough. **ALLOWED**
Not _____ to get to the airport, we missed the flight.

28 Lee's trying to reduce the significance of losing his job, but he's obviously devastated. **PLAYING**
Lee _____ the significance of losing his job, but he's obviously devastated.

29 He left the company after he realised that his promotion was blocked. **NEVER**
Having _____ promoted, he left the company.

30 There aren't so many characters in his latest play. **SLIGHTLY**
In his latest play, _____ characters.

31 The president said he hoped the two countries could work more closely together. **STRENGTHEN**
The president said he hoped _____ the two countries.

32 Paula wished she had made a formal complaint. **REGRETTED**
Paula _____ a formal complaint.

33 The new chat show is hosted by a former world-famous footballer. **PERSON**
A former world-famous footballer _____ hosts the new chat show.

34 My summer job was the perfect excuse for not going on our family holiday. **OUT**
My summer job was the perfect excuse for _____ our family holiday.

35 I wish I hadn't gone to James' party. **SHOULDN'T**
I _____ to James' party.

36 Jane's many good qualities don't include patience. **NONE**
Jane has many good qualities, _____ is patience.

37 Why would anyone be a police officer, apart from earning quite good money? **EVEN**
I wouldn't work as a police officer, _____ quite good money.

38 Experts believe that ancient peoples knew about the healing properties of plants. **THOUGHT**
Ancient peoples _____ about the healing properties of plants.

39 Unless Gavin arrives soon, we will start the meeting without him. **MEAN**
If Gavin doesn't arrive soon, it _____ the meeting without him.

40 Lydia refused to sleep in a tent. **CONTEMPLATE**
'I will _____ in a tent,' Lydia declared.

41 They ought to decide when they are going to get married. **MAKE**
They ought _____ about when they are going to get married.

42 You must never tell anyone the PIN for your credit card. **SHOULD**
Under no circumstances _____ the PIN for your credit card.

43 I don't know how my grandmother made such perfect cakes. **METHOD**
I don't know _____ to make such perfect cakes.

44 I hadn't seen Katie or heard all her news for ages. **CATCH**
It was good to see Katie again and _____ all her news.

45 They will give you all the instructions before the exam. **GIVEN**
You _____ all the instructions before the exam.

46 It wasn't until she saw Oliver that she understood why her parents were angry. **DID**
Only _____ she understand why her parents were angry.

47 John went home early because he didn't know Harriet was coming. **IF**
John would have stayed longer _____ Harriet was coming.

48 Pete and I made a snowman when we were little. **FORGET**
I _____ a snowman with Pete when we were little.

49 The jury members were told to consider their verdict very carefully. **INSTRUCTED**
The judge _____ consider their verdict very carefully.

50 People thought that eating carrots helped you to see in the dark. **BELIEVED**
It _____ eating carrots helped you to see in the dark.

Agreeing with opinions

I (completely) agree that/with …
I couldn't agree more that/with …
That's fine with me.
I think so too.
I agree that it's true that …
I am of the same/a similar opinion because …
He's absolutely right.
He has a point.
I fully support the view that …

Apologising

Informal phrases

I'm really sorry (that) …
Sorry for bothering you.
Sorry to bother you.
Sorry for any trouble.
Sorry I didn't write earlier, but I …
Sorry I haven't written for so long./Sorry for not writing
    for so long.
I'm writing to tell you how sorry I am to … (about) …
It will never happen again.

Neutral phrases

I apologise for …
Please accept my apology …

Closing formulas: emails and letters

Informal phrases

Bye for now/See you!
Love,/Take care!/All the best,

Neutral phrases

Best wishes,
Regards,

Formal phrases

(Dear Mr/Mrs/Miss/Ms Brennon) Yours sincerely,
(Dear Sir or Madam/Editor) Yours faithfully,

Complaining

Describing problems

I wish to express my strong dissatisfaction with …
I am writing to complain about …
I'm afraid I have to make a complaint.
I am writing to express my concerns about …
I would like to complain about …
We are particularly upset because, …
To make matters worse, …
Without doubt, the worst part of the whole
    incident was …
… I/we decided to contact you and complain.

Suggesting solutions

One possible way to solve this problem is to …
An alternative solution to this issue is …

Asking for action

I/We urge you to (reconsider your policies).
I/We ask/demand that you (investigate the matter).

Describing a person

The first thing you notice about (him/her) is …
(He/She) is special for a number of reasons.
He/She is the kind of person who …
The most unusual/interesting person I've ever met is …

Describing appearance

Height: of medium height/tall/fairly short/long-legged
Build: muscular/well-built/overweight/skinny/slim/thin
Age: in his teens/middle-aged/in her late forties/elderly
Facial features: round/oval/freckles/dimples/scar/mole/
    wrinkled/pale/tanned/a crooked nose/moustache/
    beard/almond-shaped eyes
Hair: balding/short/shoulder-length/long/wavy/
    curly/thick
She dresses casually/smartly/well/in black/fashionably.
He always wears scruffy/stylish clothes.

Disagreeing with opinions

I disagree that/with …/I don't agree that/with …
I am totally against …
I see your point of view but …
I'm afraid I can't agree with …
I'm not convinced about …
I don't think it's the best solution …
I must say I do not agree/strongly disagree with …
I am of a different/the opposite opinion because …
Contrary to popular belief …

Ending an email/a letter

Informal phrases

It was good to hear from you.
Email me soon.
I'd better get going./I must go now./Got to go now./
    I must be going now.
Bye for now.
Looking forward to your news/to hearing from you again.
Say hello to …
Give me love/my regards to (everyone at home).
Have a nice (trip).
See you (soon/in the summer).
Write soon.
Keep in touch!

Neutral phrases

I look forward to hearing from you/your reply.
I hope to hear from you soon.

Formal phrases

I look forward to your prompt response/reply.
I wonder what other readers think about …
I hope you will publish more articles about this problem.
I would be grateful if you could publish my letter.

Expressing doubt

I have read the advert/about your services and/but
    I am not quite sure if …
I cannot understand if …
It is not clear to me if …

Expressing interest

I am interested in …/I have been looking for …
I am planning to … and that is why I found this
    advertisement/offer/text interesting/important.
I was very interested in your … (article/ editorial/
    presentation).

Expressing opinion

I believe/think/feel (that) …
I really/do believe …
In my opinion/view,
From my point of view/The way I see it,
It seems/appears to me (that) …
To my mind, …
My opinion is that …
As far as I am concerned, …
To be honest, …
It is my firm belief that …
I am inclined to believe that …
It is popularly believed that …
Most people feel that …
I am (fully) convinced that …
I certainly believe that …
People often claim/maintain that …
Some people argue that …
Some people point out that …

Expressing preference

I really enjoy/like/love … because …
I prefer … to …
I'd like to …/I hope to …
… is great because…
I find… boring/dull.
I don't like/I can't stand/I really hate …
It's not really my thing.

For and against/Opinion essay

Introduction – for and against

What are the arguments for and against this idea?
What are the benefits and drawbacks of such a solution?
What are the advantages and disadvantages of …?
This idea can be said to have both advantages
    and disadvantages.
Let us consider the advantages and disadvantages of …

Introduction – opinion

Personally, I believe (that) …
In my opinion,/To my mind, …
In this essay I am going to argue that …
To explain the reasons for my opinion, I will explore the
    issues from the viewpoint of (an elderly person) and
    (a teenager).
It is my intention to examine this issue in terms of
    (freedom of speech) and (public safety).
This essay will look at this question from the perspective
    of (both) (customers) and (shop owners).
(Today) Many people believe that …
Let me explain why I agree with this view.

Introducing various points of view

The first (dis)advantage for (the young adult) is …
From the (teachers') point of view …

Giving arguments

First and foremost, …
One (dis)advantage is that …
It is also often hoped that (the event) will …
It is also important/vital to consider …
Another benefit/drawback is that …
Another downside is the …

Generalising

Generally/In general/By and large/As a general rule/In
    most cases/Broadly speaking/On the whole,
    everyone who …
It is often said …
It is rarely/sometimes/often/usually the case that …
People tend to regard … as …
People often claim that …
In some/certain/many/most cases …
Many/Most people/of us feel/believe/agree …
Some would say (that) …

Introducing opinions

It seems/appears that …
It would seem/appear that …
It is believed/recognised that …
There is little/no doubt that …
There is some doubt …

Expressing your own opinion

In my opinion/To my mind/In my view,
    (the advantages outweigh the disadvantages).
As far as I am concerned, …

Expressing certainty

There are undoubtedly certain drawbacks …
Without (a) doubt, there are people who believe the
    opposite.

Expressing condition

As long as/Providing/Provided that a connection
    is available, anyone can use the Internet.

Expressing cause and result

In such countries financial difficulties are common,
    so people have fewer children.
The result/consequence/outcome of (such a decision/
    choice could be (that) …)
This could lead to/result in/trigger …
People spend most of their time online today.
    As a result/Consequently/As a consequence,
    many people are losing the ability to tell fantasy
    from the reality.
Before the era of antibiotics, more soldiers died due to/
    because of disease than were killed in action.
Owing to/On account of the strike there were no trains
    between Berlin and Warsaw.
There were traffic jams in the city centre on the
    grounds/given that the protesters had decided
    to march along one of the main streets.
The man had been robbed, therefore/hence/thus he was
    penniless when he finally reached the railway station.
… is at the root of many social problems.
Many learning difficulties stem from …
The idea has its origins/roots in …
The problem can be traced back to the 1990s …
It gives rise to …

Introducing opposing opinion and contrast

On the one hand, the park is extremely popular with elderly people, but on the other (hand) they are not the ones who buy tickets.

Some people feel it is wrong for advertising to be aimed specifically at children, while/whereas others do not share this view.

Mark was not an exceptionally talented man, neverthless/nonetheless/yet/even so/still he applied for the job and to everyone's surprise, was offered the post in the IT department.

However, many people say that action should be taken straightaway.

Even though/Although many residents support the mayor and his policy, he also has many enemies.

In spite of/Despite winning in the local election, his real ambition was to work for one of the EU institutions.

But all this may be about to change.

Spain has got a population of over 46 million. By/In contrast there are only 5.5 million inhabitants in Finland.

Many accidents are caused by reckless drivers. Conversely, some are the result of overtly cautious driving.

The economy will not improve this year. On the contrary, it will deteriorate.

That said/Having said that, there are also drawbacks.

Conclusion

In conclusion/To conclude/To sum up/All in all/On balance/On the whole/All things considered/Taking everything into account/consideration, …

For all these reasons, I am convinced that …

Giving advice

You should/ought to …
You'd better …
If I were you, I would …
It might be a good idea (for you) to …
Why don't you …?
Have you thought of/about …?
It's better (not) to do …
Make sure that …
Remember (not) to do …
It's (not) worth (doing) …
I (don't) think it's a good idea.
I don't think you should …

Giving examples

For example,/For instance, …
Like …/Such as …
Especially/In particular/Particularly …
In the same way, …
Similarly,/Equally,/Likewise, …

Justifying opinions

I think so because …
In fact/Actually,
The reason why I believe so is …

Making suggestions

I think I/you/we should …
Perhaps I/you/we could …
What do you think about …?
What about …?/How about …?
Would you like me to …?
I (would) suggest/recommend organising …
You should pay more attention to …
It would be a good idea to …

Making requests

Informal phrases

Can you …, please?/Could you …?
Do you think you could …?
Let me know if you can (come).
Could you tell me …?

Neutral phrases

Would it be possible for you to …?
I'd be grateful if you could …
I wonder if I could ask you to/for …
I'm writing to ask for your help/advice …

Opening formulas: emails and letters

Informal phrases

Dear Margaret,
Hi Anne,

Neutral/Formal phrases

Dear Mr and Mrs Edwards,
Dear Miss/Ms Brennon,
Dear Mr Brennon,
Dear Sir or Madam,
Dear Editor,

Presenting arguments

There are numerous/potential/clear/considerable pluses/downsides to …

First argument

First of all, …
First/firstly, …
To begin with, …
The main/major argument in support of … is that …
On the one hand,/On the other hand, …
One argument in favour of … is that …
One of the most convincing/most persuasive/strongest arguments for/against … is …

Successive arguments

Secondly, …
Thirdly, …
Then/Next …
Another (dis)advantage is (that) …
A further benefit/drawback of … is (that) …
In addition/Additionally, …
Also, …
Apart from this, …
Moreover/What is more/Furthermore, …
Most importantly, …
Last argument …
Finally, …
Last but not least, …

Presenting different aspects of the issue

It is also important to consider this issue with regard to
    (public figures' rights to privacy).
From the perspective/viewpoint of (a teenager), …
In terms of (public figures as role models), I believe …
Another important angle on this issue is (public safety).

Emphasising what you say

Clearly/Obviously/Of course/Needless to say/Naturally,
    if everyone were allowed to buy a gun,
    the crime rate would increase significantly.

Rephrasing

In other words/To put it another way/That is to say,
    if they do not vote in the parliamentary election,
    they will not have the right to criticise
    the government's decisions.

Expressing reality

In fact/As a matter of fact/The fact of the matter is that/
    Actually/In practice a mobile would be quite useless
    if a plane crashed in the middle of the Amazon jungle.

Making partially true statements

Up to a point/To a certain degree/extent/To some
    extent/degree/In a sense/In a way it describes
    all teenagers.

Proposal/Report

Stating the aims

The main goal of this proposal is to outline/describe …
The principal objective of this proposal is to …
The report discusses/provides …
This report aims/is intended to …
In this report I intend to …
The report researches the question of …

Making recommendations

I would recommend/suggest that …
We hope that students will …
One suggestion/idea would be …
We should consider …
It would benefit everyone if …
Students should now think about …
The best solution seems to be …
There appears to be no alternative but …
Consideration should be given to …
It would be inadvisable to …
… would be counterproductive.

The best course of action would be to …
It is absolutely essential to …
One way forward would be to …
The problem could be solved by …
Another way to combat the problem would be to …

Describing benefits

… because this would allow people to …
… this would have the additional advantage of …
The students would have the chance/opportunity to use
    …
The residents will benefit from … because …
This approach will provide them with the chance to …
This solution will enable them to …
In this way/By doing this …

Recommending

Positive opinion

You'll love it!
If you like love stories, you should definitely read it.
It's a must!
I think it's worth reading because …
I was impressed by …
I couldn't put it down.
It's a classic./It's a masterpiece of its kind.
The plot is believable/entertaining/thought-provoking.
It's a highly entertaining read.
It will change the way you see …
If I were you, I wouldn't hesitate to …
I highly recommend (reading it.) …
I recommend it to everyone.
This is a film/book not to miss.
If you only see one film this spring, this should be it.
I would thoroughly recommend this film to anyone
    regardless of …
This destination would be ideal for …
X is definitely worth visiting.
If you're looking for …, then this is the place for you.

Negative opinion

One weakness (of the book/film) is that …
It is rather long/boring/confusing/slow.
The cast is awful/unconvincing.
The script is dull.
It is poorly/badly written.
Unfortunately, this film/book fails to/does not live up
    to expectations.

Adjectives

Characters: (un)convincing/shallow/plausible/likeable/ realistic/charismatic

Plot: far-fetched/bland/overcomplicated/predictable/ riveting/gripping

Special effects: laughable/cheap/staggering/amazing/ astounding/mind-blowing

Photography: poor/amateurish/breathtaking/incredible/ impressive/stunning

Acting: wooden/mediocre/appalling/natural/powerful/ spectacular

Script: contrived/confusing/convoluted/realistic/thought- provoking/compelling

Music: unimaginative/sentimental/atmospheric/ stimulating/moving/brilliant

Products: hand-crafted/state-of-the-art/streamlined/ compact/timeless/brand new /innovative/durable/ ergonomic/one of a kind/has some wear and tear

Landscape: pristine beaches/crystal clear water/unspoilt landscape/unsurpassed views/bustling markets/ tranquil scenery/dilapidated tenement houses

Review

Introduction

The film/book tells the story of …
The film/story is set in …
The events take place in …
The book/novel was written by …
The film is directed by …
It is a comedy/horror film/love story.
This well-written/informative/fascinating book …
It is based on real events/on a true story/on a book.
It has been made into a film.

Plot description

The story concerns/begins /is about …
The plot focuses on …
The plot is (rather) boring/thrilling.
The plot has an unexpected twist.
The film reaches a dramatic climax …

Describing the location of a holiday destination

… is a reef/an island off the west coast …
… is a town/region/resort on the (east) coast of …/Island.
It is surrounded by turquoise waters/majestic mountains/ lush forest …
In the southern part of the island lies the resort of …
Part of its coastline is a sandy beach.
The region is a national park.

Starting an email/a letter

Informal phrases

It was good to hear from you.
I hope you're doing well/you're fine/you're OK.
How are you (doing)?
I'm writing to tell you …
Thanks for your letter.
I wonder if you remember/have heard …
I wanted to tell you about …

Neutral/Formal phrases

I am writing in order to …
I am writing to thank you for …
I would like to express my …
I am writing in connection with … (the article/report/ editorial) …
I have just read … (the article) titled … in Saturday's paper/last month's edition of …
I am writing to ask/enquire about …
I read/found your advertisement in … and would like to…
I am writing on behalf of myself and my friends …
I am writing to draw your attention to …

Telling a story

It all started when …
No sooner had we … than …
While I (was playing), …
Just as I was watching…
As soon as …
First, …
Then, …
Finally, …
After a little while, …
Suddenly/All of a sudden, …
Unfortunately, …
Fortunately, …
It was the best/worst time ever.
We had a great/awful time when we were …
I'll never forget …

Thanking

Informal phrases

I'm writing to thank you for …
Thank you so much.
It was so/really/very kind of you to …

Neutral phrases

I really appreciate your help.
Thank you for sending it back to me.
I am really grateful for your help.
It's very kind of you.
I hope it's not too much trouble for you.
Thank you for doing me a favour.

SPEAKING BANK

Unit 1

Speculating about appearance

Offering initial thoughts

When I first saw the photo, …
At first glance, …
She/He looks quite + adj/a bit of a + noun
It looks to me as if …
My initial impression was …

Justifying your speculations

I'm assuming he's/she's … because …
It's more than just his/her …
It's more than just …/something to do with …
There's something about the …
Judging by the way he's/she's …

Rethinking your ideas

On closer inspection, I'd say …
Having said that, he/she may be …
Mind you/Then again, I could be wrong.

Hedging

It's hard to say, but …
I can't be certain, but …
I'm only guessing, but …
Going purely on appearance, I'd say he/she …
I could be wrong, but my gut feeling is that …

Unit 2

Giving supporting examples

Phrases with *example*

A typical/classic/obvious example is …
The most striking/extreme/graphic example that
    comes to mind is …
One of the most notable examples is …
I think it's a prime example of …

Alternative words for *example*

A useful illustration is …
For instance, …
A case in point is …
In my case …

Imperative verbs

Consider …/Think about …
Take a family where …
Look at my cousin …

Unit 3

Responding appropriately in conversation

Introducing a new subject

So, I hear/understand/gather that …
(Sarah) tells/informs me …
(Sarah/you) mentioned that …
Did/Didn't I hear (Sarah/you) say that …?

Correcting someone politely

Well, (yes) almost/sort of/in a way, though not exactly …
That's not quite right/true/correct, (I'm afraid …)
To be completely accurate …

Emphasising a piece of information

Well, actually, …/Yes, in fact …
As a matter of fact, …

Refusing an offer politely

Thanks for/I appreciate the offer, but …
I couldn't possibly …
That's very kind/generous/thoughtful (of you), but …

Showing interest

Is that so?/Oh really?/You don't say!
I'm impressed.
That sounds interesting/intriguing/fascinating.

Unit 4

Agreeing and disagreeing

Agreeing enthusiastically

Absolutely! I'm totally with you on that!
I've got to agree with you!
You can say that again!
You're definitely not wrong there!
You've got that right.

Agreeing in part

You're right of course, but …
I know that's true, but …
You've got a point, though …
I agree … but …
I guess you're right, though …

Disagreeing politely

Sorry, but I just don't think that's right.
I'm sorry, I really don't agree with you here.
I'm afraid I have to disagree with you on that.
Hmm, I'm afraid I'm not so sure.

Unit 5

Buying time

(Hmm,) let me see/think about it …
(In actual fact,) I've never really thought about it/
    considered it/been asked that before …
(Wow,) that requires a moment's thought …
My mind has gone blank. Can you give me a second?
(I mean,) to be honest with you …/to be frank …/to tell
    you the truth …
(Actually,) it's a kind of tough/tricky one …
(Well,) all I can say/all I know is that …
(Come to think of it,) that's an interesting/
    a difficult question …
(I suppose) it depends on what you mean/you're referring
    to …

Unit 6

Comparing photos

Highlighting similarities

These photos have various things in common, like/such as …
I can see a number of similarities between Photos A and B.
They're both …/They each have …
The photos are also alike because …
These photos resemble each other in that …
The images are related/are not dissimilar in that …
Not unlike Photo A, this photo …

Highlighting differences

On the other hand, Photo A differs from the other
    photos in …
There are other notable differences too/as well …
Another crucial difference is that …
It's also dissimilar in that …
In contrast, in this photo …
In this photo …, whereas in this photo …
This photo …, as compared to this photo …
Unlike the first image, the second image …

Unit 7

Discussing advantages and disadvantages

Presenting advantages

One of the main benefits/advantages of …
That could be an argument in favour/support of …
There are points in favour of …
… is a real plus.
… is a strong selling point.

Presenting disadvantages

I see (that) as a drawback of …
A major downside of …
One difficulty I see with that idea …
There's a strong argument against that idea, namely …
… a somewhat negative aspect …

Reaching a decision

Taking everybody's needs into account, …
Bearing everything in mind, …
Weighing up the pros and cons, …
On balance, …
If you consider all the negative and positive aspects, …
All things considered …

Unit 8

Adding emphasis

There's no question/doubt that …
The one thing that really disturbs/bothers me is …
The key thing/issue is …
What's critical/crucial is …
The crux of the issue is …/The main point is …
I'm absolutely certain/adamant in my view that …
I'm not sure/convinced (that) …
We need to be aware/cognizant of the fact that …
And don't forget/overlook the fact that …

Unit 9

Speculating about photos

Modal verbs

must/might/may (well)/could/would (be)

Introductory verb phrases

I assume/suppose that …/I presume that …
I can imagine/envisage …
It would appear/seem that …
I don't know whether/if …
It's bound to be …
I shouldn't/wouldn't think that …
I very much doubt that …
We can't rule out the possibility that …

Adverbs

(almost) certainly/definitely/admittedly
presumably, probably, potentially, tentatively,
    likely, unlikely

Unit 1

Exercise 1
1 unconditionally 2 unprejudiced
3 approval 4 disrespectful 5 hardship

Exercise 2
1 forthright 2 imposing 3 split 4 gut
5 obstinate

Exercise 3
1 d 2 a 3 e 4 b 5 c

Exercise 4
1 were constantly arguing
2 have packed 3 will be hitchhiking
4 will have made 5 are spending

Exercise 5
1 hadn't/had not been told
2 they are causing a lot of
3 had been rehearsing their roles
4 will have been redecorating our house
5 has been manipulating the data

Exercise 6
1 going 2 due 3 supposed 4 verge
5 about

Exercise 7
1 A 2 C 3 C 4 D 5 B 6 A 7 D 8 B

Exercise 8
1 would 2 takes 3 in 4 as
5 Despite 6 have

Exercise 9
1 on the point of getting
2 strongly reminds me/reminds me (so) strongly
3 put her foot down
4 has only been taking part
5 attempts to get in touch with
6 will stand by me in

Unit 2

Exercise 1
1 minefield 2 head 3 looming
4 teetering 5 feet

Exercise 2
1 leap into the unknown
2 bundle of nerves 3 common sense
4 meet the deadline 5 in the same boat

Exercise 3
1 notched 2 brush 3 flits 4 come 5 set

Exercise 4
1 must 2 can't/couldn't 3 won't
4 might/could 5 may

Exercise 5
1 must have borrowed/must be borrowing
2 won't help to improve
3 can't have been learning
4 might have come across
5 could be preparing

Exercise 6
1 a practical experience and not just theory.
2 an incredible number of uninspiring subjects
3 a good night's sleep.
4 need a help
5 a progress that students make

Exercise 7
1 A 2 C 3 B 4 A 5 B 6 D 7 C 8 D

Exercise 8
1 administrative 2 rambling(s)
3 rationalise 4 guidance
5 initiative 6 dependable

Exercise 9
1 having a good knowledge of
2 have done it in a hurry
3 went through the roof
4 might be running a
5 I could have helped you
6 be feeling more tired

Unit 3

Exercise 1
1 sizzling 2 fit 3 stodgy
4 occupational 5 processed

Exercise 2
1 nutmeg 2 soggy 3 shellfish
4 crunchy 5 glutinous

Exercise 3
1 toothsome 2 nutritional 3 cravings
4 spoonful 5 elusive

Exercise 4
1 dined 2 wolfs 3 go 4 pick 5 do

Exercise 5
1 snacking on 2 filling up 3 got rid of
4 cut back on 5 give up

Exercise 6
1 out 2 up 3 off 4 on 5 up

Exercise 7
1 C 2 A 3 B 4 D 5 C 6 A 7 C 8 B

Exercise 8
1 over 2 must 3 good/great
4 on/upon 5 more 6 well

Exercise 9
1 drink up the syrup
2 you keep/carry/go on eating crisps
3 have only flicked through it
4 much improvement in/on the freshness
5 recommend letting him make his own
6 will result in educational standards going

Unit 4

Exercise 1
1 purpose-built 2 ever-better
3 backlash 4 commercial flop
5 flick through

Exercise 2
1 prominence 2 glared 3 brainchild
4 on 5 fuel

Exercise 3
1 popularity 2 cheapened
3 carelessness 4 ingenuity 5 awareness

Exercise 4
1 us to help 2 not to be doing
3 To find 4 to vacate 5 not to conduct

Exercise 5
1 to be playing 2 as to save
3 is to open 4 To confirm
5 to have been sent

Exercise 6
1 Clearly 2 Unfortunately 3 In fact
4 Without doubt 5 Incidentally

Exercise 7
1 A 2 D 3 D 4 C 5 B 6 A 7 D 8 B

Exercise 8
1 capitalise 2 ascendency
3 Presumably 4 authenticity
5 breakthroughs 6 effectiveness

Exercise 9
1 way 2 be 3 high
4 joy/pleasure/delight 5 push 6 not

Unit 5

Exercise 1
1 covers all his expenses
2 my/me standing up for
3 his persistence 4 made a mint
5 had the guts

Exercise 2
1 on 2 with 3 for 4 up 5 around

Exercise 3
1 revenue 2 permanent 3 scupper
4 wage 5 foot

Exercise 4
1 Not knowing 2 On seeing
3 not being asked 4 Having been found
5 freezing

Exercise 5
1 succeeded in changing the relationship between
2 It is no use explaining your
3 overheard the applicants talking about the
4 Not having completed any training for
5 more and more time being used

Exercise 6
1 at sea 2 by means of 3 to no avail
4 to my mind 5 at fault

Exercise 7
1 A 2 B 3 D 4 A 5 C 6 D 7 B 8 C

Exercise 8
1 competitive 2 recruitment/recruiting
3 resourcefulness 4 adaptability
5 humility 6 willingness

Exercise 9
1 brush up on your
2 did not apologise for introducing
3 will be at your disposal
4 despises being forced to work
5 putting on a brave face
6 you see Betty sacking Ann